Christmas 1991.

Friend o' Mine

Friend o' Mine

The Story of Flyin' Phil Gaglardi

Mel Rothenburger

Orca Book Publishers

First Edition

Canadian Cataloguing in Publication Data
Rothenburger, Mel, 1944–
    Friend o' mine

Includes bibliographical references and index.
ISBN 0–920501–61–3

1. Gaglardi, Phil, 1913–   2. British Columbia. Dept. of Highways –
Biography.   3. Cabinet ministers – British Columbia – Biography.*
4. Politicians – British Columbia – Biography.   5. British Columbia –
Politics and government – 1952 - 1972.*   I. Title.
FC3827.1.G33R68 1991   388.1'092   C91–091544–X
F1088.G33R68 1991

We gratefully acknowledge the financial support of the Canada Council.

Jacket design by Arifin Graham, Alaris Design
Printed and bound in Canada

Orca Book Publishers
P.O. Box 5626, Station B
Victoria, B.C., Canada V8R 6S4

To Jacob

Contents

Preface   ix

The Prodigal Son   1

Small Wonder   14

The Man For The Job   26

The Road To Prosperity   36

A Different Kind Of Minister   49

Engineering Changes   63

Bless This House   73

Strait Talk   84

Flyin' Phil   98

The Greatest Roman Roadbuilder   110

Opportunity Knocks   124

A Helping Hand   137

The Hand Of The Philistine   149

King Lear   164

The Boys   177

The Plane, The Plane   189

A Stranger In The House   202

His Brother's Keeper   216

This Little Government   228

Square Pegs   240

Resurrection   256

Sources   266

A Personal Chronology   269

Index   271

Preface

"If I were to go outside right now and talk to the first ten people who came down the sidewalk," I told Phil Gaglardi over coffee one day in 1988, "five of them would say you're the greatest man on earth and five would say you're a crook."

Gaglardi finds the word "crook" distasteful, and bristles whenever he hears it used in reference to himself, pointing out that in all his years of politics, not a single accusation about his alleged dishonesty was proven. In fact, such charges were shown on a number of occasions to be totally unfounded. Yet he acknowledges that, to some people, the accusation is more important than the truth. On this particular day, he agreed there would be a difference of opinion, but disputed the numbers. It would be closer to eight to two, he suggested, in favour of the greatest man on earth.

In a sense, Gaglardi had the last word on that subject a few months later when he returned to politics after a sixteen-year hiatus and rolled to an easy victory in the Kamloops mayoral election.

There's no question, however, that Philip Arthur Gaglardi is one of the most controversial, most loved and hated, Canadians of our time. For twenty years his squat, barrel-like body drove through British Columbia politics like a pile driver, smashing red tape and getting more accomplished than any highways minister before or since, but just as often treading on toes and scraping scandal. His five-foot five-inch frame harbours a giant of an ego that has remained undiminished. His name evokes affection or disdain almost as much now as it did then. The passage of time since he unwillingly left politics in 1972, and his triumphant return in 1988, have only served to gild the legend.

Whenever Phil Gaglardi steps up to a microphone (having, of course, to lower it several inches) his topic has unfailingly to do with what's wrong with society and politics today. Where other politicians retire to a life of solitude, perhaps to write their memoirs, and quietly fade away, Gaglardi remains a current force and a dependable quote. Reporters rely on him on a slow news day for headlines on everything from Canadian unity to the trials and tribulations of Jim and Tammy Bakker.

At an age when many men would be content with a rocking chair and slippers, Gaglardi spends almost as much time in airplanes as he did when he was known as Flyin' Phil, the jetsetter of politics. Private business takes him to Hong Kong, Korea and other exotic locations. For years after losing his job in provincial politics, he divided his time between Kamloops and Vancouver or Calgary, flying out to work with his son Bob in the development business during the week, and back again on weekends to his old riding. More recently, his mayoral duties kept him closer to home, but on any day of the week he is ever the preacher and politician, burying and marrying, or holding court with a few of his cronies and admirers at the Sandman Inn restaurant.

He believes in himself now as he always has, sees himself as the practical little guy who could, if given the chance, sweep away the bafflegab and nonsense gumming up politics today and get back to the basics. He is, he'll tell you, big on ideas and action — two things bureaucracy feels uncomfortable with. He sees himself as a rebel, a nonconformist, an opinion largely confirmed by the way he has conducted his life.

Phil Gaglardi's story — his upbringing in a family of hard-working Italian immigrants, his lunchbucket days in the logging industry, a sudden conversion to evangelism, and an unexpected draft into politics — is a fascinating assembly of unlikely events. It's a story of heartbreak as well as exhilaration, but one always coloured by the energy and optimism of a man convinced that just about anything can be accomplished if only you have the determination and faith in God to do it.

Phil Gaglardi is most famous for speeding tickets, airplanes and patronage charges. These, however, are merely by-products of the drive that enabled him to build an impressive network of roads and bridges that linked the province of British Columbia at a crucial time in its history. Along the way, he hobnobbed with the likes of John Kennedy, John Diefenbaker, Walt Disney and many more. His fame extends far past his home province — he's known across Canada, in the U.S., Europe and the Orient. He's an honorary citizen of Palm Springs, and a sample of his handwriting is in Seattle's Balch Library along with those of people like Theodore Roosevelt, Winston Churchill, Rudyard Kipling and John D. Rockefeller. Though no major structure bears his name, there are many with his mark: the Port Mann

Bridge, the Deas Island Tunnel, Rogers Pass Highway, Second Narrows Bridge and dozens of others. His achievements are not in question; his methods were admirable or reprehensible depending on your point of view.

One of the dangers in writing a book about Phil Gaglardi is that it's impossible to please everyone. Those who love him will suggest it doesn't say enough about his concern for people and about his accomplishments. Those who dislike him will complain it doesn't show him up for the scoundrel they're convinced he is. "What about the time . . . " they'll say, recounting yet another tale of Gaglardi's adventures or misadventures.

The truth about Phil Gaglardi, as with many things, is probably somewhere in between two extremes. In fairness to him, his accomplishments have been great, while the accusations against him were consistently disproven. Yet there's no question, as he'll readily admit, that he's made many miistakes. In this chronicle of a fascinating life, I've tried to present a balance. On whichever side of the Gaglardi polarity you sit, his story is exciting because he influenced so greatly the future of B.C., and continues to represent to much of the world what the province is all about. It's time that story is told in full.

This book has been some ten years in the making; assembling a lifetime of facts about a man such as Phil Gaglardi is a daunting assignment. It's the kind of book, for this writer, that has required frequent rest periods. Several acknowledgements are deserved. The staffs of the B.C. Archives and Records Service, Vancouver Public Library, Kamloops Museum and Archives, and Pacific Press Library and Promotions Department were all very courteous and helpful. My wife Sydney was of invaluable assistance with the manuscript. The many people who agreed to be interviewed were essential to completion of the book. And a special thanks is owed Phil Gaglardi for making himself available for many hours of discussions and interviews.

Mel Rothenburger

The Prodigal Son

And God said, "Let us make man in our own image, after our likeness."
GENESIS 1.26

*When God made Phil Gaglardi, he threw away the mould. He said,
"There's not room enough for two like him."*
PHIL GAGLARDI

Phil Gaglardi sits in the coffee shop of the Sandman Inn in
Kamloops, tying into his eggs, hash browns and coffee. It's the
same motel that got him and his son Bob into trouble twenty-five
years ago — they said he was spending public money to fix up the
Highways Department yards across the street so the view from the
motel would be better.

Gaglardi is a methodical eater these days, pausing
occasionally to carefully fold his napkin before dabbing at his
mouth. He's particular about his hash browns, and doesn't
hesitate to tell the waitress they aren't quite up to snuff today. He
no longer devours a steak in four minutes flat between phone
calls or speaking engagements as he did when he was B.C.'s
minister of highways, but he still rises early. It's 7 a.m., and he's
already been up and at it for two hours. He wears, as usual,
comfortable western wear, including the familiar alligator boots.
On his wrist is an Omega watch, with a solid gold band — his
tastes are expensive. At seventy-eight, the face is older, the lines
now firmly etched, the hair almost white, but he's fit ("I've got all
my own teeth, and I'm healthy as a horse"). Three or four times a
week, he says, he strips to his shorts and jogs around his huge
office atop the Silver Threads senior citizens' tower for fifteen or
twenty minutes.

He's now retired from politics for the second time, having
declined to run for another term as mayor of Kamloops. The
mayoralty was the second political coming of Flyin' Phil Gaglardi,
and for a couple of years — from 1988 to 1990 — he kept things
almost as stirred up as he did when he was jetting around the

province as highways minister under Premier W.A.C. Bennett. It's that era he still recalls most fondly, for it was during those heydays of Social Credit when "this little fellow," as he always called himself, became a national phenomenon.

"My God!" he exclaims (Gaglardi exclaims more than he talks, with a tenor voice that has lost none of its oratorical, evangelical quality though he hasn't preached full-time for more than thirty years). "Outside of W.A.C. himself, I'm still the most remembered cabinet minister in the history of this province. W.A.C. said to me before he died, 'Phil, it was you and me, we were the ones that got things done.' "

Then, pausing over his coffee, Gaglardi adds, regretfully, "But that's all history."

It may be history, but it was history made by Phil Gaglardi, for much of what British Columbia is today has its roots in the actions of this little fellow. His life has followed at least three distinct paths, and all had an impact on the identity and destiny of the Pacific province. He moved from one unlikely career to another — redneck mechanic–logger to sermonizing evangelist to enigmatic politician. The common threads among them were his drive, ambition and cocky self–assurance, making possible both his outstanding successes and his spectacular stumbles.

Phil Gaglardi is known most for his life in politics, but his political decisions and actions were hewn from family and religious upbringing. Though he seemed an unlikely candidate to become one of the most famous, and infamous, Canadian politicians of this century, his early years growing up in Silverdale, near Mission in B.C.'s Fraser Valley, determined what he would become. That, and the fickleness of circumstance. In that tiny community of immigrant labourers and farmers were shaped his love of fast cars and other mechanical toys, his determination to succeed, and his absolute faith in himself, God and the work ethic.

In 1906, John and Domenica Gagliardi left Calabria in southern Italy looking to escape from the dehumanizing poverty of farm life in their homeland. They were both young and strong, ready to work. With son Tony and adopted daughter Annie, they sought their new life first in St. Paul, Minnesota, then in Revelstoke, B.C. They had two more sons, Frank and Joe, and another daughter, Lena. Finally, John set out alone, boarding a CPR train and heading west to Silverdale, where several Italian families had taken up farming.

Other than being overrun with dogs, this tiny settlement five miles west of Mission had the distinction of being the site of

Canada's first train robbery. In 1904, seven years before John Gagliardi stepped off the train, the Bill Miner outlaw gang brought a CPR freight screeching to a halt. As curious residents watched, shots rang out and the friendly train robber and his cohorts relieved the CPR of several thousand dollars in currency and gold dust.

John Gagliardi liked what he saw. Soil in the thickly forested valley was rich, rain for crops plentiful. The woods were alive with wildlife, while nearby the brown–green Fraser River was abundant with salmon. And that year the sun shone in an endless blue sky.

Besides the Italian families, there were Irish, Scots, Germans, Japanese, Chinese, Dutch, English and Swedish, all kindred in their quest for a better life. John Gagliardi went in with another Italian to buy a twenty–two–acre piece of land from a resident named William Clark, whose son Ken would become a close friend of Gagliardi's son Phil in later years. The two Italians drew straws to see who would get first choice of the halves, and Gagliardi won. So, on his gently sloping piece of land, he built a small but comfortable two–storey shake–covered house, with a living room, kitchen and pantry, and curved stairs leading to the bedrooms on the second floor. A pot–bellied stove provided heat. When he was just about finished, John sent for his family. On an icy, stormy January night in 1913, Domenica gave birth to their first child born in Silverdale. His mother wanted to name him Mario, but his father liked the name Philip, so the new child was Philip Gagliardi. The family name became Gaglardi when the spelling was inadvertently changed on school records by a Silverdale teacher, who took the 'Gahlardi' pronunciation and left out the first 'i' when she wrote it down. The 'Gaglardi' spelling stuck. (Phil grew up without a middle name, but when he applied for a birth certificate in his early twenties, he decided he should have one. He wanted his initials to be P.A. "I just liked the sound of P.A. Gaglardi, so then I had to attach a name to it." He picked Arthur.)

The family continued to grow, with more sons — Bert, Chuck and Jim — and another daughter, Helen, forcing additions to the first house and, eventually, a new combination store–living quarters, where they sold groceries and hardware to local families. Another son died only nine months after birth.

The newcomers didn't prosper, by any means, but there was always food on the table. John Gaglardi was used to work. An eleven–acre farm couldn't support a growing family, so he worked elsewhere. When they first arrived in Silverdale, he was able to work for a mill cutting ties within walking distance of home. But now he had to work fifteen miles away, putting in ten hours for the CPR at ninety cents a day, for the Public Works Department building roads, or in logging camps. These jobs kept him away from home throughout the week, and he would arrive home for a day off (a "day off" to him was a day working the farm) exhausted and intolerant. Often, he'd fall asleep during the rosary, and his wife would give him a prod and he'd continue. This sometimes took so long that by the time he was finished, the children were all snoring. But John was a devout Catholic, and the rosary could not be missed.

Domenica was just under five feet tall and every bit as hard a worker as her husband, putting in endless hours of washing, cooking and farm chores until her own muscles screamed in pain. Phil Gaglardi maintains a special reverence for his mother, and talks of her as being the focus for the family. "My father was a very quiet individual and mostly reserved," he says. "He wasn't a conversationalist. As far as talking with the children, I don't ever remember on any occasion me carrying on a conversation with my father of any endurance. My mother was a different personality altogether. Mother was the kingpin of the home. Mother was the most important individual in my life. She was the one who moulded whatever character I've got, and whatever principles I've got."

As John Gaglardi worked at logging and road building, his wife and children tended the farm and the store. A cow, pigs, rabbits, chickens and horses, and a barn, became part of the operation — if you didn't raise your own meat, you didn't eat any. From the ground, cleared of timber as John Gaglardi pushed back the forest little by little, there came hay, potatoes, raspberries, strawberries and vegetables. Silverdale was growing, with forty other families now industriously toiling away. Logging became the major industry, and there was also dairying, truck gardening and fishing. Civilization came: electricity replaced coal oil lamps, cars joined the horse and buggy. There was now (infrequent though it was) a police patrol. One of the few phones in the area was installed in the Gaglardi store and was used by anybody who needed it. Then came the magic of radio, and the Gaglardis would gather around to listen to their favourite program, *Amos and Andy*.

The ethnic diversity of the area carried with it some problems. Once in awhile, somebody would take offense at the "Dagos" or "Wops" but John Gaglardi told his family not to worry, that such conflict built character. One day when two rather large Swedish kids were pushing one of his brothers around, Phil

The Gaglardi family, about 1919. Left to right: Joe, Phil, Frank, mother Domenica, Lena, Helen, Tony, Bert, father John and Charlie.

decided to build some character by punching them both in the face. But such incidents were rare, and most of the time the need for cooperation kept the families working together. The children happily coexisted, attending an old, one-room school with a row of windows down one side and a forgiving teacher. Families of all origins depended on each other through the lean times. The Gaglardis were a little too neighbourly for their own good, readily handing out beef or whatever goods another family might lack. Phil's oldest brother Tony was in charge of the store below their living quarters, and their mother baked bread to sell over the counter. To a large extent their hard work simply paid for their generosity, so the store wasn't a profitable venture.

As the children got older, English replaced Italian as the main tongue spoken in the Gaglardi home, though the children still spoke a lot of Italian to their mother. When John Gaglardi heaved his strong, stocky body into his chair at the end of a day, he liked to read himself to sleep with an Italian-language newspaper published in Vancouver. He could read and write in Italian, and communicating in his native language after a day of hard work in an English-speaking world relaxed him. He liked to smoke, or chew snoose. Sometimes he played the one tune he knew on his accordion.

This simple, tough life was an early lesson in capitalism for a growing boy. He learned that you helped others out when they needed it, but your first responsibility was to pull your own weight. "Right from day one we were taught the work ethic and that the only way we achieved anything was by deserving it," says Phil Gaglardi. "We were also taught that possession was an objective and the only way to possess anything was to go out and earn enough money to purchase whatever it was that you wanted to possess. So I think we learned free enterprise right from day one."

Though John Gaglardi was unable to show his children outright affection, he sometimes kissed them after they went to sleep. And he was not without a sense of humour. But he had an explosive temper that broke out quickly when his children did something wrong. Then he'd tie the offender in a chair as punishment or, worse yet, lift him up by the ears, which was John Gaglardi's special method of discipline. When Tony, who was as impish as Phil, didn't get around to weeding the garden one day, his father hit him with a sledgehammer handle. Another time, Tony decided to wake up his father during a rosary by yelling in his ear that the barn was on fire. All he got for that prank was a tongue–lashing. Their father often didn't stop to find out which child was responsible for a wrongdoing. Younger brother Bert once broke a butcher knife, so he hid under the veranda in fear of the consequences. When John Gaglardi came home and discovered the knife had been broken, it was Phil, not Bert, who got hoisted off the ground by the ears. On several occasions, Phil's earlobes were left split and bleeding. He would carry the scars for a lifetime. Phil's father concluded that his young son would never amount to anything.

Years later, when Phil got into politics, and was busy night and day paving the province's highways, his father told him, "Phil, you're working too hard." John Gaglardi's boy, when he heard those words, thought to himself that he'd finally made good.

"My dad used to tell me I was the most useless individual in the family. I was the black sheep. After I was made a cabinet minister I used to visit him. By that time he was in a wheelchair from rheumatism and sciatica. There was very little conversation, but I'd talk to him for a few minutes. On my way out one day he told me I was working too hard. That's about the closest to a heart attack I ever had because a kind word from him was the last thing I ever expected."

Despite this lack of warmth between father and son, Phil Gaglardi respected his father for the hard worker and good provider he was.

Frank Gaglardi's memories of his brother in those days are

of a friendly and energetic kid. "Phil was always a real socializer, he was always accepted by everybody, right from the time he was young. He could make friends with anybody in three minutes. But at the same time, he was mischievous."

Though he sometimes played hooky, feeling he learned more from his mother, and found it impossible not to tease the teacher, Phil really did like school. "I got a strap every day two years running because the teacher thought I was a bit of a rascal, and I was."

It was his mother, he says, who taught him most about helping thy neighbour. If a neighbour needed help, you gave it without expecting repayment. That's the way you all survived. "If anybody knocked on her door and asked for something to eat she never turned them away. She never seemed to run out of generosity."

She apparently never ran out of patience, either. Often Phil would go wandering the woods with his big mongrel dog, Sport. "One time a wildcat jumped off a tree at me," Gaglardi recalls. "The dog leaped up from the ground and caught that cat in the throat and actually cut its throat. Often when I got a bit tired from walking I'd sit or lay down and fall asleep. Sport would lay on me, protecting me just like a person would. An amazing dog. I love dogs. They were my best friends, although we only kept one at a time because it was expensive to keep dogs, especially a big one like Sport was."

During such adventures in the woods, Phil tended to miss dinner, so his mother would save him a meal for when he got home. Phil had a strange habit of standing on one of the stumps left from the big cedars being cleared from the farm, and talking to the trees as if they were people. Only a mother could understand this. "I had many idiosyncrasies, and she seemed to understand me more than anyone else did." Mario (as his mother still called Phil) admitted himself he was the kind of person you either loved or hated. But, he would tell you, he was sincere!

All the children worked outside the home as well as on the farm at an early age. Phil was only ten years old when he got his first summer job at a cedar mill as water boy, getting ten cents an hour to put out the fire every time a spark hit the sawdust. Later he lied his way into a job manhandling a jackhammer at a quarry, though he'd never done it before. When it came to machinery, he was the boss! He prided himself in his ability to pick things up after watching somebody else do them a couple of times. Some people found him a braggart, and he was. Modesty would never be one of Phil Gaglardi's failings, but he preferred to think of it as honesty. According to

Phil, if he was good at something, and he talked about it, that wasn't bragging, that was just telling the truth.

As an adult, he would become famous for his fast driving. His love of speedy cars started early, and he had his first driving experience at the age of twelve. It happened one spring day in 1926 as he was wandering along the road between Silverdale and Mission, a thing he often did when there were no chores or games to hold his attention. On the side of the road, a Chev was stuck in a wodge of dark Fraser Valley mud. Its despondent, besotted driver sat on the running board, toasting his hard luck with hard liquor and awaiting the Lord's assistance. Instead, he got young Phil Gaglardi, a cocky round-faced little kid dressed in old boots, rumpled shirt, coveralls and a baseball cap. A kid who got behind the wheel, rocked the car out of the mud and drove the drunk home to Mission.

The boy's mechanical abilities soon became more and more evident. He began spending a lot of time tinkering with whatever engines he could put his hands on, including the family car. He worked on them in the barn with a screwdriver and some wrenches, sometimes making spending money, more often tuning up neighbours' cars for nothing. He enjoyed driving cars as much as he did repairing them. He got hold of an old Ford motor and chassis, put it into good running condition and lead-footed around the back roads of Silverdale. They called it The Bug. One day he was tearing down a hill when a wheel sped past him. It was one of the rear wheels from his Bug. Soon after, Frank and Tony went to work and laboriously cut The Bug in half, thinking it was a great joke.

One of the family's times of togetherness was Sunday morning. At the excruciatingly ungodly hour of four o'clock each and every Sunday, John Gaglardi would roust his family from the security and warmth of their beds, no matter what the weather, harness up the horse to the wagon while Domenica fed them breakfast, and take them six miles to six o'clock high mass. But the family's devotion to Roman Catholicism was to change dramatically. It came about in a roundabout sort of way through the visit of a man named Pat Marian — Mariano in Italian — who had known the family in St. Paul. During his visit in Silverdale, Pat Marian and Annie Gaglardi fell in love, and they got married and moved back to Minnesota. One day in St. Paul he wandered into services at a Pentecostal church, a frantic sort of religion based on being "born again." Marian was converted, and soon, so was Annie. With a vengeance.

Annie was so excited about this change in her religious life that her letters home concerned little else. Writing about it wasn't enough; Annie had to tell them about it, so she returned to Silverdale on her personal mission to convert the whole lot of them. Sitting across from her father at the long family dinner table, she catechized him unmercifully: although Catholicism teaches that Christ died for our sins, Christ must be accepted as your saviour, and that could not happen without a proper religious experience. Jesus said to Nicodemus, "You must be born again." She explained the Day of Pentecost, when a small band of men and women, following Jesus' direction that they wait in Jerusalem for the promise of the Father — a Holy Spirit baptism — gathered and prayed, and how they heard a mighty sound from heaven, and saw tongues of fire, and they were filled with the Holy Spirit and started talking in other tongues as the Spirit gave them utterance. This was the core of Pentecostal belief and practice, Jesus being our justification and our sanctification, our holiness, our purity. We must forsake liquor, and tobacco, the theatre and even cosmetics. We must be born again.

This was a lot for a rough Italian immigrant, and a Roman Catholic at that, to soak up. Annie talked her mother into going to a service at the Foursquare Pentecostal church way off in New Westminster, and the singing, clapping, praying and crying seized Domenica Gaglardi's mind and emotions as though the Lord had grabbed her by the scruff of the neck. Her husband, curious as hell about this, went with them the next Sunday. That's how the Gaglardi family was converted from devout Catholicism to devout Pentecostalism. And how John Gaglardi, a drinking, swearing, hard–working Catholic, became a teetotalling, clean–talking, hard–working Pentecostal. He also changed his ways with the children after his conversion . . . he stopped hoisting them by the ears.

The children, though they immediately benefitted from this change in their father, didn't automatically convert along with their parents. Each person must go through the same experience, and some of the kids were slower than others to take it up. Phil was the slowest.

Joe, however, made the change, taking part in a river baptism near where they lived. One summer day not long after, Joe was working at a logging show along with his brother Frank and brother–in–law Bud Charlong, Lena's husband. He was standing on a load of logs, watching the big timbers come down the skyline. One of them, unknown to anyone, had been cracked in falling. The brakes on the skyline failed, Bud, who was operating the donkey, couldn't control it, and the big timber struck the spar tree, split and smashed into Joe, caving in his left side. A rib snapped off and sliced through the top of his heart like a knife through a tomato. And Joe was dead at eighteen.

Phil was in Alberta when he got the news. The kids usually quit school after grade eight to go to work, so when school had ended in Silverdale that spring, Phil went out into the workaday world at the tender age of fourteen to make a living, riding the rails to Alberta where he got work as a hired farm hand for the wheat harvest. Now, Joe was dead and he had to go home. When Phil had left Silverdale, Joe said to him, "Phil, you'll be back home on the next train." Phil joked, "Joe, all I have to do is think of you and I'll go farther away." Phil thought of that exchange as he headed home to his brother's funeral, and wished it could have been different. There are so many things you want to tell people, and you never do it, and suddenly it's too late.

When the Great Depression came, the Promised Land became tight-fisted with its bounty. People lost their jobs, the food disappeared from the table. While others desperately searched for work and sustenance, John Gaglardi continued to hold down one job after another, working from sunup to sundown, providing as always. And, as always, when neighbours were in need, they could count on a share of the Gaglardi beef, and unlimited credit at the store. The store went broke, but John Gaglardi refused to declare bankruptcy, insisting instead on paying back every penny. So he worked harder than ever.

As they struggled through that period, Phil came into his working prime. Some of the boys worked with their father on various jobs, but Phil went out on his own, using his mechanical skills to real advantage. In logging and construction camps he honed his natural ability into an artform, nursing and cajoling the big trucks and bulldozers into action, often creating his own parts as he went along. He became a gas mechanic and a diesel master mechanic, and a good one. He could operate the big machines, too. He drove truck or jockeyed bulldozers all over the Fraser Valley and Vancouver Island. He drank, smoked and swore, and he danced and had girlfriends. He and one or two of the boys would get some wine and go to a dance, and they'd sometimes drink a little more than they should and not drive very well, but they stayed out of trouble. Gaglardi says he never became the alcoholic some claimed he did, and never even got falling-down drunk. He just lived the life of a red-blooded Italian-Canadian boy, like he always had. He stopped growing at five feet, five inches tall, a

*Phil Gaglardi
in his 20s.*

victim of his genes. He determined that his height would never get the best of him, nor allow others to get the best of him. What he lacked in height, he'd make up for in strength, energy and living. After all, his legs reached the ground, didn't they?

But nothing could prepare him, or any of the family, for the loss of their mother. One autumn she became ill. Through the winter months, she steadily deteriorated, and it was discovered she had cancer. She hung on until the following spring, with the entire family helping look after her at various times and trying to fill the gap her sickness left in the day-to-day functioning of the household, for John Gaglardi still had to go to work every day.

Bert Gaglardi was positive a temporary healing took place. "She had a lump in her stomach and she had been passing blood. One day we were praying for her and she felt just like fire had touched her stomach, and then the lump was gone, and her colour all came back. The doctor came to see her and he said, 'I don't know what happened to it, but the lump is gone.' "

Yet her weakness continued, and her will to live drained from her with her strength. They prayed for hours. One day in

1935 the family was called to her bedside. She had always experienced premonitions, and she felt her time had arrived. For a reason known only to her, she suggested to Phil that a good career might be to go into the church. Her fondest desire had always been that some day one of her children would preach the Gospel. It was about the last thing Phil Gaglardi had in mind for himself. He still hadn't converted to Pentecostalism as the rest of the family had. But what's a twenty–two–year–old son to tell his dying mother? He heard himself telling her he would one day preach the Gospel.

Since the conversion of the family to Pentecostalism, a new church had been established in Mission. The family attended this church now, and it was pastored by a young woman named Jennie Sandin who had a car that was badly in need of fixing. Phil, home from a job north of Vancouver, went along and took a look at the car. He fixed it, and Jennie Sandin thanked him for it, but that was about all.

She was four years older and a head taller than Phil, of Swedish origin, and very definite about what she wanted to do with her life. Like Phil's parents, Jennie Marguerite Sandin's mother and father had immigrated to Canada, lured by a land promotion, in search of a better life. Like so many other immigrants, they had spent years of impoverishment on the Saskatchewan prairie.

She remembers back to when she was twelve, and the incident that changed her life. Somehow, perhaps in one of the sloughs near their home, she got an infection in her foot that spread so badly into her leg a doctor advised amputation. By that time, she was in so much pain she looked forward to even that remedy. Two Pentecostal evangelists prayed and talked to her about healing. Even after Jesus was crucified and gone, his disciples carried on the healing. The evangelists told her about how, in Acts, Peter and John came across a man lame from birth, who asked for alms, and Peter said, "I have no silver and gold, but I give you what I have; in the name of Jesus Christ of Nazareth, walk." And he did.

The sermon frightened her, but early the following morning, she says, she heard a voice telling her, "In the name of Jesus arise and walk." She stood and walked for the first time since the onset of the infection, and two days later the skin was perfectly healed. That day, a Sunday, she went to the new church and became a Pentecostal. She trained at the Glad Tidings Bible Institute in San Francisco and accepted Mission as her first pastorate.

It wasn't easy. Pentecostalism was still years away from its back-to-the-Bible populism, still viewed by many as radical, ephemeral, spurious. Speaking in tongues, many even believed, was demonically inspired. Pentecostals were dubbed Holy Rollers and Holy Jumpers for their highly animated ceremony and stress on divine healing. "We were supposedly of the Devil, we were heresy, we were regarded as a little strange."

Jennie Sandin and a girlfriend named Frieda Schultz talked a local man into renting them quarters for their church and gradually built up a following. Among the first families to attend were the Gaglardis. First the parents with Helen, Lena, Frank and Bert. Domenica would say to Jennie, "Pray for Mario."

Phil kept coming around to fix that car. One day he even came to a service on his own. She talked to him, as only a religious zealot can, about the winning of the world to Christ. Phil began to see there was more to life than drinking, dancing and carousing. More, in fact, than being a mechanic, even though you were the best. " 'Born again' was a term I'd never heard, but there came a day when I came face to face with the fact that God was a reality, that the word of God was a true book, and I decided that I would become a born-again Christian and I did. It was the accepting of a new way of life and I definitely had an experience that gave me a new outlook."

Soon he was doing street singing with Jennie, belting out old-time religion with his powerful voice while she accompanied him on her guitar. In church, the girls continued to flirt with him, but he and Jennie progressed to going for long drives. When he asked her to marry him, she told him he would have to become a Pentecostal preacher first.

That's how Phil Gaglardi changed from a hard-working, smoking, drinking, swearing mechanic to a hard-working, non-smoking, teetotalling, clean-talking. . . . Well, one day he invited his boss, Jim Dollar, up onto the big seat of his bulldozer with him and announced he was quitting to go to Bible college to become a preacher in the Pentecostal church. "God," said Jim Dollar, "is taking away the best mechanic and bulldozer operator I ever hired."

Small Wonder

Though thy beginning was small, yet thy latter end should greatly increase.
JOB 8.7

I used to get mad at God for making me short. So I made up my mind that if I was going to be a shrimp, I was going to be the best little shrimp God had ever made.
PHIL GAGLARDI

The story of David and Goliath was one of Phil Gaglardi's favourites. For the soon-to-be pastor, small in stature but big in ego, it was a parable of his own life. Phil Gaglardi, in a sense, was David taking on Goliath every time he set a goal for himself. He simply did not believe that, once he made up his mind to do something, he could possibly fail. Far from humbling him, his newfound religion and the dedication of his life to evangelism gave him even more self-confidence and determination, for he concluded that in acting on God's behalf, he acted with the power of God backing him up. As with everything else, he gave his own unique spin to stories from the Bible:

> In the case of David, he was just a shepherd boy tending the sheep at home. And the seasoned warriors were being challenged by Goliath standing out there on a vantage point, swinging his arms around, challenging all the big Israelites. None of them were courageous enough to walk out and to meet the challenge. And David happened to stray into the camp, and when he heard the challenge, he said, "Well, I'll take that fellow on." So Saul said, "Fine, go ahead, take him on." And they put a large coat of arms around him and on top of him and cinched him up and away he went. And he couldn't get anywhere on that kind of basis, so he ripped it all off. He said, "My strength isn't in the shield, my strength isn't in the sword, my strength isn't in the armour, but my strength is in the living God." Friend o' mine, it has always been thus, and so, David marched out and took his sling because he was used to it. And when the giant saw him coming, why he rocked with laughter. But what the giant failed to recognize was that heaven was behind this young stripling. The

man who puts his trust in God is just exactly as strong as God is.
That is pretty strong. And so, David met the giant and he slew him.

That was Phil Gaglardi, tackling anything that came his way, including a total change in his way of living, from the rough–and–tumble workaday world to Bible seminary in Seattle. It was a shock to his system — "worse than a shock" — to go back to school and back to the books, and to sit in a classroom soaking up religion. He never, though, had any thoughts about quitting. "It was new to me, but the moment I landed there, I was a speckled bird, I was a standout."

He needed every bit of strength he and God could muster, because the experience at Northwestern Bible College taxed his mental resolve to the limit. "You better believe I suffered for it. It was just a different set of muscles that I didn't know how to handle." He sang in the class choir and as a soloist, and opera teacher Giussepe Bellotramo told him that with that powerful voice he could be making $50,000 a year in opera within two years (though the teacher wasn't sure he had the brains or discipline to go with the voice). That was far more money than he ever hoped to make even in the bush, but he hung in at the seminary. When the class held its graduation ceremonies, he was chosen to sing the solo, "The Holy City."

Phil Gaglardi emerged from Bible college on the verge of mental collapse. He had never thought much of preachers. Like politicians, they were full of hot air. And now he was a preacher, about to face the physically and emotionally demanding world of evangelism. The reality of evangelism was that on the one hand, it was exciting to go around campaigning for people's souls; on the other, it was frustrating, exhausting and poor. You went into the ministry because you felt you were called by God. And you depended on Him to look after you. Sometimes He chose not to put very much on the collection plate.

As he started his ministry, Rev. P.A. Gaglardi was moved from one place to another, doing two- and three–week evangelical campaigns. In his first campaign, lasting three weeks, he was paid $6, about what John Gaglardi made in a week twenty years before. But the novice preacher swallowed his discouragement and campaigned in North Vancouver, Cranbrook, Terrace, Chilliwack, Mission and in Washington state, his persuasive voice ringing out to the crowds to be born again, to accept the Lord as their personal saviour.

And how he loved to preach, to command the attention of hundreds of people. Though he now wore the trappings of a minister, there was still a hardhat, at least symbolically, on his head, and he combined an earthy, rural, working man's language and outlook with the word of his God. He translated the "begots" and the "ye shalls" and "saiths" into the language of the guy with the lunchbucket and shovel. Instead of lecturing, he told stories. "You've heard people say, 'Brother can you spare a dime,' haven't you? Well, that's just what this fellow was doing to Peter, see? And Peter said to him, 'Just hold everything there a minute, fella!' "

Of course, some of the colourful language of the bush was no longer appropriate at the pulpit. Incredulity was expressed with "Jumpin' Jehoshaphat" or "Juda's Priest!" Anything that wasn't true, instead of being described as the leavings of an uncastrated ox, was "poppycock," "hooey," "pure hogwash," "a pack of nonsense," "a bald-faced untruth." If something was really fouled up or annoying, it was "cotton picking" (which was also handy for references such as "keep your cotton-picking hands off"), "lousy" or "cockeyed." Something might be "this cockeyed business" or "this blasted thing." If an idea was particularly stupid, it wouldn't be "worth the powder to blow it out of the room." Sprinkled liberally among his exhortations were personal acknowledgements to his listeners as "friend o' mine" or "my friend." Working with his limited but special vocabulary, he wrapped his tongue around the English language and blasted it out with a syntax all his own, punching syllables with inflections and pronunciations Noah Webster could never have imagined. An individual (a person was never just a person) was, in a full-flight Gaglardi sermon, "an in-dee-vid-u-al" who may, or may not, possess "in-gen-oo-i-teh," and who should make a "con-tri-buu!-tion" to "so-ci-e-teh." It was a resonant, entertaining, pleasantly rasping voice that was fun to listen to no matter what the message, and whether you agreed with him or not. This preacher needed no microphones; his voice rolled around inside his lungs and rumbled out into a room, bouncing off the walls like an electronic impulse.

> *I think I had a feeling most of my adult life, even my young life, that I was going to be a spokesman, because of my ability to express myself verbally in a very dramatic manner and in a manner that always attracts people's attention. There are speakers who speak and nobody pays any attention, but that's not the case when I speak because I believe in what I'm saying and I say it emphatically and therefore people listen . . . . It's an amazing thing because it isn't something you can manufacture. It's either part of you or it isn't.*

Phil explains his common-man approach to revealing the

wonders of The Good Book. "I've always remained not a religious religionist but taken a very practical type of outlook and always been able to bridge that gap between the religious world and the practical workaday world."

The basis of his message was the individual, the freedom of choice given to man by God, the importance of knowing that good deeds and words weren't enough to get you into heaven, but that you had to accept the Lord Jesus Christ as your personal saviour. "For what shall it profit a man, if he shall gain the entire world, and lose his own soul?" "There's a spot for you in heaven," Reverend Gaglardi would tell the multitudes. "It's easy, all you have to do is do it, ask him to reserve you that spot. Look up at the ceiling some time and take a look at that little old light bulb. It doesn't come alive, it doesn't do what it can do, until somebody turns on a switch. That's what God does, He turns on our switch. He says just ask for forgiveness, confess your sins, and he's got a spot for you."

Jennie Sandin transferred from the Mission church to Langley, down the Fraser Valley toward Vancouver. The couple decided they would be married on December 8, 1938, and services were arranged in Vancouver's Broadway Tabernacle Pentecostal church. The twenty-five-year-old novice pastor and his twenty-nine-year-old bride-to-be arrived a couple of days in advance to complete arrangements, and the pastor of the church asked Phil to check out his car. Phil spent his last few dollars tuning up the pastor's car and fixing the brakes. He was down to his last five-dollar bill, and fully expected it to be refused when he offered it as payment for the wedding service, but the pastor took it. Resigned to starting married life without a penny to their name, the couple opened their wedding presents, and there, in an envelope, was $15. As usual, the Lord was looking out for them.

Phil Gaglardi not only inherited the Model A Ford he'd kept running for Jennie Sandin, but her big church in Langley. Having his own church didn't make things come much easier, though. They ministered largely to a farming community, and these were very practical people who found it tough to accept there was much good in praying and singing when you could be out tending the crops or milking the cows. These were the people the pastoring couple had to depend on not only to join their church, but to support them with donations of farm goods. So they had to rely on their practical style of preaching in order to convince the farmers they needed God for the rain, the sunshine and the soil to grow those crops, to provide the trees to build their homes and barns. One way of proving they were worthy, practical people as well as pastors with a message was to pitch in and help out with more than words.

> *One individual never came to church but his wife always did. He stated constantly that he would never come. One day, driving down the road, I saw him in the field digging potatoes, for he was a truck farmer. I saw when I drove by that he was on the field, and I thought well maybe this would just be a marvellous opportunity of reaching this man. I went home and picked up a fork and drove back, and walked out into the field without saying a word and started to dig potatoes. But he never said anything for awhile until I caught up to him. And he looked over to me and said, "What do you think you're doing?" I said, "I'm digging potatoes. As long as I'm not bothering you, I don't mind helping you out." Well, the atmosphere was pretty charged. But after a bit he started to soften up and that ended up in that man's salvation.*

Phil was called upon to organize a big camp meeting in Langley. It was a daunting assignment, and he and a friend took out a $1,500 bank loan for expenses. Everything seemed in order when a church official called Phil to say the Pentecostal Assemblies could no longer back the conference because he was spending too much money. "I said, 'If this doesn't come out on the right side of the ledger you just leave me alone and quit bothering me, I will climb off of the pulpit, and I will step on the seat of a bulldozer and I'll work until I make enough money to pay every bill.' " This was Phil's first disagreement with church bureaucracy, but certainly not his last. "I found myself at cross-purposes numerous times because I did things that nobody else ever did." The camp meeting was a huge success. Fifteen hundred people attended every day for three weeks; at the end of it, Rev. Gaglardi didn't have to climb back on a bulldozer. He had generated enough money to pay all the bills and turn over a nice profit.

When World War II started, Phil tried to join up as a pastor, but at the time they didn't need any pastors so he stayed at home, joined Civil Defense and helped sell war bonds. He also helped organize a citizens' committee that eventually got Langley a hospital. And he and Jennie had a son, Bob. They stayed there five years and then were put back on the evangelical campaign trail. At a closing meeting in Langley, one of the flock stood up and complained that it had taken their pastor five years to improve the grammar of his sermons, and now he was leaving. They moved to Silverdale and rented a house from one of Phil's brothers, and Jennie stayed at home with Bob while Phil went out campaigning again, two, three and four weeks at a time. "It wasn't the most enjoyable part of our lives." But Phil and Jennie had another son, Bill.

Then the church started asking the pastoring couple to go to Kamloops. P.S. Jones, the Pentecostal district superintendent, was anxious to get a new pastor there. The Kamloops church had been started in 1931 by Jones' daughter Joyce and none other than Jennie Sandin, before she went to Glad Tidings Bible College. Since its opening, the church in Kamloops had been going through an average of a pastor a year. Phil could see why. He'd done a campaign in Kamloops, had seen the sagebrush, clay and barren hillsides, suffered under the heat, and concluded that a jackrabbit would have to pack a lunch to head across that country. Frankly, he was hoping for something better.

Jones, however, kept bringing the matter up. Since itinerant pastoring out of Silverdale wasn't something anybody would want to turn into a lifetime career, Phil thought over the possibilities. He'd always been attracted to the idea of a radio ministry, saving souls over the airwaves — he had the voice for it, after all — and had done some radio ministry in Chilliwack. He wrote a letter to Ian Clark, owner-manager of CFJC, the Kamloops radio station, explaining to him the request that he, Phil Gaglardi, come to Calvary Temple. He wanted to come, he said, but was reluctant to do so unless he could establish a daily radio program. An absolute necessity. Clark thanked him for the kind offer but no, he couldn't do that. Sunday was okay, but every day was impossible. Reverend Gaglardi wrote another letter. He had to have a daily religious radio broadcast between seven and eight in the morning. If he couldn't get it, he wasn't coming, and Ian Clark would be to blame for the Pentecostal church not getting a new pastor. Clark, himself a deeply religious man, recalled, "It wasn't long before Phil was at my office door, desperately wanting air time on CFJC. I doubt that he had any funds to pay for time, yet I couldn't avoid his sparkling, exuberant personality so I decided to go along with him."

Phil Gaglardi was now out of excuses for not going to Kamloops, so he, Jennie, Bob and Bill packed up a lunch and headed across country.

Kamloops in 1944 was a rough, tough Interior city of a few thousand people at the confluence of the North and South Thompson Rivers. Like so many other B.C. cities, it owed its beginnings to the fur traders who had arrived a century before.

Those early settlers who had stayed had become cattlemen. Cattle and forestry were now its main industries, and heavy machinery rumbled through its streets. The treeless, sagebrushed hillsides that so daunted Phil Gaglardi were fringed with forest and pocked with countless lakes for which the local chamber of commerce claimed the grand title, "Sportsmen's Paradise" and "Home of the World Famous Fighting Kamloops Trout."

The church, if somewhat run down, was a pretty, steepled old wooden structure built a block up from the town's main street in 1887. Known as St. Andrews Presbyterian until its merger with the Methodist church in 1925, it became Kamloops United before that church's move to new quarters. An adjoining hall was built in 1912. The Kamloops Pentecostal church purchased it from the St. Andrews and Caledonian Society and there it sat, the white paint peeling off its wooden siding, red shingles fading in the blistering Kamloops sun.

The first thing Phil and Jennie decided to do was set up housekeeping in the church in order that all their energies, and the meagre resources of the church, could be put into their new ministry. The congregation numbered a dozen, with about twenty-five children in Sunday school — not exactly a booming success. A complete renovation program was called for. The original auditorium had been used for basketball and other indoor games, and was in terrible disrepair. Phil wanted to restore it to use as the main church, and he sketched out his plans and called in his brother Tony to help him get the work started.

Phil and Jennie and the boys lived in the basement in a couple of bedrooms and a small kitchen, with no bathtub or shower. The old wood and coal stove couldn't warm the cement floor or keep the snow from sifting under the doors and windows. Phil and Tony and a couple of Tony's men went to work on the auditorium. Another brother, Chuck, helped out, too. It took six months. They built a new basement under the auditorium for the Sunday school. The inside of the church was restored and modernized, while a new coat of white paint went on the outside. The red roof was bright and new once again. The local newspaper, *The Sentinel*, was moved to remark that "perhaps never has a pastor been closer to heaven than Mr. Gaglardi when he painted the apex of the steeple."

Money was often a problem. The church board would say there was no more money, and Phil would go out and put to work the powers of persuasion he had learned in his years of living frugally from one day to the next at the whim of a congregation, and he'd get more money to carry on the work. The Lord, he was confident, always provided. One time when it seemed work would be stopped, he and Jennie took the money they had been saving for a refrigerator and put it into the church, and the work continued. During all this time, in the midst of all the construction work, the ministry was carried on. On the day six months later when the congregation gathered to rededicate the building in the name of Calvary Temple, Pentecostal Assemblies of Canada, the place was packed with 250 people. The church board presented Phil and Jennie Gaglardi with a brand new fridge.

The radio ministry Phil Gaglardi had hounded Ian Clark about became the foundation for their church work. Phil chose 7:15 each morning for a fifteen-minute broadcast and it wasn't long before the whole town knew about Phil Gaglardi and the Calvary Temple. They heard him over their morning coffee, and on their way to work. He'd sing a couple of songs and then he'd talk, sending that voice through the mike as if he were standing on a stump back in Silverdale. He dispensed Christianity with the secular, practical flavour he had honed in the Fraser Valley. He called the program *The Chapel in the Sky*. On Monday, it was Christian News Report. On Tuesday, a program for shut-ins. On Wednesday, Prophecy; on Thursday, Personalities You Should Know; and on Friday, Science and the Bible. And there was no better way to evangelize than through the radio. God ordained that people worship in a church, but with radio you could reach more people in one broadcast than you could preaching in a church for a year. Ian Clark, who acted as announcer for the program introductions, said, "Financially, I never knew or cared where we stood. Sometimes I would question Phil on this aspect and, in his kind way, he would berate me for not fully accepting his conviction that 'the Lord would provide the funds. . . .' And the surprising thing is that the Lord did, time and time again."

Jennie had her own radio program. Every Saturday morning, she became "Aunt Jennie" with songs and Bible stories for the children. It proved popular, and helped their determination to build the congregation and save souls through the young people of the community. If evangelism was the main work of Calvary Temple, children were its main target. The Gaglardis believed that if you got to people when they were still young, you had them for life. "Suffer the little children to come unto me, and forbid them not, for of such is the kingdom of God." Peter was told, "Feed my lambs." Then, "Feed my sheep." So as Phil worked on the adults to save their souls, he began working on them to bring their children to Sunday school. It took awhile to get the point across. He'd stand in the newly renovated auditorium with its newly finished floor and walls and its new heating and lighting systems and harangue them about the need to reach out to young people with the Gospel. Soon he was hanging around schools, talking to children as they left on their way home. "Hi, I'm Phil Gaglardi," he'd tell them, then talk them into coming to his Sunday school. Then he'd talk to the parents, who'd say they had no way of getting little Johnny there and Phil ("heck, everybody calls me Phil") would say no problem, he'd pick him up bright and early Sunday morning and take him off their hands for a few hours. Sunday morning a car would pull up to the house and little Johnny would go off to Sunday school. Reverend Phil would gather them together in his church and tell them a story, and after he'd finished that he'd lead them in a song, maybe "God Bless Our Sunday School" to the tune of "God Save the Queen." Then maybe a song with hand gestures to get them moving and keep their attention.

Jennie, who acted as Sunday–school superintendent, was the administrator. Phil figured there was no woman in the world more capable than his wife when it came to organizing something and teaching young people. "An angel couldn't always understand her — you'd have to be a pretty capable individual to do that — but she is a very capable and powerful woman." Just to organize Sunday services meant calling dozens of volunteers to help with the services, teach Sunday school and drive the buses.

The buses themselves became sort of famous. Soon there were so many kids coming to Sunday school that private automobiles weren't enough. So Phil began buying buses. Eventually, he had thirteen of them, a regular bus line. He kept them running and Jennie kept the drivers driving, and the place was packed out every Sunday with young people. He got the buses the same way he'd gotten everything else — by relying on the Lord to convince people it was in their best interests to give to the church. He got one bus for $1,100, just half price ("I said to the Lord, 'Lord, I want that bus'"), with plates and insurance thrown in. Funds were found for another when his son Bob donated $4 from his piggy bank to get the fund started at a church service. Phil Gaglardi's unorthodox methods didn't always work. Allan MacLeod, then the young secretary-treasurer of the Kamloops school district, received a phone call from the pastor in response to a newspaper advertisement announcing the sale of an old school bus. "He phoned saying he wanted the bus for the

The famous fleet of Sunday-school buses outside Calvary Temple in the late 1940s, with inset photo of Jennie and Phil Gaglardi. This picture was used as a postcard.

church. I said he'd have to tender a bid the same as anybody else. He said, 'You let me know what the highest tender is and I'll go a hundred dollars more.' I said no damn way."

The fire marshall looked at the flock crowding into the church and ordered the pastor to put a stop to it — he was breaking regulations. So the church was enlarged again. "God didn't send me here to preach the Gospel to have a fireman come down and tell me I can't do it."

The fact that the church had to be enlarged seven times in six years, that people were being turned away at the doors every Sunday night for lack of room, that Calvary Temple had the biggest Sunday school in Canada, that "The Chapel in The Sky" was one of the most popular and familiar radio programs in the Interior, didn't convince everybody in the Pentecostal Assemblies of Canada that this was the way to do things. When some purist would question him on this, Phil Gaglardi would have to explain that a person who criticizes the way another fellow is doing something should know what he's talking about. If a person hasn't had the experience and hasn't been successful at something himself, he should let those who know something do the job.

Phil Gaglardi and several other ministers of the Pentecostal Assemblies of Canada flew to Europe to represent Canada at the International World Conference of Full Gospel Churches in Paris.

After the conference Phil visited several other countries, preaching and singing. His audiences nicknamed him Gigli, after Beniamino Gigli, the great Italian tenor. The small–town Canadian pastor didn't know Gigli "from Adam's off–ox." Gaglardi was impressed on that trip with the food shortages due to the war — he came home several pounds lighter than when he left.

While Jennie stayed in the background quietly organizing, Phil Gaglardi was now a man of the community. He preached on anything that seemed current, including, when a shortage of beef preceded horse meat going on sale in butcher shops, a service on "Is it lawful to eat horse meat?" with a special invitation to butchers. ("If you want to eat food with God's stamp of approval, just like you might want a genuine General Motors part for your automobile, then you should eat meat from animals with cloven hoof or that chew their cud; if not, eat dog or monkey meat if you want.")

The effervescent pastor gained a reputation throughout the town as somebody you could go to for help. That resulted in the phone constantly ringing, and the door being regularly rapped on by people with sad stories for the man they knew wouldn't turn them away. Whether it was a young person in trouble with the law or a man out of work, he tried to help them all and did a pretty good job. One day an unemployed young drifter named Jimmy Pattison showed up at the church looking for a handout. Gaglardi gave him airfare home to Vancouver. Many years later, Pattison became a multi–millionaire.

Gaglardi didn't believe in making people wait. He got the problem cleared up as fast as he knew how and went on to the next one. Sometimes, however, the people he was helping weren't the ones who needed it most. Bert Barrett, a carpenter, moved to Kamloops for its dry climate, and bought a house on 6th Avenue inhabited by a drunken renter who refused to vacate. Barrett insisted. The drunk beseeched Gaglardi to help him stay. It sounded like a good story, a poor unfortunate unemployed citizen trying to keep a roof over his family, so Gaglardi went to the man who was selling Barrett the house, and there was a lengthy delay as Barrett tried to take possession. Meanwhile, Barrett and his own family had to live in the annex of a run–down hotel. Barrett became a career Gaglardi–hater after that.

Yet if Reverend Gaglardi's assistance was occasionally misdirected, his energies were often invaluable. In June 1948 he climbed onto a bulldozer and spent four days tirelessly shoring up dikes in one of the town's regular battles against the floodwaters of the North and South Thompson Rivers.

As the ever-growing congregation packed Calvary Temple's new balcony, and filled every pew and every chair set up in the aisles, Phil Gaglardi become more and more a local celebrity. He was asked to run for the chamber of commerce executive. He eventually agreed. Surely a man of such dynamism and grass-roots popularity had political potential. He was asked to run for alderman, even for mayor. He declined. His work, he declared, was in the church. If ever he had any time left over after his commitment to evangelism, maybe he'd think about it, but he really wasn't interested in politics.

The Man for the Job

Go ye into all the world, and preach the Gospel to every creature.
ST. MARK 16.15

There were two things in life I always despised: the preacher and the politician.
PHIL GAGLARDI

By 1952, the coalition Liberal–Conservative government that had ruled in Victoria for a decade was dishevelled and shaken by a growing predilection of the two partners to scrap in public. Post–war prosperity had carried the province through several years of economic development and job security. The Red Scare that accompanied the Korean Conflict seemed to guarantee that the Co–operative Commonwealth Federation and Labour parties would dwell forever in the political wilderness. The coalition kept up a steady and effective flow of propaganda on the benefits of maintaining the two–party government in office working for the good of all British Columbians.

One would have thought the coalition secure for many years to come. Yet decomposition had actually set in quickly after the 1949 general election, in which Liberal Premier Byron "Boss" Johnson led the coalition to a resounding majority with thirty–nine seats — twenty–three of them Liberals — compared to only seven for the CCF plus one Labourite and an independent. The partnership had held together because there was little discernible difference in their political philosophies and because they had a common cause: early on, the war, and later, keeping the "Socialist Horde" from power. But the Liberals and Conservatives were always, deep down, reluctant partners.

Conservative leader Herbert Anscomb, the coalition's finance minister, desperately wanted Johnson's job.

Giving focus to this natural and increasing discomfort was a new government hospital–care plan that was quickly recognized as an expensive mess. The advance annual premiums that were supposed to finance the scheme proved impossible to collect, resulting in huge deficits. Johnson moved to raise the premiums and add a daily "co-insurance" hospital bills to try to bring the scheme out of its multi–million–dollar debt. Anscomb denounced Johnson's new plan as a foolish venture into socialism, and the brawl was on.

When the premium amendment came up for debate in March 1951, a renegade Conservative MLA named William Andrew Cecil Bennett demanded the entire government resign, announced he was quitting his party to sit as an independent, then left the House, walked downtown and went to a movie. Though his fellow MLAs wrote off Bennett's political career and returned to their feud, he soon persuaded Point Grey Tory MLA Tilly Rolston to defect with him.

As the CCF began fingering its political abacus, daring to hope its ascendency might be nigh, a new political movement began attracting attention. The B.C. Social Credit League was a byproduct of what had generally been regarded as a crackpot aberration imported from Alberta. It traced its origins to the Dirty Thirties and before. A British engineer, Major Clifford Hugh Douglas, had begun searching in the 1920s for a financial depilatory that would dislodge the traditional marketplace restraints in which poverty festered. He came up with what he called the A plus B Theorem in which A included the wages paid to workers, and B the bank charges, cost of materials and any other payments needed to make a product. A plus B equalled the price of the product. Douglas reasoned that since A wasn't enough to pay for the product, some method was required to make it affordable to those who produced it. Douglas proposed that it would work if the government ordered all prices reduced by a certain amount and made up the losses caused producers with interest-free credits. Inflation would be controlled by the amount of credits given out.

Early in 1935, Douglas was invited to Alberta to explain his system to the United Farmworkers of Alberta government. A fifty–seven–year–old high school principal, radio evangelist and neophyte politician named William Aberhart didn't believe in A plus B, but did believe Social Credit held the secret to prosperity through tidy legislation and efficient, honest, Christian government. When the UFA wouldn't adopt Douglas' report, he quit to form a Social Credit League. Aberhart sold his party in a visceral rather than intellectual pitch, telling voters Social Credit was the sound, scientific alternative to the effete UFA. The Alberta public, desperate for a new order, bought his classic trust–me strategy and the ablution they believed it offered to the extent of fifty–seven of the sixty–three seats in the Alberta legislature in the 1935 general election. "Bible Bill" Aberhart never did risk Douglas' proposals, staying in office with the aid of wartime prosperity until his death in 1943 during a visit to Vancouver.

He was succeeded by Ernest Manning, another radio evangelist, who undertook the final transformation of Social Credit from a funny–money party to a more traditional right–of–centre political movement with religious roots. Alberta Social Credit now saw itself solely as a nonpartisan Christian movement practising clean, honest, highly efficient government, a generation removed from A plus B and the marching green–shirted British fanatics of early years.

Before Alberta struck oil in the mid–1940s, the resource–rich hills and valleys of British Columbia had beckoned many a Prairie farmer to seek out a better standard of living. In almost every community in Canada's westernmost province could be found a family or two of carpetbag Albertans. It was only natural that Social Credit should find fertile political soil in B.C., and it had been quietly incubating since 1932 when the Douglas Social Credit Group was founded in Vancouver. Aberhart visited B.C. frequently to encourage the formation of Socred groups.

One of the many expatriate Albertans living in B.C. was Lyle Wicks, a native Calgarian now working in Vancouver as a streetcar driver. In 1949, supported by the Alberta party, he led a breakaway faction out of the B.C. section of the Social Credit Association of Canada to form the B.C. Social Credit League. The old group foundered while the League, with Wicks as president, struggled and nurtured a dedicated cell of workers. Organizers would go into a community, seek out Alberta transplants, and set them up as Social Credit volunteers. Small but active units were set to work in community after community.

W.A.C. Bennett, the Kelowna MLA who had twice refused a Conservative cabinet post and twice been rejected for the party leadership, bumped into Social Credit as he was casting around for a political home following his disaffection from the Tories. Wicks met with and gradually came to see "the Okanagan cherub," as Bennett was called, as the potential star personality the Socreds lacked. Bennett weighed carefully the potential of Social Credit versus a new free–enterprise party he might set up himself, but he liked what he saw in Alberta, a pay–as–you–go government that paid its debts and balanced its budgets. In December 1951 he came off the fence and quietly joined the Social Credit association in his home riding. Bennett's enemies in all parties confidently noted that he'd finally gone over the brink; he'd sentenced himself to political oblivion.

Bennett's conversion to Social Credit sent the Alberta party neons into violent ticks. So Wicks was called on the carpet of Ernest Manning's expansive Edmonton office to face a grommet of anxious party hierarchy, the national council of Social Credit. With Wicks were three of his B.C. executive members: Peer Paynter, a farmer and carpenter from Saskatchewan who had been with the B.C. Social Credit movement in Vancouver for years; Hugh Shantz, a Vernon grocer; and J. Alan Reid, like Wicks a former Albertan, who had worked with Aberhart and now ran a sawmill in Salmon Arm. They were told in no uncertain terms that the leader of Social Credit in B.C. must be someone with solid experience, someone from Alberta. That person was to be Reverend Ernest Hansell, MP for McLeod. Ignoring the fact that the leader of a provincial party should be elected to the provincial legislature, and that Hansell almost certainly could not satisfy the B.C. residency requirement in time for the next election, Manning and his hierarchy proposed that the B.C. executive manoeuvre Hansell into the party leadership, in return for which Alberta would continue to provide support. Paynter, Shantz and Reid immediately capitulated and argued on the side of the Albertans. Totally daunted, Wicks agreed to an offer he hardly felt able to refuse.

The importance of finely tuning the Social Credit party machinery (everywhere its adherents insisted it was a movement, not a party) quickly became evident when, in the middle of January, the Coalition in Victoria fell thrashing to the ground in a mortal convulsion. Herb Anscomb, the B.C. Tory leader and Coalition finance minister, was suddenly fired by Johnson after a silly disagreement over who got to make an announcement on the results of a meeting in Ottawa about tax revenues. The other three Tory cabinet ministers quit and all the Conservative members, plotting putsch all the way, crossed the floor to replace the CCF as the official Opposition.

The Coalition was dead.

Since the Liberals, backed by three pure Coalitionists, retained a majority on their own, Johnson attempted to carry on.

Meanwhile, Lyle Wicks had been chafing under the Alberta directive, and called a meeting in Penticton of his B.C. executive to discuss the leadership issue. It was a rough one, raging until three o'clock in the morning. Paynter, Shantz and Reid stuck by their guns in supporting the Alberta position that Hansell should get the leadership. But three other members didn't: Eric Martin, a

Vancouver accountant; William Chant, a retired farmer and former Alberta cabinet minister, now living in Esquimalt; and Rudy Rudolph.

When it came to voting, Wicks sided with Martin, Chant and Rudolph in deciding to reject Alberta's generous offer. As far as the B.C. executive was officially concerned, Hansell was not a suitable leadership candidate. British Columbia would choose its own.

This battle won, Wicks drove north to Kamloops before heading back to the coast. The president of the Kamloops constituency association of the party, Walter Smith, had mentioned to Wicks several weeks before that he figured he had a potential candidate for the next election. Smith, like Wicks, had deep Social Credit roots, having headed the Socred organizing committee in Vancouver in 1947. After moving to Kamloops where he worked as a building contractor, he had continued his active involvement in the party. The man he had in mind for a candidate was Phil Gaglardi. Who could possibly be better suited to the Christian democratic grassroots movement of Social Credit? So Wicks drove into Kamloops and met the little guy. Gaglardi seemed to Wicks to be rather unapproachable. "Putting it quite bluntly, I wasn't a big enough frog in the pond. I was just a bus driver from Vancouver. He really wanted to be a candidate because he was outgoing and flamboyant, but he had reservations because of the church. Make no mistake, Phil wanted to be persuaded. He was a reluctant bride." The meeting was inconclusive, and Wicks decided thirty-nine-year-old Gaglardi was waiting to be won over by the right man and the right party. Soon, W.A.C. Bennett would turn out to be that man, and Social Credit the party.

Back in Victoria, Johnson's Liberal remnant wasn't faring well. A commission to investigate the hospital insurance program, chaired by Kamloops Liberal MLA Syd Smith, tabled a report scathingly denouncing the system as costly, inequitable and over–administered, and recommended sweeping reforms. Before the politicians were forced to do anything about it, the session came to an end on April 10. That same day, an election was set for June 12, 1952. It would be fought under amendments to the Provincial Elections Act providing for a system of alternative voting. Instead of marking a single X on their ballots, voters would rank the candidates according to preference. If no single candidate in a riding received a clear majority on the first count, the second preferences of those who had voted for the lowest candidate would be counted up, the lowest candidate dropped, and so on until a clear winner was declared. The system had been pushed for years by Liberal and Conservative conventions, supposedly to enhance democracy by eliminating the election of candidates and governments by a minority of voters. But CCF leader Harold Winch condemned the system as an attempt to ensure his party would never get into power, and he was right. It was designed to avoid the splitting of the free-enterprise vote. It went on the theory that a voter whose first choice was, say, Liberal, would almost certainly take the Conservative candidate as second choice. The sole socialist party, the CCF, would be the loser.

Shortly after the session ended, the B.C. Social Credit Party held its convention in New Westminster. There was an amazing turnout of 740 delegates, plus another 300 visitors. It opened with the by-now traditional Socred song, "O God Our Help in Ages Past" and turned into a bitter on-floor and behind-the-scenes dogfight over the party leadership. The Alberta faction succeeded in getting a motion passed that a campaign leader only, not a party leader, should be chosen at this point. Their strategy was obvious: Reverend Ernest Hansell of Alberta could then lead the party in the campaign. Delegates gave Hansell, who couldn't run for election in B.C. because of the one-year residency requirement, the temporary job. But the party leader would be chosen by those Social Credit candidates elected June 12.

Now came the job of rounding up candidates. Two weeks after the provincial convention, on May 5, Social Credit called its nomination meeting in Kamloops. Smith had done a solid job of organizing in the Kamloops riding, and seventy-four voting delegates and fifty visitors showed up at the meeting. Twenty-two of the twenty-four Socred groups in the riding were represented. Peer Paynter was there as returning officer, and J. Alan Reid chaired the meeting.

Phil Gaglardi was there, too. Harangued by Smith, and visited by Alberta party president Orvis Kennedy after Lyle Wicks and Eric Martin, he'd finally relented and joined the party six weeks before the nominating meeting. But join was all he'd do. "At least come to the meeting and say grace," said Smith.

A wary Gaglardi showed up, still pulled between his commitment to his church and the magnet of politics. The Pentecostal Assemblies of Canada discouraged its pastors from involvement in politics on the grounds nothing should detract from their dedication to their calling. Gaglardi didn't argue with that line of thinking. He is adamant that he had no respect, in his earlier days, for either preachers or politicians. "There seemed to be so much hypocrisy in those two areas of life. There was a lack of sincerity, not as individuals, but a lot of difference between what they said and what they practised. There's a side to religion that, in my opinion, is very hypocritical." Gaglardi didn't think of himself as a preacher, just a practical man teaching the word of God. Politicians: "If ever there was a windbag, there was a politician. I felt a politician was an individual who ninety–nine percent of the time never keeps his word. He's always playing the game of getting elected."

Yet there was something in Gaglardi's blood that attracted him to the political arena. He told people he didn't know beans about any Social Credit, but they insisted he was the man who could win the seat for the Socreds. He had not met W.A.C. Bennett. "I'd only heard of him and his reputation was not unscarred because at that particular time he was a maverick." Phil Gaglardi felt people were fed up with anything connected to the Coalition. He couldn't tell you what the A plus B Theorem meant, but he felt the Alberta government was "a good straightforward and honest government."

He asked Jennie about being a candidate, and she said if he wanted it, to go ahead. But he couldn't reconcile the conflict between politics and his church work. Thinking back to that time, his wife said: "It was a really tough time for Phil because he had never taken part in politics. So when the meeting finally came, he thought, 'If it's not God's will, don't let them nominate me.' "

Though his name was prominent among potential candidates, he arrived at the meeting without having arranged anything for his candidacy. He didn't like to step out into the open and declare himself. In later years, this trait would be regarded by many as coy and even devious; this night, he seemed to make a genuine effort to reject the crown of thorns he saw politics as being. Seven people were nominated at the meeting, including Reverend P.A. Gaglardi, the man they'd invited to say grace. He declined. James Ayres, the nominator, insisted that the nomination stand. Reid agreed with Ayres. Gaglardi was going to be nominated whether he liked it or not.

Each candidate was given five minutes to talk. But, while the others told why they wanted the nomination, Gaglardi told why he didn't want it. "I am a man of God," he told them, "and I have a big job to do in this city and district. A lot of people have told me that, if I take this nomination, I would have to give up my church. But if I am elected the Social Credit candidate, I am not going to give up my church. I think I would be the poorest pick that you people can have for Social Credit . . . I would like to have my name withdrawn."

Sitting down beside Jennie, he whispered, "Pray I lose."

It took an hour and a half to complete the balloting. One by one the candidates were eliminated. When Paynter announced the last ballot, Gaglardi was a clear winner. Whether by reverse psychology, or party members' determination not to let a good candidate get away, Phil Gaglardi was their man.

Gaglardi's nomination filled out the ballot. Running against him were R.E. Emery of North Kamloops, a CNR carman, for the CCF; George Greer, president of the Kamloops and District Board of Trade, for the Progressive Conservatives; and Syd Smith, the incumbent MLA, for the Liberals.

Gaglardi felt it important to tell people how he'd gotten into the election. "I did my very best to keep from having to accept," his familiar voice explained in a radio broadcast over Ian Clark's CFJC radio station. "Though I have always felt that I would do all possible to help humanity wherever I may be, even to the last my refusal was not accepted and I was drafted. I took it as though it were in the plan of things for my life, and now that I have, I will do my best for the most people who wanted to see me here."

Not exactly modest, but then, as Phil Gaglardi had always said, if you're telling the truth it isn't bragging.

The Gaglardi camp embarked on a high-profile campaign designed around the personal popularity of its candidate as much as on Social Credit. You didn't need to talk about party politics when your candidate epitomized the party. "The Man For The Job," read the ads, and "Social Credit, You Won't Regret It."

Hansell visited for a campaign rally which, of course, opened with the singing of "O God Our Help in Ages Past." The newspaper advertisements announcing the meeting ended with "Checking facilities for halos available."

Herbert Anscomb paid a visit to Kamloops on behalf of Tory candidate Greer. Harold Winch came for the CCF, saying in Kamloops that a Social Credit victory would put B.C. under the domination of Alberta. The Socreds, he said, were Nazis and Fascists.

Kamloops Tory MP E. Davie Fulton said: "As far as Social Credit is concerned, it's difficult indeed to get anything out of the platform, but they do say they are the only Christians in British Columbia. You would think the rest of us were heathens."

Actually, the Social Credit platform was quite well enunciated. It had nothing to do with funny money, but its claim to Christian purity was emphasized again and again. It was a simple, three-point platform: "Acceptance of the right of the individual, pay-as-you-go, and no monopolies." "Individual rights" wasn't as blasé as it sounded, for the Coalition had come to symbolize for suspicious voters an inaccessible stone wall in Victoria to which only the well-heeled corporate elite were admitted to cook patronage deals. "Pay-as-you-go" sounded like a steal from Johnson's last hopeful budget, to which he'd stuck the same label, but it followed the Alberta budget strategy of debt reduction, lowering of taxes and increased public services. A major plank was the improvement of B.C.'s terrible road system. Only ten percent of its 22,500 miles of roads were paved. The government said it would take sixty years to pave them all. Above all, Social Credit wasn't a party, it was a movement. Parties were corruptible; a movement was saintly. "A great crusade for a way of life," Hansell called it.

The leaderless Socreds were written off by all the other parties as hopeless, but, undeterred, they plodded onward, singing "O God Our Help in Ages Past" and promising integrity. Bennett campaigned tirelessly throughout the province, driving from one rally to another, speaking in support of candidates he'd never heard of, let alone met. Some were literally last–minute candidates, urged or shamed into running because no one else could be found. The Socreds were doing well, but nobody gave them much chance of putting MLAs in Victoria. After all, they had never elected even a single member in the province.

On June 12, in a warm B.C. spring, the voters tramped to the polling stations to try out the new transferable voting system. Smith and Gaglardi happened upon each other on the street and the Liberal told Gaglardi to prepare for the worst beating of his life. Gaglardi told Smith to wait for the vote results, then they shook hands.

The election was chaos. By the next day, only four candidates were elected: Hugh Shantz in North Okanagan, Ralph Chetwynd in Cariboo, Ken Kiernan in Chilliwack and W.A.C. Bennett in the South Okanagan riding. To the astonishment of the people of B.C., especially the politicians, all four happened to be Social Credit members. And Social Credit was ahead in ten more ridings, but the CCF led in twenty–one. The Liberals were leading in nine, the Conservatives three and Labour Representation Committee candidate Tom Uphill, the mayor of Fernie, also led.

One of the Socreds ahead after the first count was Phil Gaglardi in Kamloops, who polled 2,823 to Smith's 2,580, Emery's 1,217 and Greer's 898. Smith led in the early returns, but by 11 p.m. on election night Gaglardi had pulled ahead.

If not for the alternative voting system, the CCF would have formed a minority government. The new ballot was doing its job, but it was doing it for Social Credit instead of the old–line parties. Although CCF led in the popular vote, with almost thirty–one percent, it hadn't elected a single member.

The second count wasn't completed until July 3. Social Credit, with support from sects and Catholics, was confirmed the victor in fourteen seats. CCF had crept up even at fourteen also. It was already obvious that both the Liberals and Conservatives were being stripped of power and given the heave-ho by the voters. The alternative voting system that was supposed to save them was, instead, turning against them. Conservatives were giving their second votes to the Socreds, denying the Liberals office. And the CCF, with their just-not-quite-enough first-vote popular tally, were handing over their second votes to Socreds at an alarming level, ignoring party strategists' pleas to "plump" their ballots by not X-ing a second or third choice.

After the second count, Gaglardi still led with 3,251 votes to Smith's 3,160 and Emery's 1,360. Supporters of the CCF's Emery went to Gaglardi on their second choice in significant numbers. Although 407 CCF votes were plumped, 672 gave their second vote to Gaglardi. The next day, Gaglardi was declared the victor on the third count, 3,923 to Smith's 3,376. The don't-know-beans Socred had won with 53.75 percent of the count after three tries.

As the final counts came in, the Pacific province sat back exhausted, and amazed. Gaglardi was "flabbergasted." With only 27.2 percent of the popular vote, Social Credit, the leaderless nobodies, had won nineteen seats. The CCF had eighteen, with 34.3 percent of the popular vote, the Liberals six (and 25.3 percent) and the Conservatives four (and 9.7 percent). It was a phenomenon in which dozens of coincidences and close calls combined to give Social Credit victory — if any one of them hadn't materialized B.C. would have had its first socialist government. There was, of course, the new voting system that denied CCF its long-awaited rise to power, and the desertion of Bennett and Tilly Rolston from the Tories and eventual association with Social Credit. There were recounts, last-minute candidacies and one court challenge, all of which added up to those nineteen seats.

The defeated included Premier Byron Johnson, Health Minister Douglas Turnbull, Agriculture Minister Harry Bowman, Tory leader Herb Anscomb. Among the winners were CCFers Winch and Robert Strachan, a Nanaimo unionist. And Lyle Wicks for the Socreds in Dewdney, J. Alan Reid in Salmon Arm, Robert Sommers in Trail and Rolston in Point Grey.

Once again, the Socialist Horde had been thrown back from the gates of power in Victoria. But instead of the Liberals or Tories carrying the banner of Free Enterprise and The Truth, it was a strange assortment of individuals preaching a new conservatism and calling themselves the Social Credit movement. They were the new keepers of the gate against The Horde.

The Road to Prosperity

And ye shall know the truth, and the truth shall make you free.
I JOHN 8.32

If I'm telling a lie, it's because I believe I'm telling the truth.
PHIL GAGLARDI

Now that he was a politician, Phil Gaglardi didn't quite know what he'd do about it. He stopped taking payment for his Calvary Temple work, and Pentecostal Assemblies agreed to appoint an assistant pastor to help out during his absences in Victoria, but he still intended to keep the church as his priority. He wasn't alone in his uncertainty about the political future. The novice Social Credit caucus didn't even have a leader yet. Assuming the party was called upon to form a government, that person would become premier. A caucus meeting was called for July 15 in the Hotel Vancouver for the purpose, and the backroom manoeuvring began in earnest. W.A.C. Bennett was a favourite among the movement's new blood, but the old guard, ever abetted by the Alberta establishment, carried ambitions for an aspirant of its own, maybe the ever-hopeful Peer Paynter, though the electors had been uncooperative by denying him a legislative seat.

All nineteen Socred MLAs-elect, as well as the defeated candidates, made it to the meeting, gathering expectantly like grade schoolers on the first day of class. Gaglardi wasn't overly impressed with them, but then, some weren't all that impressed with him, either. The MLA-elect for Kamloops struck Wesley Black, a schoolteacher elected in Creston, as being extremely talkative with other caucus members. "The main idea, in my opinion, was Phil was trying to muster support for P.A. Gaglardi as the leader."

Gaglardi sized up his Socred brethren askance. "I don't think I was too inspired. I think that I really felt that W.A.C. was a very fine man. I liked him right from the start. There were others there that I liked as well, and enjoyed, and there were some that I had reservations about, which is natural."

Lyle Wicks chaired the meeting, and immediately made it clear that, as stated in the pre-election resolution, only elected candidates would be allowed to vote for a leader. But as a compromise, non-elected members could be nominated. Bert Price, a shoe repairman from Burrard riding, his running mate Eric Martin and Ralph Chetwynd were nominated but didn't stand. Instead, Martin nominated Bennett, whose challengers turned out to be Peer Paynter (the only nominee who hadn't been successful at the polls), J. Alan Reid, Delta MLA-elect Tom Irwin and Phil Gaglardi.

A candidate needed fifty percent plus one vote to win, and there are two stories on what happened. One is that Bennett won it on the first ballot with a clear majority of 14 votes, while Paynter got two and the others one each. The other, Gaglardi's version, is that Bennett squeaked by him by only one vote. Although the ballots were destroyed, scrutineer Claude Powell, the provincial Socred association's treasurer, later signed an affidavit confirming that Bennett won it with a clear majority. Since the rules of the election required a clear majority for victory, Gaglardi's story is even more unlikely.

Wicks, the other man who had access to the ballots, has strenuously backed up Powell's count, saying Powell clearly told him Bennett got more votes than all the other candidates put together. Gaglardi's mistaken impression may have resulted from a communications problem when Wicks told him the result: while Wicks told him he had received one vote, Gaglardi may have thought he said he lost by one vote.

"It may be in all honesty he repeats that (the one-vote-loss story), I don't know, but I did try to straighten him out," said Wicks.

Gaglardi admits he may, indeed, have received only one vote, but he's adamant Wicks told him he lost by only one. "It's no big deal. The man (Wicks) who told me (that I lost by only one vote) denies it, but that's OK. I know what I know. I was glad I didn't win."

If the caucus had a difficult job in picking a leader, the leader had an even tougher one trying to pick a cabinet from a collection of strangers. Gaglardi, despite his avowed disinclination, was a contender. "After the caucus, W.A.C. came to me and he said, 'Phil, I think I would like to have you if you would consent.' I said, basically, 'I don't want anything. I would like to stay in Kamloops and do my job.' "

Two weeks later, Gaglardi received a wire back in Kamloops

from Bennett asking him to meet the leader in Victoria's genteel Empress Hotel at 1:45 p.m. on August 1. If he saw any other Socreds in the hotel, he was to pretend he didn't know them. Several caucus members received similar messages, with varying times for their appointments. Bennett had been busy setting the stage for his party's appropriation of power, and the going was not easy. Since the Socreds had won only one seat more than The Horde, and had received less of the popular vote, their ascendency to government was by no means assured. Bennett was holed up in his Empress suite quietly but firmly putting pressure on Lieutenant–Governor Clarence Wallace to call upon the Socreds.

Gaglardi made the long trip from Kamloops to Victoria by car. Bennett had hinted about the public works portfolio and Gaglardi still had misgivings about the offer. It was a long way from the stump farms of Silverdale to the halls of power in Victoria. On the way down to the capital, he stopped near Mission. At the top of a hill, he parked and entered a little cemetery. Beside his mother's grave, a few steps from the gate, he knelt and prayed that he was doing, would do, the right thing.

On August 1, Bennett "interviewed" one by one the caucus members he had called to Victoria. He walked up to Gaglardi and told him, "You are my minister of public works." It was the first time Gaglardi had been told for certain which portfolio was his. "I hardly even knew what the Public Works Department was."

Gaglardi, thirty–nine, joined an amorphous assortment of people invited into the cabinet: Wesley Drewett Black of Creston, provincial secretary and minister of municipal affairs; Tilly Jean Rolston, sixty–five, housewife and former teacher, minister of education; Eric Charles Fitzgerald Martin, forty–six, a former banker and civil servant, MLA for Vancouver–Burrard, minister of health and welfare; Robert E. Sommers, forty–one, a Trail teacher and trumpet player, minister of lands, forests and mines; William Kenneth Kiernan, thirty–six, a garage owner from Chilliwack, minister of agriculture; Lyle Wicks, thirty–nine, the Vancouver streetcar driver and longtime Socred, minister of labour; Ralph Chetwynd, sixty–two, Cariboo MLA, public relations officer for the Pacific Great Eastern Railway, minister of railways, trade and industry and fisheries. Bennett chose two non–elected people for key posts: Robert W. Bonner, a thirty–two–year–old Conservative he asked to join Social Credit and the cabinet as attorney general; and Einar Maynard Gunderson, fifty–two, an accountant Bennett had met years before when he was getting started in the hardware–store business in Alberta. Gunderson would be finance minister.

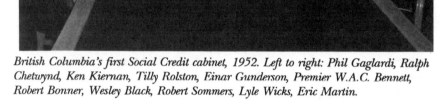

British Columbia's first Social Credit cabinet, 1952. Left to right: Phil Gaglardi, Ralph Chetwynd, Ken Kiernan, Tilly Rolston, Einar Gunderson, Premier W.A.C. Bennett, Robert Bonner, Wesley Black, Robert Sommers, Lyle Wicks, Eric Martin.

Finally, Wallace called Bennett. If there were a swearing–in tonight, would Wallace still have time to leave for the Okanagan immediately afterward? Bennett assured him all was in order. Wallace told Bennett to have his cabinet ready for swearing–in at 9 p.m., before the last ferry to the mainland.

So it was that at nine on a Friday night, the members of the new government arrived at Government House in a half–dozen taxis, ready to be sworn into office. "It will be the policy of our government to give fair treatment to all and special privileges to none," stated Bennett in his speech. "In this task I want to make it clear that our government will not be a government of the right or of the left. A Social Credit government will be a middle–of–the–road government."

At eleven the next morning Bennett led his ministers two abreast out of the hotel, down the sidewalk past the yachts in the Inner Harbour, and through the gardens and capacious lawns of the Legislative Buildings, a miniature army of raw recruits nervously marching toward the sweet ambrosia of power. Inside, Bennett presided over his first official cabinet meeting. Gaglardi wore a light suit, loud tie and basket–weave shoes for his first day on the job. After they posed for pictures, the new premier got down to business. He ordered them to study hard for their jobs and know them well enough to be able to bring solutions rather than problems to cabinet. "Each minister should run his own department," he said.

The first business to be tackled would be hospital insurance, the mess that had helped bring down the Coalition. "We'll get at that right off the bat." Bennett's answer was to make participation voluntary and to cut co-insurance to a dollar a day. Amnesty was granted to those who hadn't kept up payments. Suddenly, hospital insurance was a non-issue.

Then, Bennett's newly named executive assistant, Ron Worley, showed each minister his office. Several ministers weren't sure what to do next. Phil Gaglardi didn't have that problem. All his doubts about politics were immediately removed. "I went over and sat in that cotton-picking chair and from then on I was the boss."

From that day on, Gaglardi had no trouble justifying his dual roles as preacher and politician. The more Christians in all phases of life, the better, he decided. "Why does the Devil have to be running everything? I prayed very seriously. I said, 'But, Lord, how can I preach the Gospel in politics?' The Lord said, 'You can preach the Gospel anywhere.'" Gaglardi resolved to mention the Gospel whenever he made a political speech.

He wasn't commonly given to self-doubt, though he always confessed the chance he could make a mistake. He brought to the job, he was confident, more than any professor could offer. He brought the hard lessons learned in the workaday world and in the service of evangelism.

> *You must realize that one of the things that is very, very tragic about all governments is that there's little genius that you can transport from your practical background into the political arena. A real smart businessman may make the worst politician in the world. The only individual that can make a real success in the political arena is an individual who has an ability to be all things to all people. And I don't mean a compromiser. I simply mean you have to have the ability in politics to relate to ordinary grassroots people, you have to have a feeling inside about political affairs.*

Green or not, Gaglardi wasted no time in getting down to the business of operating a Public Works Department. Central to Bennett's vision for a twentieth-century British Columbia was a modern road system. As a Tory backbencher in 1942, Bennett had served on Premier John Hart's Post-War Rehabilitation Council, whose job it was to take the pulse of the provincial economy. As he roved the province with the wayfaring council, Bennett saw that the means for wresting B.C.'s wealth from the mountains, rivers and valleys lay in binding them all together with concrete and asphalt. He resolved to make the opening of the interior and the north of B.C. a policy priority. In 1952 British Columbia's roads were sadly wanting. Where they existed, they were characterized by frightening inclines, hairpin curves, rocks and dust. The Coalition had built the Hope–Princeton, but it was one of the few modern pieces of highway the province owned, and it wasn't in good shape. Even newer highways, like the John Hart Highway in the northern interior, required a strong constitution, and other routes, like the Fraser Canyon, tested a driver's mental stability. Author Bruce Hutchinson was a friend of Coalition public works minister Ernie Carson, who had grown up in the Fraser, and called him "the most respected public figure in the province, a man who rebuilt the provincial road system on a scale which (Governor James) Douglas could never have imagined." But despite his unabashed admiration of Carson, and his love of the interior of the province, Hutchinson's descriptions of B.C.'s roads speak for themselves. In his 1950 book, *The Fraser*, Hutchinson described the canyon highway north of Yale: "In places only a fragile barricade of dry walling stands between the automobile driver and the river, far below. On many a turn he looks straight down on the swirling water and perceives that it is tearing at the foundations of the road, spreading its bars of sand broadcast against the cliffs, eating them away again, licking at the roots of trees to suck them into its vegetation in ceaseless struggle against its prison. And over it, as if they would fall inward at any moment, lean the angry mountains."

Ernie Carson had developed a plan for massive highway upgrading, but never got a chance to implement it. Bennett wanted the old highways upgraded, and new ones built to fill in the gaps. He wanted a highways system where cars could safely travel at fifty or even sixty miles per hour, and he handed this job to Gaglardi. The Coalition had seen the need, Bennett had the vision, but the day Phil Gaglardi sat in his chair and became the boss, it was as if nobody had ever before noticed that B.C. was full of potholes. "Before I got in there, B.C. ended at the Pattullo Bridge," says Gaglardi of the state of the highway system, in his characteristic hyperbole.

The public works portfolio was a major plum because Bennett, in setting the program as a priority, was saying to Gaglardi, go to it. While other cabinet ministers, like poor Lyle Wicks in labour, and Eric Martin in health, neither of whom wanted the portfolios they got, had to take people's money away and toil in altogether thankless jobs, Gaglardi was allowed to spend money on projects that would be visible to all as examples of Social Credit-inspired prosperity. But Bennett refused to give a blanket go-ahead to the year's public-works program laid out under Johnson's Coalition regime. The merits of each project, he said, would be investigated. And it would be pay-as-you-go the whole way. "Social Credit is opposed to heavy borrowing," Bennett declared, "especially in a period of inflation. As much as possible, we will pay as we go." The promise of tight spending control would be kept. His order to Gaglardi: build more roads for the same money, or less.

Gaglardi soon found being Santa was rewarding but not easy. He was like the winner of a modest lottery being besieged by people wanting first crack at the windfall. He and Neil McCallum drove off on a tour of Interior highways that took them from the Kootenays to the sunny, orchard-laned communities of the Okanagan, then north to Prince George. He listened to people's complaints, but was careful to put the necessary strings on his promises. Studies would come when there were engineers available to do them. Work would get done when the money and equipment were there. Pay as you go.

The state of Vancouver Island highways was due for discussion at a meeting of the Victoria Chamber of Commerce in the Empress Hotel, and Gaglardi and McCallum ended their week-long whirlwind highway stump to return to the capital. In his first major political speech since the election, Gaglardi brought the two hundred chamber members up to date on progress but stressed he could make no new commitments. "Vancouver Island will get its just share, but we must think provincially. You would not want me to develop one region to the detriment of others."

He gave notice of his priorities. "Ministering to highways is important and vital — but ministering to souls is the highest calling of man."

This was welcome fare to a bored and cynical press gallery used to suffering stuporous speeches with all the fire and interest of cold soup. Here was a politician, they sensed, who would always be good for a quote. Reporters listen for quick, catchy phrases they can put into the first sentence of news stories to make readers want to know more. Gaglardi was a bonanza of them, no matter what the subject. Nothing, in his view of the world, was ordinary or impossible. An event might be "the greatest tragedy mankind has ever known," or it might be "the most fantastic." To you and me, at first blush, it might be a bit sad or a bit unusual, but to Phil Gaglardi the world was a

cornucopia of wonders. If something was true, it wasn't just one
hundred percent true, it was one thousand percent true. At least.
But if he wasn't absolutely convinced it was true, it had happened a
certain way "to the best of my ability" or "as far as I know." A sort
of CYA disclaimer. But if he knew for sure, he would dare his
listeners to "check the record," whether or not there was a record to
check. He disdained "woolly–headed do–gooders" and "bleeding
hearts" who, likely as not, must be "smoking something" or "should
see a psychiatrist." He didn't just do his job, he "tackled" it, he
"rolled up his sleeves" and got to work, and he insisted everything
be done "on a proper basis." He was square with God, slept well at
night, and didn't own a pair of bedroom slippers.

In his short time in office, Gaglardi was proving himself to
be both a captivating speaker and an able politician. One of his
secrets, when he stood up behind a podium, was that he poked as
much fun at himself as he did at others. Far from suffering from
his shortness, or resenting it, Gaglardi revelled in it. A master of
the short–joke putdown, he called himself "this little fellow,"
referring to "this two–by–four body," or saying something like, "I
can get into Volkswagens easier than most, but not everyone
wants to get into Volkswagens." As he would step up to a
microphone, he would say something about his inevitably taller
host, or if there was a local beauty queen at the head table,
remark that, if he were a few years younger and a lot taller, he'd
be talking to her instead of to the crowd. And his audience would
laugh, feel immediately at ease, and the focus was all on Phil
Gaglardi and his candid Gaglardi–isms about what's wrong with
the world and what he was doing to fix it. In those early days of
his political career, that ingenuous approach served him well. As
he put it, "My aim is a square deal for all, and with God's help I
hope to satisfy as many people as possible."

The Interior trip had provided only a hint of the magnitude
of his job. The cries for help were coming from every city and
backwater nook in the province, and Gaglardi was kept busy just
promising action: on Vancouver Island, in the Fraser Valley,
Vancouver and the Okanagan. He promised studies, look–sees; he
would go after federal money. His fast action and decisions made
him immediately popular with municipal leaders. After years of
frustration in attempting to get a study done on a new route and
crossing of the lower Fraser River, Richmond and other
communities south of Vancouver were almost incredulous when
Gaglardi agreed to spend $27,000 to do it. Richmond reeve E.R.
Parsons called it "wonderful."

Bennett came up with a solution to the dilemma of having two non-elected cabinet ministers. It just meant a little juggling. He persuaded Columbia MLA Orr Newton and Similkameen MLA Reverend Harry Francis to resign, with Bonner and Gunderson stepping in to contest by-elections in their respective ridings. Francis, a Pentecostal minister like Gaglardi, was convinced to accept a new post in Revelstoke.

Gaglardi admits he was asked to talk to Francis, and that he offered to look after him if he resigned, but contrary to CCF accusations at the time, he didn't force Francis out. "My role in that was to talk to Harry and I did, but never on the basis that has been suggested. I simply said to him it would be a noble thing to step down, and I also believe that I said to Harry, 'I'm sure that there's something we can do for you. I can't promise you anything right at this time, but I'll do everything in my power to see that you're looked after.' I don't make any bones about that. He was one hundred percent agreeable."

Despite the controversy surrounding the by-elections, both Bonner and Gunderson won, and Bennett was left still only a few members short of a majority government.

On February 3, 1953, the twenty-third Legislative Assembly opened. It was a colourful affair. Veteran legislative correspondent James K. Nesbitt described it: "It was the most exciting legislative opening in years. Everybody wanted to see what Social Credit MLAs look like, and so crowds turned out, and were mildly surprised to see they look like everyone else. All the usual pomp and circumstance was observed. Lieutenant-Governor Clarence Wallace resplendent in court uniforms, a military band, a gun salute, ADCs with swords and medals, an army guard of honour, RCMP in scarlet and blue."

Tom Irwin was elected speaker. The throne speech, read by Wallace, promised prison reform, more highways, a cut in auto-licence fees and a solution to Doukhobor unrest. The entire ceremony took exactly one hour. Now it was time to shuck the pleasant trappings of state ritual and get down to the business of the legislature: accusation and insult. The place was a zoo, a den of political cutthroats throwing words like harpoons, cudgelling each other with derision. The inexperienced Socreds were as Christians being heaved to the lions, and the opposition members, seasoned in legislative tactics, gleefully ground their incisors.

The public and press may have liked what they saw in Phil Gaglardi thus far, but the CCF was unconvinced. By the time the MLA for Kamloops made his maiden speech on February 25, he had been accused of misusing government aircraft and of holding back monies allotted to his department in order to show the public a big surplus. No one could imagine then that such accusations would dog the little minister for all the days of his political life. But when he stood to deliver a long and churlishly eloquent speech in the legislature that first time, he made it clear he was not one to be daunted by criticism. After some opening niceties about his premier and government, Gaglardi opened fire on the airplane issue, inviting his critics to look at the logs. "I say without fear of contradiction that every trip taken in the plane has been considered one of absolute necessity!" he told the legislature. If the CCF could not prove their accusations, said Gaglardi, they should resign.

Finally, the public works minister got onto the real purpose of his speech, which was to review his department's program. It was almost anticlimactic after the spirited defence of his use of airplanes, but it did contain announcement of a record road–building program costing almost $39 million, including $6.5 million from the federal government for work on the Trans–Canada Highway. Gaglardi covered every possible detail of his department's plans for the coming year, touching on new bridges and buildings as well as highways.

"I might further state that this is the largest public works program ever to be undertaken by any government in the history of this province and we are determined to endeavour to carry it out without an increase of our provincial debt or the borrowing of a five–cent piece," he declared as he wound down to the conclusion.

Despite all the ballyhoo, the 1953 session wasn't very productive. Little legislation — and nothing of major importance — was approved. Gunderson's budget reflected the avowed pay–as–you–go policy. It came in at $184.4 million, $5 million less than the last one. And from the time of the previous government's last budget to the end of 1952, the net debt had been sliced by $21 million to $169 million.

With the support of the Liberals, the government survived two nonconfidence motions on minor issues. But it couldn't last forever. Bennett and his cabinet would later insist that they had no thought of intentionally forcing an election by providing for their own defeat in the legislature, but political historians have had their suspicions.

Tilly Rolston had come up with a new method for school financing. What became known as the Rolston Formula shifted the burden of education tax away from the rural areas and onto more densely populated regions. The opposition was unwilling to let the Rolston Formula be tested. The CCF's Randolph Harding described the formula as "a terrific body–blow to the educational system." Even the Liberals would not support the Socreds on this one — former education minister W.T. Straith considered the proposal flimflam.

Yet, on March 24, as the sitting opened for the day, Bennett called for second reading of Bill 79, an amendment to the Public Schools Act — the Rolston Formula. The opposition pounced, united in their condemnation. The result was foregone. "I think this session from the first day was destined to come to this hour," Bennett told the House.

The government fell, 17 votes in support, 28 against, including Socred MLA Bert Price. The House adjourned March 27, Lieutenant-Governor Wallace refused to call upon Winch to form a government, and the election was set for June 9.

Gaglardi was nominated without opposition in Kamloops, and this time he was anything but the reluctant candidate. He had enjoyed his taste of politics, and wanted more. He had found little difficulty in maintaining his church ministry along with his public works portfolio, and he liked the travel, the political repartee and the attention. He conducted a spirited campaign, though he spent much of it away from his own riding, making appearances in support of other Socred candidates. Gaglardi promised to avoid mudslinging, saying the Social Credit party was nonsectarian, nondenominational, and nonracist. "I love the Jews," he declared at one point.

There were three new party leaders in the battle. Following his failure to convince Wallace to put him and the CCF in power, an exhausted and heartbroken Harold Winch resigned after twenty years in opposition. School principal Arnold Webster took over, and Arthur Laing quit his federal seat to lead the B.C. Liberals after their house leader, E.T. Kenney, quit. The new Conservative leader was Nanaimo insurance agent Deane Finlayson, thirty–three. Unlike the 1952 election, this one would see only the Socreds with experienced leadership.

As with the 1952 election, 1953 saw the use of the single transferable ballot. Bennett, with his short–lived minority government, hadn't had a chance to scrap it. Had it not been in use, Social Credit would have swept in with a majority by midnight on June 9. As it was, only four Socred members were elected with the necessary clear majority, while two CCFers were declared elected. In Kamloops, Gaglardi easily outdistanced the field with 3,452 votes compared to a combined total of 4,141 for his opponents. There was no doubt who was going to be the next MLA for Kamloops.

While Gaglardi was busy thinking about which roads to build next, the rest of his fellow Socreds sat wondering for four weeks if they were going to be the government again. It took that long to complete the counting. At the final count, Social Credit held a majority with 45.54 percent of the popular vote and twenty–eight seats. The CCF trailed with 29.48 percent and fourteen seats. The Liberals, wiped out on the first count, had come back with 23.36 percent and four seats, while the Tories managed only 1.11 percent and one seat. Tom Uphill, the perennial winner for the Labour Party, rounded out the House. Two cabinet ministers, Tilly Rolston in Vancouver–Point Grey (running against Laing) and Einar Gunderson, switching from Similkameen to Oak Bay to take on Finlayson and Liberal Archie Gibbs, were defeated. Rolston died soon after of cancer. Gunderson lost again in a Victoria by–election, but stayed with Bennett as a financial adviser.

The new legislative session got underway in September, and it was lively but undistinguished. Despite the best efforts of the opposition parties, the Socreds thus far enjoyed a reputation as an honest government. When Bennett claimed that his government had reduced the provincial debt by $36 million, Gaglardi defended the premier with his usual assurances of truthfulness and integrity. He explained that the Liberals had spent $10 million to pay off debts just before leaving office. It was $10 million that should have been left to the Socreds, he said, so Bennett had a right to claim credit for it as part of the new government's debt–reduction program. Then, in an apparent attempt to explain any discrepancies between statement and fact, he made one of those comments that live after a man. As members of the legislative press gallery scribbled furiously, he told the House, "If I'm telling a lie, it's because I believe I'm telling the truth."

While it bemused the government's critics, it made perfect sense to Gaglardi. And, while stated with his own unique turn of phrase, his strange assurance was a sort of statement of mission of the entire Socred government. It was an admission of fallibility but an offer of the best attempt at honesty the Socreds could make.

For the most part, the public accepted the somewhat limited warranty and appreciated its candour. The 1953 provincial election, in fact, set a pattern that would persist in B.C. politics into the 1970s. Born of turbulence, the province's Socred government would endure and seemingly flourish in it. As a people's government of the centre, it held the loyalty of the great bloc of moderate British Columbians disenchanted with the corporate interests of the right, and afraid to experiment with the left. While W.A.C. Bennett was the mastermind of this populist revolution, Phil Gaglardi was the standard–bearer, the quintessential iconoclast who represented for voters a sort of folk hero. For the duration of B.C.'s first Socred government, two men — Bennett and Gaglardi — dominated the affairs of the province. Alone but never aloof, Gaglardi embodied for the public those things essential to sustain not only electability, but genuine affection — he was fearless, decisive, and he was tough. He made many mistakes, but through twenty years of scandals and controversies, British Columbia's common men and women admired, forgave and believed in him because they identified so easily with him. After all, would he tell a lie unless he thought he was telling the truth?

A Different Kind of Minister

Whither have ye made a road today?
I SAMUEL 27.10

As a dual minister, my job will be to put the highways in such shape that motorists will avoid the language which would deny them access to the highways of heaven.
PHIL GAGLARDI

Clearly, in many ways Phil Gaglardi was a different kind of a cabinet minister. His religious zeal, his infectious energy, his natural curiosity and his boundless ego attracted both instant fans and lifelong enemies. He didn't like to let rules and traditions get in his way when he decided something should be done. An inveterate early riser, he was up by 5 or 6 a.m. and would hit the floor working before he even had his first shot of coffee. Dressed in a suit of grey, black or dark blue — sometimes in plaid — cut to the peculiar shape of his body, with well-buffed, pointy-toed shoes, gold cufflinks and an Omega watch, he'd head to his office for a flurry of phone calls and quick consultations with his deputies. He didn't like the desk in his office, so he designed a huge replacement, built by a government carpentry shop, that curved into an L with a credenza down one side and across the back. He loved his new desk. He could roll out highway maps among the papers, documents, drawings, three telephones, Bible and collection of souvenirs (which would grow to ridiculous proportions over the years) without getting everything mixed up.

He might have breakfast, he might not. At times, he tried to cut down. His usual weight was around 175, but it went as high as 190, as low as 150. Often, a good lunch would be his first meal of the day. Preferably, it was steak — "and it must be top-notch Kamloops beef" — with ice cream and strawberries for dessert.

Once or twice a week he lunched with Bennett. Though he was friendly with other cabinet ministers, he seldom socialized with them. "I was a lone eagle, I didn't fraternize. I was always by myself."

Gaglardi didn't enjoy legislative sessions or cabinet meetings, preferring to be off looking at roadwork or to one of his two or three public-speaking engagements that invariably crept into the day's schedule. In the House, he was bored by the inane debate unless he was personally engaged in it. When he was, his oratorical dexterity made him legendary. Like Bennett, rather than shrinking from heckling, he enjoyed it, and no one was quicker with the good comeback than Gaglardi. When he spoke, there was no mistaking who had the floor. He could be heard not only upstairs in the public rotunda, but outside in the corridors. Gaglardi invariably ignored the long and detailed reports from his department, telling MLAs he'd give them mimeographed copies and spare them "the boring details." At times, he didn't even read his own department's reports. He called the opposition CCF "bugs" and they called him "an ignorant clown."

When he didn't have the floor, he soon became restless, combing what was left of his hair, excavating lunch with a toothpick, or even snoring. After a few minutes, he'd wander out into the legislative corridors to chat with whoever happened to be about, or sneak back to his office to get in some more work.

He preferred to work in Victoria Mondays, but work out of Vancouver or elsewhere the rest of the week. Whether in Victoria or on the road, he'd go until midnight, then get in a few hours sleep, to start all over again. Gaglardi not only loved to work, he encouraged his workaholic image. "I work for a living," he said over and over and over, in interview after interview. "I don't even own bedroom slippers and never sleep more than four hours at a stretch. I never learned how to play."

To Phil Gaglardi, work was his relaxation. He enjoyed breaking rules, and he liked notoriety, but even he was never entirely sure what drove him other than that.

> *I don't think I've ever been excited in my life about anything. I have never accepted one piece of feeling exultation over any type of achievement. No matter what I've achieved, it has always been accepted on as low a basis as eating a sandwich. I don't know why. I have no sense right to this day of feeling that I have attained something that was otherwise not capable of being accomplished, yet I've done so many things that people have said could never be done. I think the entire motivating force of Phil Gaglardi has to be my feeling that I am an individual placed in society to fulfil an obligation.*

In the first crucial years of his political career, Gaglardi's top adviser was Evan Stennett Jones, an engineer who had left his

native England for Canada at nineteen and served in the First World
War with the Canadian 68th Battery and Fifth Canadian Seige
Battery. After the war, he worked for a time on the Canadian
National Railway, then became a civil engineer with the government.
He was appointed deputy public works minister while the postwar
highways–reconstruction program was in full gear. The brash young
public works minister trusted the mannerly Englishman implicitly,
and Jones became the ultimate loyal deputy. When it came time for
Jones, already in his sixties when Gaglardi entered politics, to retire,
he stayed an extra three years.

   While Jones gave Gaglardi the benefit of his years of
experience in making crucial decisions, there was another person
who was just as essential to B.C.'s version of the Tasmanian devil.
That person, responsible for trying to organize Gaglardi's day, was
an attractive, intelligent thirty–five–year–old named Edith Scarff,
who became and would remain his faithful secretary. There were
many others who served Gaglardi well — deputy ministers and
engineers, civil servants and constituents — but none more loyally
than Scarff. Single and ambitious, she had worked for a brief time as
an assistant to the public works minister's secretary, but had quit for
a better–paying job as an Eaton's assistant manager.

   But when Gaglardi's confidential secretary, Amy Wills,
retired in 1953, he called Scarff in and offered her the job.

   "I'm neither a Socred nor a Pentecostal," said Scarff. "Surely
you know a good Pentecostal."

   "Amy Wills recommended you," Gaglardi replied. "That's
good enough for me."

   Gaglardi hired a lot of people that way. He met them
somewhere, decided he'd like to have them work for him, and
hired them when an opening came up. His personal assessment of
their abilities was what counted, not hiring procedures or
seniority. His intuition was good, but his charge–ahead style got
him in trouble over the years as political enemies laid charges of
patronage in hiring. Nevertheless, he put together a new working
team for his department, and he didn't mind bragging about
them any more than he minded bragging about himself. "My
department is filled with good men," he'd say. "I picked them, I
trained them."

   If Gaglardi didn't like an applicant, he didn't waste the
person's time with promises to keep a resume on file. "If you
were the last man on the face of God's earth I'd never use you,"
he'd tell those who didn't measure up.

   The other person responsible for office detail was Ray

Baines, a Victoria journalist hired a couple of years after Scarff. Baines, interviewed by Gaglardi just as Scarff and many others were, became the department's information officer. The idea for the position came from Gaglardi's deputy, Evan Jones, but Baines in some ways was just another secretary. While Scarff handled constituency matters, Baines took care of departmental details from his office down the hall in the Government Building across the street from the legislature. In the beginning, Baines was technically an administrative assistant, although "who I was assisting was not clear."

While Gaglardi was highly accessible to reporters — a wedge was jammed symbolically under his office door to keep it open throughout the day — his civil servants got into the habit of checking with him before answering reporters' calls. On occasion, he was accused of "muzzling" his senior employees. Gaglardi says it was government policy that the ministers do all the talking. "I never muzzled my men. They could say anything they liked about me."

Probably no legislative reporter knew Gaglardi better than the veteran James K. Nesbitt, who joined the press gallery in 1936 as a young scribe for the *Victoria Times*, and saw four B.C. premiers — T.D. Pattullo, John Hart, Byron Johnson and now W.A.C. Bennett — come to power. A forty–two–year–old bachelor when the Socreds unseated the Coalition, he found no problems working with them. But the scoop mentality was alive in those days, perhaps even more than now, and the patina soon wore off Gaglardi's accomplishments as reporters pounced on his more outrageous statements, and gleefully transcribed the opposition's indignation. It would become, as Nesbitt put it, "fashionable" to malign Gaglardi. The attacks came not from the Interior and rural press, but from the Big City boys in Vancouver and Victoria. Socred members found a generally warm reception from reporters and editorial writers in their own ridings, but cynicism in the *Sun, Province* and *Victoria Times* and *Colonist*.

While Gaglardi appreciated the difference between reporters and editorial writers or newspaper owners, he came to dislike the press in its broad context, specifically the Vancouver–Victoria press. His wife Jennie disliked them even more, and she eventually came to regard reporters as the enemy. "I used to cry over those headlines."

The press carried out its watchdog role well in some respects, but, on occasion, Gaglardi had every right to be cheesed off at the treatment he got from them. One day, for example, the *Vancouver Sun* asked him to have his picture taken at Lions Gate Bridge in Vancouver. Gaglardi had twenty minutes to spare around 10 a.m. so he met photographer Brian Kent at the entrance. The photographer asked Gaglardi to pose with a paper and pencil for something "different." The result was a photo of Gaglardi published the next day, standing on the bridge, supposedly counting traffic. At that time, there were a lot of public complaints about traffic volume on the bridge, but 10 a.m. was a slack period. Gaglardi was taken to task in editorials and in the legislature as not having the brains to take a count at peak flow. After he good-naturedly chastised *Sun* publisher Stuart Keates at a Vancouver Chamber of Commerce meeting a couple of weeks later, Keates wrote Gaglardi an apology. Gaglardi wrote back: "Dear Stu, awfully nice of you to apologize, but I think the only way this could be done properly would be to give it exactly the same prominence on the front page as you gave the picture." The apology was never published.

Gaglardi tried to count his blessings, knowing the importance of media attention to a politician. Say anything you want, but just spell my name right, he implored. Sometimes they didn't even do that, mutilating it to Galardi or Gaglardia, or inadvertently using the original Italian spelling of Gagliardi.

His experience with hotliners like the gritty Jack Webster ("always a very good friend of mine") wasn't much better, though he enjoyed the chance to talk even if it was to defend himself. "Open-line radio shows are the most overstated and overrated gimmicks radio people have been able to invent," he said.

Throughout his political career, though, he continued to get favourable attention from magazine writers. *Maclean's*, the *Star Weekly*, *Toronto Globe and Mail* magazine and others profiled him. He appeared on *Front Page Challenge* three times. *Coronet* magazine called him "the fastest moving man in Canada" and probably "the next premier of British Columbia," maybe destined for national prominence.

For most of the years he was in government, the public paid scant attention to Gaglardi's detractors in the Big City Press. Even his opponents had trouble questioning either his hard work or his competence. Gaglardi operated as a sort of super works foreman, getting right into the dirt with the men who drove the trucks and ran the bulldozers. His love of machines, of the practical aspects of construction, made him identify much more closely with the slob hefting a shovel than with the engineer holding a pencil. He didn't always know his way around new equipment, but he practised until he learned, just as he had as a kid in Silverdale. Out on a highway site, he'd climb up on a machine and play with it until, often with some helpful advice from the operator or foreman, he'd figure it out. Touring his projects, he could knowledgeably assess progress and demand to know why something hadn't been done. He asked questions not only of foremen, but of labourers, and if he didn't think a man was doing his job, he'd say so.

"What is that guy doing in second gear?" he demanded one day as he pulled his car up in front of a bulldozer. "We'll never get any highways built that way." And he walked over to the bulldozer and chewed out the operator.

"He was always looking under leaves. It kept everybody on their toes," said Fraser McLean, who became assistant deputy minister under Gaglardi after a time as mechanical superintendent. "He talked to everyone it suited him to, not necessarily through channels. His only channel was a direct route." Gaglardi's deputies soon learned not to exaggerate, because Gaglardi's knowledge of the field would catch them.

It was obvious that a bold new highways program employing exciting new methods needed a better system of communication than the one the department had been working with for years. The bottleneck that slowed decision-making and hamstrung the operations of the department was partly caused by poor communications among the various divisions. A province-wide radio system of repeater stations was set up to get around the problem of line-of-sight signals. Now, a department man out in his car in the Prince George area, for example, could call into the Prince George repeater and ask to be patched into Kamloops. Any emergency, whether it required moving equipment in to take care of heavy snowfall or rutted roads, could be quickly met. The system, supplemented by a teletype network, was connected to the department's aircraft as well as its vehicles. Wherever Gaglardi was, in the air or on the ground, he was a call away from contact with any department employee in the province. He had a radio in all of his cars. He was Car 1, and when the boss came on the air, everybody else went silent for awhile. The boss could be rather abrupt.

One day, district engineer Jake Krushnisky was in his car when Gaglardi called him on the radio from the department's Kamloops office. "Be in my office in two minutes," Gaglardi told him.

"But I'm in Dallas," replied Krushnisky, driving through a Kamloops suburb a few miles from the office.

"Five minutes," barked Gaglardi.

When Krushnisky hustled into the office, Gaglardi chewed him out for a routine complaint made by a local service club, then dismissed him. But as Krushnisky left, Gaglardi said, "By the way, we really appreciate the job you're doing for us."

"He always left things on a positive note," explained Krushnisky.

If the minister wanted to give somebody hell, nothing would stop him. Flying over a highway project near Hope, he noticed a couple of trucks pulled over to the side of the road. He ordered his pilot to land at a strip, caught a ride to the site, and demanded to know what they were doing. When they told him they'd only just pulled over for a break, Gaglardi suspended them.

The works foreman in him sometimes yielded bizarre results. Family members Joyce and Larry Strohmeier tell an anecdote about Gaglardi driving down a highway near Kamloops and spying two men standing by an unfinished fence. He stopped, told them they were fired, and received only laughter in return. Peeved, he returned to the department's office in town and told an underling to fire the two men who were out on the fencing job. But his department didn't have two men out on a fencing job. The pair were farmers repairing their own fence.

Gaglardi's quickness in acting on requests became legend. Friends say he had a tendency to accept the first version of a complaint at face value, and it was a weakness because that version wasn't necessarily the right one. But when it was, the public loved him for it. Taxpayers with such minor problems as sidewalks, or something more major like potholes, felt free to go directly to the minister. And more often than not, he'd get them what they wanted.

A Fort Langley man named Charles Perkins came to Gaglardi with an odd request. His son had been killed in the war, and a hundred-foot fir tree had been designated as a memorial. But it was about to be cut down to make way for highway construction. Could Gaglardi save the tree? "Don't worry," the minister told him. "Leave it with me." And he ordered his engineers to put a curve in the highway so it would miss the tree.

Some days, it took more than speedy action by the minister and his crews to rectify a problem. In May 1953, just before the election of that year, an early dry spell raised clouds of dust on some of the roads in the Kamloops area. People complained, so Gaglardi phoned the engineer in charge, who said the only way to fix things up was to dump gravel or pour oil on the roads. Both would take a while and cost a lot of money.

"If it rained it would help a lot," the engineer said.

"I'll see what I can do for you," said Gaglardi.

At 8 p.m. that day it snowed.

A similar thing happened for the opening ceremonies for one of his projects. Nasty weather cleared just in time to make the celebrations a success. After that the highways minister took to praying for good weather for all of his openings.

Gaglardi's methods were sometimes confusing to the public, not to mention his employees and fellow caucus members. As the Trans–Canada Highway project between Hope and Vancouver crept along, people started noticing that several bridges were being built long before there were any roads to take cars to them. Gaglardi had promised a four–lane highway, and it seemed odd that all that concrete was being poured before the appearance of any asphalt. The minister worked with whatever money he could squeeze out of the finance minister. If a bunch of bridges looked ridiculous sitting out there without roads, well, then, it might help if the coffers could spit out some money for them a little quicker.

Gaglardi pushed projects to the limit so that there would be no choice but to do more. When the Yellowhead Highway was under construction north of Kamloops, the new pavement sailed along in a straight line, cutting through the old zigzag road until it suddenly ended, where the contract finished up. People complained to Gaglardi, who went up for a look. Gaglardi called Krushnisky to come up and take a look, too. Showing the engineer the problem, Gaglardi instructed him to push the highway through and worry about the cost later. When Krushnisky telephoned deputy minister Evan Jones in Victoria to tell him about the visit to the North Thompson Valley project, all Jones wanted to know was, "How much did that trip cost us?"

Indeed, building a highways system in B.C. was a costly business. Geography made it so. There were thousands of miles of roadway to build and maintain. Each year, some of it had to be paved; most had to be graded and gravelled. In B.C.'s 366,000 square miles, Gaglardi was in charge of more than twenty thousand miles of road, only about two thousand miles of it yet paved, less than nine thousand gravelled, the rest dirt. There were already more than three thousand bridges, and more had to be built. B.C.'s terrain made road construction costs at least double what they were in other provinces, blessed as they were with prairie flatlands, and the puny hills that passed for mountains in the east.

Gaglardi took offense at suggestions that his highways program of the first three years was haphazard. Though it might appear that way, he knew where it was going. It was just a question of when he would get the money. "I think you will find that our construction program is perfectly planned," he said in a report to his Kamloops constituents, "and although it may appear

Official photo of Phil Gaglardi shortly after taking over the new Highways Department portfolio in 1955.

lopsided, when we get the unfinished pieces completed the plan will be easily recognized."

Tom Miard, who arrived in Victoria in 1954 as assistant deputy minister and became deputy four years later, said Gaglardi got a lot done "and worried about money later. He knew what was going on." And, added Miard, he was "good at not answering," a talent any successful politician requires.

After the first few years, the money for highways was easier to come by, but the matter of costs was one the opposition frequently raised. If they couldn't question Gaglardi's success in getting things done, they could try to cast doubt on what it was costing the province. In one election campaign, for example, Tory leader Deane Finlayson ("a great guy," according to Gaglardi) took issue with the minister's cost overruns. "It is hard to compete with this man in the business of pouring out words," said Finlayson in Kamloops. "He starts too early in the morning." He cited several major projects he claimed had gone over budget, and noted that Ottawa was paying more than $100 million of the $190–million cost (it eventually hit $209 million) of the B.C.

section of the Trans–Canada Highway. "Ottawa supplies the money and Gaglardi takes the credit."

Gaglardi and the feds often didn't get along. When Gaglardi proposed a 50–50 provincial–federal split for an expanded B.C. highways system, he was, in essence, told where to place his request. His running battle with Ottawa over who should be footing the bills, and who should be getting the credit, paralleled Bennett's own funding fights with the feds. But in the early 1950s as Social Credit was solidifying its hold on government, many major projects were barely on the drawing boards or at the idea stage. His 1954 highways program was more than $40 million, in 1955 it topped $50 million, and a year later, a record $84 million. Projects in those years included a start on construction of the long–awaited Upper Levels Highway between Lions Gate Bridge in Vancouver and Horseshoe Bay, the new Agassiz–Rosedale toll bridge, work on the Big Bend Highway, a survey for a Yellowhead Pass route, the new bridge on Oak Street in Vancouver to replace the old Marpole span (a project that came about only after protracted arguments with Ottawa over funding), plans for a Kitimat–Terrace highway and other northern routes, start of work on the Second Narrows Bridge ("Some people want to sit around arguing and haggling over where it's going to be. We can do that after the bridge is built.") and plans for a floating bridge across Okanagan Lake from Kelowna.

Gaglardi's "state of the highways" address for 1954 had more impact for its visions of the future than for its immediate projects. He did more than outline the year's spending program. It was time, he said, to start thinking about super highways fanning out from Vancouver south, north and east. A four– to six–lane highway could connect the proposed Oak Street bridge to the United States. "The travelling public could come up from the American border into the city of Vancouver within twenty minutes. Then, just envision, if a road were built into the Squamish area, how all of this traffic could pour up into that great tourist–resort area as well as through a four–lane highway up as far as Hope where the highway system splits and one ribbon goes up into the Canyon area and the other the Hope–Princeton," he boomed enthusiastically across the House. It would be, he said, a "veritable speedway." The highway south would require a new crossing of the south arm of the Fraser River, but he foresaw no problem with that. What more could the critics who claimed lack of planning in his department want than a network of six–lane highways? "And there's no politics in it. Just real, old–fashioned planning."

Gaglardi was always on the lookout for new concepts, and willing to listen to those who had them. A lot of his ideas never got past the drawing boards. Ferries between Vancouver Island and the mainland, he suggested, might some day be replaced by fast-moving hovercraft. That was superseded by much more ambitious dreams, ones he didn't necessarily expect to see in his lifetime. One was that people would drive from Vancouver to Victoria on a series of bridges. Another was that they would drive in a plastic tunnel under the water. Sections of the tube weighing "maybe one hundred tons each" would be sunk sixty feet below the surface of the water, and would be anchored to the bottom by non-corrosive cables. Buoyancy would exert a steady upward pressure on the cables even when the tube was fully loaded with vehicles, holding it stationary. Tamco Engineering Consultants in Montreal were encouraged to "play around with the idea."

By 1985, Gaglardi figured, drivers would be able to take a nap on long trips, thanks to an electronic track device set in the pavement that would guide the cars by setting up an electronic beam. The car would hook onto the beam and the driver could change directions with the push of a button. "The Buck Rogers era is coming to pass," he said. Today he says, "It's a hundred percent still valid."

But Gaglardi knew technology often ran far ahead of will. New ideas take time to be implemented. "When you build a system dependent on certain things, you must make changes gradually." Other ideas were more easily copied, and Gaglardi eagerly soaked them up. He liked to say he went all over the world for ideas. To Italy where they had the best engineers for concrete. To Germany for steel, where the idea for the expansion-joint decking on the Port Mann Bridge was found. He went to Holland to look at a new method of building roads through boggy terrain, to Japan to look at equipment plants. He preferred to check things out himself. In one two-day trip, he left Vancouver in the morning, looked at a transit-car prototype in Winnipeg in the afternoon, and inspected a hydrofoil, hovercraft and a cableway system in Montreal in the evening. Early the next morning he was up to look at a monorail, then flew to Pittsburgh to inspect a Westinghouse skybus system. He arrived in Detroit in late afternoon to check out a Teletrans system of elevated passenger cars. That evening, he was back in Vancouver.

Flying places, in fact, was one of Gaglardi's favourite pastimes. Obviously, he wasn't watchdogging thousands of miles of road, while personally approving major equipment expenditures, from behind the wheel of an automobile. He needed a much faster, more efficient way of getting around, and he had his Coalition predecessor, the late Ernie Carson, to thank for the answer. While Gaglardi is credited, if that is the correct term, for the creation of the provincial government's aircraft fleet, it was actually Carson who inaugurated it. When Carson had grown frustrated with the immense difficulties his senior personnel had in keeping on top of highways problems in the province, he saw air travel as the solution. So his Public Works Department bought itself an Avro Anson, a Second–World–War spruce–framed plane the pilots called the "Bamboo Bomber." Though Carson seldom went into the field himself, his engineers used it frequently for inspecting highways.

The idea of an airplane being at his beck and call was attractive indeed to the nimble, speed–loving Gaglardi. While the Anson was technically available to any cabinet minister who needed it on government business, Gaglardi himself used it by far the lion's share of the time. The use by engineers decreased markedly. Not only did he maintain the Anson at Sidney's Patricia Bay airport, he kept a Chrysler (inherited from Carson, and later traded in for a two–door Chevy Impala) at the hangar while he was out of the capital, and a new government–owned Buick at the Vancouver airport for his frequent trips there. When in Kamloops, he drove a Chevrolet station wagon. All were radio–equipped. "I kept in touch wherever I went."

Gaglardi was not about to give up his Calvary Temple ministry, and neither was he about to spend weeks on end away from his family. With the airplane, things worked out much better than the train travel he put up with for much of the time after he was first elected. Jennie acted as his Kamloops secretary, booking appointments for weekends and often Fridays in Kamloops. That way, he was able to spend his weekends at home, while continuing to carry out both church and government business.

His use of the planes brought him fairly constant criticism over the years. In October 1954, for example, the daily newspapers in Victoria and Vancouver published articles inferring that Gaglardi manipulated flight plans to suit his own trips home to Kamloops. Liberal leader Art Laing asked some questions, but found nobody willing to make a big deal out of it.

Another cabinet minister, Robert Sommers, was getting himself into deeper trouble than Gaglardi ever did.

Rumours were circulating about forest–management licences being "purchased" by forest companies from the government. Since the entire cabinet dealt with licence applications, it seemed highly unlikely anybody could be on the take, but Bennett had the rumours investigated. No evidence was found to back up the stories.

Lillooet Liberal MLA Gordon Gibson, Gaglardi's legislative sparring partner, a bullmoose of a man who had parlayed a family logging show on Vancouver Island into a fortune, had heard the same scuttlebutt. Gibson, whose favourite vices included good cigars and two bottles of Seagram's rye per day, was what they call a "character," rough, smart, shameless, a man who felt at home telling tales over drinks in a bush camp or at the Terminal City Club. He was a strong opponent of the forest-management licence system, which he felt was working against small loggers. After unsuccessfully trying to persuade both Sommers and Bennett to stop issuing them, Gibson charged in the legislature February 2 that Bennett had mishandled the granting of the licences. He claimed big forest companies were profiteering by selling huge quantities of shares after receiving their licences. The licence was money in the bank before a tree was cut. The obstreperous bull of the woods renewed his attack February 14 and again the next day, this time suggesting something shady had been going on in the way forest-management licences were issued.

"Maybe it is the colour of a man's eyes. Maybe it is the colour of a man's hair. But I doubt it. I firmly believe that money talks and has talked in this, and I want that answered by the minister!"

And now it was February 17, and Gaglardi was assigned damage control. As it happened, it would be his last speech as public works minister; a bill creating a Department of Highways had been introduced, and Gaglardi was slated for the new job. Highways had by far taken up most of Gaglardi's time, and there was a clear need for a split into two departments. William Chant, former Alberta cabinet minister, was in line to take over the old portfolio.

Gaglardi's theme that day was familiar: there was some kind of a plot to discredit the government. "I never in my life had to sit and take the kind of abuse we have been subjected to in the last few days. Well, it's not going to stop this government from giving clean, honest government," he thundered across the floor at the opposition benches during his forty-five-minute attack. "Is there some kind of a sinister plot leading up to something?" Laing ("a very good friend of mine") "rhymes with bang, which is just a loud noise." Noting that both he and Gibson ("a good friend of mine") were known for their stentorian voices, Gaglardi remarked, "I sound like a zephyr alongside that cyclone. Why, I bet that when he went into the forests and made his money, he just blew the trees down!"

Judge Arthur Lord was appointed to look into Gibson's charges. A hearing was called and Dr. C.D. Orchard, the deputy forests minister, told Lord he was aware of no dishonest dealings on forest–management licences. Gibson's lawyer stated the "money–talks" charge was not aimed at any individual, but at the way in which the licence policy favoured big loggers. On March 9, Lord announced that there had been no wrongdoing in the granting of licences.

On March 10, Gibson resigned his Lillooet seat to take the issue directly to the public.

Bennett asked Phil Gaglardi and Bob Bonner to engineer the by–election in an effort to defeat Gibson. They went into the Fraser Canyon riding and talked strategy with the Socred candidate, Don Robinson, a PGE railway engineer who had unsuccessfully challenged Ernie Carson in 1952 (Gibson won the riding in 1953 after Carson's death). Robinson would later make his mark on the list of famous and infamous Socred quotations with "Rome was not built in a day, but it might have been if our premier had been in charge." But in August 1955 Robinson was not nearly so profound. In fact, Gaglardi and Bonner decided there was no way the election could be won if Robinson ever opened his mouth. So at election meetings, Robinson would stand up, say who he was, and sit down. Then Gaglardi and Bonner would take over.

The strategy of running a phantom candidate worked wonderfully well. The Socred Robinson beat Gibson, getting 1,709 votes to Gibson's 1,282. The CCF got 844, the Conservative candidate only 201. The forest–management licence issue had been put to rest effectively, if temporarily.

Engineering Change

Then saith he unto his disciples, the harvest is plenteous, but the labourers are few.
MATTHEW 9.37

An engineer is a very staid, solid individual who deals with facts but without imagination.
PHIL GAGLARDI

If B.C.'s massive roadbuilding program was to continue apace, some fundamental reorganization was necessary. Obvious, at least, to Phil Gaglardi, based on advice from his deputies. The changes he wrought in the newly created Highways Department in 1955 and 1956 would illustrate Gaglardi's ability to engender fierce loyalty or intense trauma. The results of the political and administrative style that came to the fore during the shakeup were in keeping with a general tendency of people to love him or hate him. Many of those he worked most closely with became highly motivated by his peripatetic nature and take-charge style. It drove chief engineer Neil McCallum to distraction.

Since change is often traumatic even when guided by a gentle hand, Phil Gaglardi's no-nonsense realignment of departmental duties — necessary though it was — was doubly upsetting to some of the targets. A dismantling of empires was required. On the one hand, the highways operation was overloaded at the top. On the other, it was fractured into ten divisions in all, created in 1949. It hadn't worked well. While technical details from all these divisions had to be funnelled through Victoria, creating a huge bottleneck, each worked independently. The various branches — construction, bridges, location, surfacing — didn't know what the others were doing. The only time they connected, it seemed, was when they rubbed each other the wrong way. The Keystone Cops were running an $84-million construction program.

There weren't enough engineers, men or machines, either. Day-labour, machine-rental work helped, because that avoided the need for full location surveys, detailed estimates and "finishing" — removal of all debris. The lack of detail work necessary for day-labour or non-contract construction alleviated the shortage of engineers, but the equipment was still a problem. There seemed to be little control over department-owned equipment, and it was badly abused. The whole situation, to Gaglardi, was "an administrative monstrosity."

He was particularly galled at the power of the chief engineer, who seemed to have more influence than the deputy minister. The wrong people were in charge. Gaglardi and the engineer, Neil McCallum, who (unlike deputy minister Evan Jones) was as headstrong as Gaglardi, were destined to clash. Their incompatibility had been obvious from the day Phil Gaglardi took over the department. "About three weeks later I was ready to explode. One day Neil McCallum comes to me and he says, 'You're making too many decisions.' I said, 'What do you mean?' He said, 'You're supposed to be the titular head of this department. We're supposed to make the decisions.' I said, 'The premier told us to run our own departments.' I said, 'I'll run this department. And furthermore, Mr. McCallum, you stick to engineering.' "

There was room for only one boss in Gaglardi's department. McCallum recognized the conflict just as quickly. "The chief engineer had more authority than Gaglardi wanted him to have."

Reorganization had been on the books prior to 1952, but the election of the Socreds, and the arrival of a new minister, put it on hold. While Gaglardi didn't come up with the plan for reorganizing the department, he saw the need. As minister, it was up to him to implement the changes and accept the fallout, so he waded in. Jones recommended the ten divisions be scrapped and replaced with four regions, in Kamloops, Nelson, Prince George and Vancouver-Victoria. Contracts would be called in Victoria, but coordinated through all of the regions, and the bureaucratic tangle would be streamlined. In some respects, it was a decentralization, but it would keep Gaglardi in firm control. Construction departments would be set up in each of the regions, and each construction engineer would have earth-moving machines, paving machines, gravel crushers and other major pieces of equipment at his disposal to give the department full construction capability on its own. It wouldn't eliminate contractors, but it would give the department tremendous capability in keeping work on schedule.

The scheme, in one fell swoop, would kick the building program from second into high gear, giving it much-needed torque in processing contracts and in keeping projects in overdrive. It would necessitate some shuffling of personnel, and therein was the rub. Only four of the divisional engineers could be promoted to regional status. The other six, who had been used to bossing their own turf, would be subservient to the promotees. The effect would be felt right up to the highways office across from the legislature. More authority would be put into the hands of the deputy minister. The chief engineer, who had chaired the Highways Board, would be less responsible for policy and more responsible for engineering detail.

In November 1955, a couple of weeks before Gaglardi unveiled his major road plans for the new year, he announced the new organizational structure.

McCallum suspected Gaglardi was using the opportunity to take some of his authority away. When the plan was ready, a meeting of divisional heads was called in Gaglardi's office. The bridge, construction, paving and chief engineers were there, along with the right-of-way agent, the deputy minister and Gaglardi, who announced that Jones would hand out copies of flow charts.

"I'm going to reorganize this department," Gaglardi began.

The atmosphere was decidedly cool throughout the meeting, but it quickly became apparent that the changes weren't debatable. McCallum believed Gaglardi didn't think much of engineers. The elevation of Jones over McCallum in influence, Gaglardi's hands-on decisions and the pint-size minister's disposition toward practical experience rather than book-learning probably combined to create that impression. Indeed, Gaglardi's blue-collar background ingrained in him a deep appreciation for men with callouses on their hands. Like many in the Socred cabinet, he viewed academics with suspicion.

Gaglardi rejected any notion of a dislike for engineers, maintaining he had nothing but respect for them. He simply believed engineers worked within a set of parameters from which they could not possibly escape.

An engineer is not required to have vision. Why does an engineer need vision? All an engineer needs to know is what is the tensile strength of a piece of steel or what type of material do I use in this type of soil after the soil has been tested and so on. An engineer is a man who comes up with the figures that he gets out of a book, that he's been trained to follow just exactly the same as a train is told to follow on a track. That's what all professionals are taught to do. If you can find a professional that has vision plus the ability of what his profession requires, then you've found a genius, and they're very, very scarce. An engineer can't have too much flexibility, so there's no use looking for those things in an engineer.

McCallum stewed about the realignment of the department for several weeks. Above all, he was angered that Gaglardi hadn't consulted him.

There was another issue. On February 2, Gaglardi announced in the legislature construction of a tunnel under the south arm of the Fraser at Deas Island. Delta MLA George Massey had promoted the idea for years. The cost would be between $15 million and $17 million (it actually ended up at $25 million). A new highway from the Oak Street bridge to the tunnel might up the total cost to $30 million. "Here now is the start of the great dream of a highway from the city of Vancouver to the American border, of four–lane width with limited access," Gaglardi enthused. He was quoted elsewhere, erroneously, as calling the tunnel plan a triumph of "imagination over engineering," an apparent distortion of other comments he'd made.

Gaglardi's decision on the tunnel did ignore a three–year study by a committee of provincial and municipal engineers that recommended a bridge over Annacis Island. McCallum, as chairman of the committee, argued strongly for the Annacis Island route, six miles east of Deas Island. The latter wasn't even mentioned as a possibility. The committee, which included provincial, Vancouver, Burnaby and New Westminster engineers, supported Annacis because of its southeast, corner–to–corner direction that it felt would best serve Lower Mainland traffic. In choosing Deas Island, Gaglardi accepted the recommendation of a separate study done by the Foundation of Canada Engineering Corporation Ltd., one of the largest engineering firms in Canada.

"They said that the location of a crossing at Deas Island combined more advantages from the point of view of traffic, development of the area, navigation and ease of construction, than crossings considered at Tillbury Island, Annacis Island or Port Mann," explained Gaglardi.

A choice made on the basis of sharply differing consultants' reports, and on just as sharply divided public opinion, was bound to be politically thorny, but Gaglardi was never one to shrink from such decisions.

Neil McCallum continued to argue strongly for the Annacis route, contending that the Deas crossing would funnel traffic into Vancouver's crowded downtown streets. The highways minister was unmoved by his chief engineer's pleas.

The hostility between the two men had made for an intolerable working situation. What to others was candour and flamboyance, to McCallum was pushiness and ego. What to Gaglardi was red tape that needed cutting, was to McCallum sensible guidelines. McCallum felt Gaglardi complained too much about the amount of work not getting done, and bragged too much about projects his staff should get credit for. And not being a shrinking violet himself, McCallum did not suffer easily under such a style of operation.

Gaglardi readily acknowledges the underlying hostility between him and his chief engineer, but says McCallum's main problem was getting used to having less influence on policy.

> *Evan Jones came to me time after time and said, "Mr. Gaglardi, watch your step because the chief engineer is after you." I could have easily fired him because I had all the necessary evidence that would allow me to do that, but it never entered my mind – he was a good engineer. Don't forget that what was eating him was that he was in the department long before I was and I took some of his authority away. I know that the chief engineer travelled the province and he used to endeavour to poison the minds of the regional engineers and district engineers.*

Gaglardi says other engineers paid little attention to such criticisms, but McCallum was not entirely alone in his unhappiness with his employment. On February 1, 1956, two other departmental engineers handed in their notices. Doug Willis, the chief paving engineer, and assistant paving engineer Joe Cunliffe had been thinking of starting their own company anyway. They decided to quit to establish Willis and Cunliffe, consulting engineers, in Victoria.

Two days after Willis and Cunliffe, McCallum pulled the plug. It was a memorable day for him, because he had a bad case of the shakes. His disbelieving secretary finished typing up his letter of resignation, handing it to him and shaking her head as she left. Nervously, McCallum read over the letter.

"We have lost several valuable members of the organization who feel it is hopeless to try and carry on, and therefore I have no alternative but to resign from the position of chief engineer, which, under existing conditions, has become untenable for me." The letter asked for his release effective March 31. Officially, his reason for leaving was the reorganization of the department. But the last straw was the Deas Island decision.

McCallum's hand shook as he began scratching his signature at the bottom of the letter, and he garbled it badly. "Sorry, I'll have to ask you to retype this," he told his secretary.

A fourth engineer was unhappy. Lloyd Willis, divisional engineer in Penticton, had hoped for a promotion in the reorganization of the department, but Jones told him he would be demoted to district engineer. Lloyd Willis quit February 9, professing the "highest respect" for McCallum and claiming that "the conditions under which we're expected to work have become untenable." Yet another engineer, J.A. Millikin, quit to go into private business.

By now, the band of dispirited socialists, ill–tempered Liberals and the lone hangdog Tory that formed the opposition was howling. They harassed the government in the legislature for days.

"I don't know what is going on in the Highways Department, but I am sure it is something serious," complained CCFer Arthur Turner. "They (engineers) don't just leave."

Rae Eddie (CCF — New Westminster) said the Deas Island decision was behind the resignations, that it was a "complete reversal of the technical–planning committee recommendation. The tunnel will not do the job it was supposed to do."

Gaglardi denied the tunnel had anything to do with resignations. "There is no rumbling dissension, conflict or walkout in my department," Gaglardi declared. Defending the reorganization, he repeated that it would clear out the "bottleneck" at head office.

By the end of February 1956, with the estimates through the House, the noise was dying down and Gaglardi got on with the job of planning the controversial tunnel. But as the session waned, contents of the government airplane log books were revealed, showing that Gaglardi had taken to the air for a total of 132 hours during 1955, including 41 flights to Kamloops. Asked previously in the legislature whether the department's planes had been used for non–departmental reasons, Gaglardi said they hadn't. But the logs showed relatives and constituents hitched rides at various times. On one Vancouver–to–Kamloops flight, he took with him a pair of Pentecostal ministers visiting from Oregon.

Other ministers were making use of the two planes, but Gaglardi took 134 of the total 305 flights.

It's not inconceivable that, under his tailored Western suit, Gaglardi is covered in feathers. He loves speed, on the ground or in the air but, mostly, the man loves to fly. When he dies, he wants to be flying. Lord, take him home in the cockpit of a fast plane. In retrospect, the airplanes were inevitable. His need always to work, his impatience with specifics, his hyperkinetic fixation with being everywhere at once, dictated a constant battle against time and space. Airplanes were the best that technology could give him to work with and, having been handed access to them, he would always be on a search for better and faster flying machines. He appreciated a good airplane as much as he did a good truck or a bulldozer. When he flew, Phil Gaglardi was a happy man.

> *My saying is that I was born in a hurry and I've been in a hurry ever since. You'll notice that I'm not a tall man; I'm a short man, I never even allowed myself the pleasure of growing up. I went out and started to work long before I grew up and I think I stunted myself. I asked the president of the United States (John F. Kennedy) when I was in Washington, D.C., once making a speech, I said, "Mr. President, I would like to fly in one of those missiles because I would like to fly at 50,000 mph and no RCMP chasing me." I get a feeling that I'm out to get to where I'm going – speed fits with me, speed is that for me. If I'm travelling at the maximum rate that I can travel at, that suits me one hundred percent. Travelling at 41,000 feet just under Mach 1, nothing suited me better than that. I like to see scenery, but I never take any long period of time to absorb anything.*

If you were a constituent, and you needed to go to Vancouver, and Gaglardi heard about it, and he said to you, "I'm flying down and there's room on my plane," you'd appreciate it, and you'd say, "There's a heckuva guy." You probably wouldn't complain if the person sitting next to you was Jennie or Bob or Bill Gaglardi, or a friend of the Gaglardi family. And that's the way it was in Kamloops. "If the airplane was going to Vancouver, he'd take along people he didn't even know, old–age pensioners, if he had a seat available," said Lou Iverson, one of his pilots.

Gaglardi was in Chicago when news stories about his prodigious use of the government airplanes broke, but he jetted back by commercial airliner a few days later. He claimed all his trips involved government business, and the extra passengers had nothing to do with the decisions to fly or the destinations. "I'd like to know when a cabinet minister isn't on business."

He said the planes cost his department only $8,000 to operate in 1955 but, predictably, cries of outrage came from the ever–bilious Art Laing, who called the cost claim "preposterous" and said Gaglardi, his family and friends accounted for sixty percent of the total flying time logged by the government planes in 1955.

By May, Gaglardi was still flying around the province as usual, unencumbered. He had a lot of work to do spending $84 million on roads in a year. Completion of the Vancouver–Revelstoke system, with 150 miles done during the year, was expected. The rebuilt Southern Trans–Provincial Highway, which would eliminate the Cascades as an obstacle, was expected to be finished in three years. Crews were going full steam on the Cache Creek–Prince

George route, with completion expected in two years. And, four years down the road, Prince George to Prince Rupert would be done.

Election speculation grew that spring and summer. On the one hand, W.A.C. Bennett titillated the province by announcing his next election slogan, "Vote for progress, not for politics," and on the other he castigated the press for attempting to create "political instability" with election rumours. The official fourth birthday party of the first Socred election victory came and went in June. Finally, he called an election for September 19, 1956.

This was to be Bob Strachan's first campaign as CCF leader. Strachan had originally come to Canada from Scotland to work on farms and at other labour jobs, gradually working his way west to B.C. In Powell River, he became a carpenter, and was eventually elected B.C. president of the Brotherhood of Carpenters and Joiners of America. He joined the CCF in 1945, gaining a seat in his second try in 1952. Once again leading the Liberals was Art Laing, and the Tories, former fighter pilot Deane Finlayson.

Gaglardi's opponents in Kamloops were union organizer Vic Mauro for the CCF, and rancher Tom Wilson for the Liberals. Nobody expected Gaglardi to be beaten, and it was a relatively quiet campaign until a week before election day. The highways minister was speaking at a Social Credit rally in Nakusp in the Kaslo–Slocan riding when John Wood, a social worker, stood up to question him on the Socreds' $28 homeowner tax–rebate scheme. "I understand the money is to come from the natural resources, which all of the people own. I want to know why I don't get a share," demanded Wood, a renter.

"Why don't you buy a house?" Gaglardi was quoted in newspaper reports as saying.

"I can't afford to buy a house. I work for the government," Wood shot back.

"You're a civil servant."

"Yes."

"You're lucky the Social Credit government is in power. If a Liberal, Conservative or CCF government was in power you would be fired on the spot."

Sandy Harris, a Silverton resident, was surprised at Gaglardi's remark. "Are you inferring you will fire Mr. Wood?" he asked Gaglardi.

"Absolutely not. If anybody feels I inferred that, I apologize. I wouldn't say anything like that. Social Credit is for freedom of speech for everybody."

But Wood wasn't satisfied. He complained to the New

Denver branch of the B.C. Government Employees Union. Wood also swore out an affidavit and sent copies to his department head and the Civil Services Commission. The affidavit recalled their "jocular" exchange at the meeting, but claimed Gaglardi wanted him transferred and fired.

Gaglardi, once again, had to profess innocence.

"That's another one of the type of tactics that the opposition parties are using in this campaign. This fellow Wood is travelling around all the meetings up in the Kaslo–Slocan area and is trying to break up the meetings with these leading questions," Gaglardi stated.

On September 19, 1956, Phil Gaglardi polled 4,594 votes, compared to only 1,888 for Wilson of the Liberals and 1,058 for Mauro of the CCF.

Gaglardi was the first MLA to be declared elected. Thirty–eight other Socreds were elected or reelected. The CCF elected only ten. There were two Liberals, no Conservatives, and Tom Uphill. Liberal leader Laing and Tory leader Finlayson were both defeated. "Fascism," said Finlayson, "has come home to roost in B.C."

Among the new Socred members was a high school physical–education teacher named Dan Campbell, representing the Island riding of Comox. Campbell and Gaglardi were not destined to get along very well over the next sixteen years they served together, but Gaglardi tells an intriguing story about Campbell. One night after the legislature wrapped up, Gaglardi went to dinner at a favourite restaurant along the waterfront.

This particular time when the House closed, everybody went their different ways, and Dan lived up island somewhere and he used to have a room in one of the motels. After I'd finished dinner I jumped in my car and parked in behind the department, and then I walked around a little, passing the motel that Dan lived in. When I went by I had a feeling that I should go in, and into a certain room, and I couldn't buy it because I just didn't feel that it would be proper to do so. I just kept on going, and then all of a sudden this thing grabbed me again and I don't know whether it was once, twice or three times before I went into the room. I knocked and there was no answer, but the lights were on so I went into the room and there were clothes on the floor, nobody in the bed, so I walked in, went into the bathroom, and here was Danny Campbell laying in the water, passed out, water up to just his nose, that's all; any time he could have slipped under, and he was unconscious, that would have been the end of him. So I grabbed the plug and pulled it out. I grabbed a big towel and I picked him up and laid him on his bed. I had the towel under him, and I wiped him off as good as I could, tossed the bedclothes back and laid him in his bed, and pulled the covers back over him – he was stark naked – and I put the lights out, closed the door and walked home. I don't know as I ever told him.

In that anecdote lies another clue to the personality of Phil Gaglardi. He could, at one level, fearlessly effect radical change and make key decisions no matter what the fallout to himself and others. His words often stung when they should have soothed. And there's no doubt that his ego was far bigger than his physique. Yet he could quietly pull a man from danger without even telling him about it.

Bless This House

No man can serve two masters.
MATTHEW 6.24

*A Christian is a servant and the best way he can serve God and humanity
is in government. I have always devoted myself to God and the people.*
PHIL GAGLARDI

The house of the Lord just never seemed to be big enough, so it
kept getting additions. As the congregation of Calvary Temple
grew, the Lord kept providing. Church members gave of their
time and their labour, and somehow the lumber, the nails, the
wiring, materialized. Seven times in six years Calvary Temple
became too small for the ever-expanding flock. Seven times it was
enlarged. It was now a truly worthy temple of God. Outside, the
"modern" squareness of the additions was a rather sharp and ugly
contrast to the gentle, quaint lines of the original heritage
building. But there was, within, an auditorium with a thirty-foot
ceiling. A new wing, with blood-red, wall-to-wall carpeting,
included pews that could seat 850. The platform held a baby
grand piano and electric organ. And there was a theatre-size
lobby for after-meeting gatherings, and a knotty-pine panelled
basement that could hold as many as needed for Sunday school.
Reverend P.A. Gaglardi's study was furnished with a mahogany
desk, cement-topped coffee table, grain-edged cedar and
mahogany panelling and a public address system. There were
study rooms, a kitchen, prayer room, baptismal pool, radio
broadcasting room (he still broadcast his programs over CFJC
radio, but now he had to tape them), nurseries for infants of
church-going mothers.

The latest addition was worth $150,000, but the actual dollar
expenditure was considerably less. The Lord provided labour and
free or wholesale-cost materials. ("I never ask for a nickel, but the
money seems to come in somehow.") The entire building was now

worth $300,000, and Reverend Gaglardi planned a big celebration January 4 and 5, 1958, to mark the official opening.

It started on a Saturday afternoon with the arrival of guest speaker Robert G. LeTourneau of Longview, Texas, a man after Reverend Gaglardi's own heart. Phil had met LeTourneau during visits to Texas looking at heavy equipment, and they were good friends. LeTourneau made his fortune in the manufacture of earth-moving equipment characterized by simplicity of mechanism and low maintenance. He was a devoutly religious man. LeTourneau was fascinated by the B.C. highways minister, at one point offering him a six-figure salary to take over as manager of the Texas operation. Gaglardi briefly considered it and then turned him down, but they remained good friends. The equipment-making evangelist was named the U.S. Man of the Year, and the roadbuilding evangelist wanted him to be special guest at the opening of his expanded Temple. So LeTourneau flew into Kamloops on one of the several private aircraft he used for evangelical trips throughout the continent.

Fifteen minutes later, a chartered Convair arrived from Vancouver with thirty-two guests of honour, including B.C. business and professional men, education minister Les Peterson, and Canadian Chamber of Commerce chairman Ralph Pybus. "Kamloops is for Christ," said Reverend Gaglardi. "Just watch our dust."

The ceremonies began that evening with a barbecue dinner for six hundred guests. LeTourneau spoke on "Religion in Business." Civic leaders were there, and the next day so were Lieutenant-Governor Frank Ross and Premier Bennett. All in all, Kamloops thought it was a fine way to open 1958, the province's centenary.

Among the things that didn't escape the notice of the more cynical members of the opposition in Victoria was the fact that the major contractor, Dominion Bridge, and designers Choukalos, Woodburn, Hooley and McKenzie of Vancouver, both did government work. They noted that Canadian Pacific Airlines had provided the $680-an-hour Convair free of charge. They noted that there were many engineers and contractors in the audience at the opening.

The following week, Strachan raised it in the legislature. "Are these firms making contributions because he was building a church or because he is the minister of highways?" he queried. "If they are donating low-cost materials for the building of a new church, then are they willing to make similar allowance for other similar projects?"

Cranbrook CCFer Leo Nimsick, in a budget-debate speech

February 17, suddenly departed from anything to do with the budget and stated from his prepared notes, "Regarding reports of the opening of the minister of highways' church at Kamloops, one would assume it was a government institution, by all the dignitaries who were present."

Speaker Hugh Shantz immediately banged his gavel. "You're out of order! That has nothing to do with the deliberations here!"

And, of course, it didn't, but members were used to employing the budget speech to get anything they wanted off their chests. Nimsick angrily refused to yield, and the day's proceedings degenerated into shouting matches between government and opposition members.

"The boast of the minister of highways that fifty percent of the cost of the church was donated, partly by the supply of goods wholesale, is rather intriguing as I have noticed so many groups trying to build modest churches in comparison and they are unable to get such concessions," said Nimsick.

Gaglardi didn't get a chance to answer Nimsick that day, but he did when his own turn came during the budget debate. And when he did, Bennett was moved to tears. As Gaglardi spoke, Bennett turned his back on the opposition, facing the highways minister in the row of cabinet desks behind him. The premier's face contorted slightly with emotion, and the tears brimmed.

"In all my years of public life I've never heard anything as dreadful or despicable. I label it a tragedy," intoned Gaglardi. Those who attended the opening of his church should be thanked, instead of having their motives questioned, he said. "God bless these men, we need more like them."

He wasn't interested in the motives of the contractors who contributed to building his temple, as long as they did it. Phil Gaglardi was two different people: one was a highways minister and the other was a pastor. If people helped him out as pastor by helping out his church, he said, they could expect nothing in return from Phil Gaglardi the cabinet minister.

Gaglardi says he had no dealings with contractors working on the church.

> *My brother Tony was the superintendent. I made it my business to stay away from the job. Whatever was donated to Calvary Temple was not anything that I was connected with nor knew about. I have absolutely no knowledge of that. If I were to stand on a stack of Bibles fifty feet high I know of absolutely no donation that was ever made to Calvary Temple by a contractor. The first collection that was taken in Calvary Temple as a church was during that opening function*

*and that collection was $1,700, and the place was jammed, and
I stated – even though Calvary Temple was in debt at that time
around $90,000 – that every dollar of that would be used for
missionary purposes. Because of me being the minister of highways
there were people there from everywhere, all kinds of contractors.*

Gaglardi says the $90,000 debt was rung up through a line of
credit he personally signed for at the bank. It was eventually paid
off by the church. "I did not own one nail in the church and
received absolutely nothing for my being pastor."

The day after his spirited defence in the House, the legislature
got down to the boring job of voting on departmental expenditures
to carry them through for another year. Gaglardi settled into his
chair, closed his eyes and took a nap. The controversy, though, had
reprised the issue of mixing politics with religion.

The combative Nimsick had nothing against Gaglardi
personally, but he felt Gaglardi had a conflict of interest between
church and politics, and that it was one of his biggest problems.
"He'd barge in where angels fear to tread, and he'd get caught up
on it every time, because there was always somebody willing to
squeal. He was a pushy guy. He'd do things without authority,
he'd take on things on his own, and this got him into trouble. He'd
shoot from the hip all the time, but being a fundamentalist, to many
of his followers it didn't matter what he did, he could do no wrong."

Concern about Gaglardi's ministerial role extended into his
own party. Dan Campbell thought it was a conflict, as well. "I've
never been a believer in mixing religion and politics. Gaglardi and
I never did get off on the right foot on that score."

Those kinds of comments amaze Gaglardi. "There was
absolutely no possibility of conflict of interest as far as me and my
ministry as a minister of the Gospel, and if it ever came to it,
which it never did, there was never any challenge on that score –
I would have stepped out of the ministry of highways more
quickly than I ever would out of the ministry of the Gospel. At no
time did W.A.C. ever come to me and even as much as suggest
there was anything I was doing that could be misconstrued."

With 1958 the one–hundredth anniversary of B.C.
becoming a British colony, the province was in an upbeat
mood. The rest of the world was embroiled in the Cold War as
U.S. President Dwight Eisenhower and upstart Soviet Premier
Nikita Khrushchev traded threats and competed in the space
race. Russia was busy handling rebellious Poland and Hungary,
while the Americans and British were threatening to send troops
into Lebanon to quell a Moslem–Christian war, and Dominican

President Hector Trujillo was giving Washington a headache with talk about Central American independence. In Ottawa, Prime Minister John Diefenbaker's Tory government was battling a recession with a peacetime–record $648–million federal deficit.

Such problems seemed mundane to British Columbians as they approached spring breakup with plans for province–wide celebrations, special community projects, Centennial caravans, treasure hunts, beard–growing contests and, above all, a boom in tourism. But the latter was to be dealt a dangerous blow from an unexpected quarter.

Ferry service between the mainland and Vancouver Island was provided by the Canadian Pacific Steamship Service and Black Ball Ferries Ltd. Their unions, the Seafarers International Union, Canadian Merchant Services Guild and National Association of Marine Engineers, muttered dire mutinous warnings while the stubborn ferry owners told them where to cast off. In mid–May, the frustrated sea dogs of the SIA struck the CPSS, wiping out service between Vancouver and Victoria and leaving the Black Ball run from Vancouver to Nanaimo as the only ferry link. A few days later, seventy–two–hour strike notice was given to Black Ball by the Merchant Services Guild and Marine Engineers.

The economic implications of a total blockade were unpleasant. The provincial government couldn't touch the Canadian Pacific fleet because it was under federal labour jurisdiction so, in full consultation with the unions and management, Bennett and his cabinet invoked the Civil Defence Act, taking control of Black Ball and preventing a shutdown. It was a dramatic move, but it worked temporarily.

A few weeks later, Black Ball workers defied the Civil Defence Act and struck. A court injunction forced them back to work and back to the bargaining table.

The dispute turned Bennett's attention to the importance of the ferries in the province's transportation system. He had been working on the idea of a government ferry service for almost a year, and now seemed a propitious time to make a move. The ferries were, basically, an extension of the highways, a sort of conduit for cars between the island and mainland. Bennett became convinced that the quality of ferry service should not be at the discretion of unions or of private–enterprise employers. Bennett put Phil Gaglardi in charge of planning for a government–run ferry system. Gaglardi, in turn, hired Seattle naval architect Phil Spaulding as a consultant. Spaulding was a key advisor to the highways minister in working on creation of a new ferry system.

Gaglardi, however, was to be tied up for most of what was left of 1958 with another problem, one that shook him to the bone both politically and personally.

On Tuesday afternoon, June 17, 1958, work on the new Second Narrows Bridge in Vancouver was progressing smoothly. The project, predictably, had been born out of controversy, with Gaglardi making the decision to replace the old Second Narrows span instead of twinning the Lions Gate suspension bridge. Lions Gate could be twinned later if more capacity were needed there, he said. "If that's not enough we can fill in Burrard Inlet."

The decision was based on a recommendation from Col. W.G. Swan of Vancouver, whose engineering firm estimated that a six-lane cantilever bridge and approaches could be built at Second Narrows for $3 million less than it would cost to twin the Lions Gate, would do more to relieve traffic congestion, and would add only seven minutes' travel time between the North Shore and downtown Vancouver. By midway of 1958, with the bridge well under construction, estimated completion cost had risen to $27 million.

Delayed for several weeks by a misshipment of steel, it was once again moving toward the South Shore. Far out in Burrard Inlet, a two-thousand-ton section of the bridge dangled from a temporary support toward a second false pier. Within twenty-four hours, it would reach that second support.

The falsework had been constructed by driving wood pilings into the bottom of the inlet. Short steel beams were laid across the pilings, then longer I-beams on top of those. Two cross-braced vertical struts rose from there to the span.

The bridge was crawling with workmen: painters, engineers, steelworkers. Steel was hauled out onto the bridge by a train, and unloaded at the end of the span by a huge crane that lifted the girders into place. A girder was just about ready to be moved into place when there was what one worker later described as a "muffled thump."

The sound was heard by hundreds of people on and near the bridge, and the scene that followed was viewed from as many angles. Each was as terrifying as the other. One witness described the sound as that of giant, shunting railway cars. Another as a "loud click," another "a bang."

The two temporary legs of the outermost section of the bridge buckled inward. Then the end span tumbled toward the water. As it did, a dozen or so men went with it, along with the big crane and locomotive. All of it hit the water with a huge splash and the roar of an avalanche.

As the first section was falling, it tipped the outermost concrete piles forward. The second section headed into the drink. When the structure hit the water, a huge geyser-like cloud of smoke and mist bellowed into the air. And, after the terrifying noise of the collapse . . . silence.

The minister was in a cabinet meeting and couldn't be disturbed, Edith Scarff told Vancouver radio reporter Roy Jacques, who was on the phone. This was one call Mr. Gaglardi would want to take, the reporter suggested. His bridge had fallen down.

The secretary tried to get the call through to Gaglardi. As it happened, he was just walking into the cabinet meeting. Reporters met him at the door, and gave him the news.

"The Second Narrows. It's collapsed. Do you have any comment?"

"I said, 'Oh, yeah, and another elephant flew by.' "

But it was true. Gaglardi informed Bennett, who told him to get over there quickly, and to report back to him. Scarff had arranged for the pilot, and the Widgeon float plane was waiting, engines revved. It took only a few minutes to fly across the strait, but they were anxious moments. No details had been known by the reporters and not much more by his own department. Only that the span had collapsed and that there were undoubtedly fatalities.

When Gaglardi got there, he ordered his pilot to take a sweep over the scene before landing on the water. From the air the crippled span looked like a toothpick toy knocked over by carelessness. Yet the extent of the disaster was only too evident. The steel girders, bent and twisted, drooped into the inlet. The crane stretched out from the wreckage. In the water, dozens of boats darted about searching for the dead or drowning, while rescuers were busy in the tangled mess of steel. On the temporary wooden dock beside the new structure, blanket-covered bodies could be seen, side by side.

The Widgeon landed on the water and those inside began helping as best they could. Gaglardi hurried to the dock. Bodies were still being recovered from the ruins, and he stared in horror at the deck of the tug *Davis Straits*, stained red with the blood of the five men fished from the water. Divers brought up another body. It had no head.

W.G. Swan and his partner Anthony Wooster were both on the scene. Swan estimated damage from the collapse at $2 million, with cleanup costing another $1 million. It would probably take six months.

Gaglardi went directly from the dock to North Vancouver General Hospital, then Vancouver General. He visited every

injured workman who was able to see him. One of them was
George Schmidt, a young steelworker who had lost his leg.
Schmidt was awake and cheerful, talking about how lucky he was.
He pulled down the sheet and showed Gaglardi where his leg had
been torn off. His attitude helped cheer the highways minister
enough to get him through the rest of the night. Next morning
Gaglardi called the families of the dead workers and offered to help
in any way he could.

Eighteen men died in the collapse of the new Second
Narrows Bridge. Some drowned, most died from multiple
injuries. Twenty others were injured. A diver lost his life when he
was swept into the wreckage while searching for bodies.
Suspicions about the cause of the tragedy surfaced immediately.
Strachan called for an investigation not only of the collapse, but
of the entire Highways Department and all of its bridge projects.
"Only a full–scale investigation of this department can give the
people of British Columbia the necessary assurance that the
present department is organized efficiently," he claimed.
Referring to the Neil McCallum controversy two years earlier,
Strachan said Gaglardi had been the cause of the resignations of
several top Highways Department engineers, and that major
changes were needed.

It was a shameless political ploy, and Gaglardi told him to "put
up or shut up . . . Why should I resign? I've got nothing to run from.
All I am is a bystander." Strachan's inferences anger Gaglardi even
today. "I couldn't believe that a politician of any kind could have the
nerve or the viciousness of being able to state what Strachan stated
on that occasion, me being charged where I had interfered with the
engineers to the degree where I weakened the span and this was the
result of it. I was absolutely dumbfounded."

But the *Vancouver Sun* joined the call to make Gaglardi the
goat. Said the *Sun* in a front–page editorial: "Highways Minister P.A.
Gaglardi has said that the whole Second Narrows Bridge will be
'thoroughly checked' to make sure it is safe after the collapse of the
outer sections. By the same logic, all other engineering works carried
out under his regime should be examined for the same reason.

"Too many good men have resigned from the government's
engineering staff. Too much talk has been attributed to the
flamboyant highways minister about 'the triumph of imagination
over the cold, hard facts of engineering.' In all the rush and
bustle and the flying from place to place, some things may have
been forgotten or gone astray."

Still in Vancouver, Gaglardi was stung by the *Sun* commentary.

"As soon as I saw that paper, I went to the telephone and I phoned the premier and I read the editorial to him and I said, 'I want to have an investigation immediately, right now.' I don't even think I needed a telephone for him to hear me. There isn't a word in the English language that could express the feeling to read an editorial on the front page that you were to blame for all those deaths. It just about drove me to the wall. God bless me, can you imagine phoning up a wife and saying to her, 'I'm sorry about your husband,' and here's the front page of a newspaper saying you're responsible?"

Bennett had already decided on a royal commission, and Attorney General Bonner agreed.

Gaglardi returned to the scene of the disaster the next night. "I walked out there on that deck at six o'clock and I cried for an hour. I felt so absolutely terrible, not because I was to blame for anything, but because I was responsible, it was my department, and, God bless me, you just don't expect things like that. If I wasn't made of steel plus more steel, I'd have jumped off that bridge, I'd go crazy. I feel like breaking down even now, just thinking about it."

Chief Justice Sherwood Lett was named as a one-man inquiry commission, and he immediately started his investigation. He hired engineering advisers, secretaries and lawyers to look at the disaster from every possible angle. John Farris, QC, was appointed to act as chief counsel for the commission.

Lett was given the widest possible leeway in his investigation. The cabinet approved an order in council setting his powers "to inquire into any and all circumstances surrounding, leading to or having any casual connection with the collapse."

Farris asked Gaglardi to open his file of correspondence on the bridge, and the highways minister did so, ordering his staff to give Farris total cooperation.

With the tragedy of the Second Narrows collapse fresh in mind, Gaglardi nevertheless prepared for the culmination of another important bridge project. Travelling north from Penticton, Highway 97 wandered along the western edge of Okanagan Lake, where it abruptly ended on the lakeshore at Westbank, starting up again on the opposite side. Through the years, a small fleet of ferries chugged back and forth between Westbank and Kelowna, carrying up to a couple of dozen cars each. Way down in Victoria, those ferries seemed quite adequate, and the idea of building a bridge across the lake a bit strange. But people in the Interior saw the need and logic for an Okanagan Lake bridge connecting two halves of a growing and attractive area. Premier Bennett, of course, had a personal

With Princess Margaret at official opening of the Okanagan Lake floating bridge, 1958.

interest in getting a bridge built to his home town, and encouraged Gaglardi to get it done.

The job was done by constructing a lengthy fill approach from Westbank, and stringing floating sections between it and a liftspan on the Kelowna side. The official opening was set for July 9, 1958, and Princess Margaret, after whom Bennett named the bridge (rejecting a proposal to name it after himself), was there for the ceremony. With Gaglardi standing proudly at her right side, she snipped a ribbon to open the innovative new span to traffic.

Meanwhile, the Second Narrows inquiry ground on through the summer and fall. As witness after witness came before Lett, the cause of the tragedy of the Second Narrows unfolded. Excess weight had not been a factor, but weight had. The girder hauled out for placement, plus the crane, locomotive and two train cars totalled about 230 tons, normally not enough to cause problems. While there was a slight wind, that shouldn't have been a problem, either. The trouble was with the temporary support holding up the half-finished outer span. It couldn't handle the weight. Stringers had buckled, and the I–beam verticals had caved inward, causing the outer section of the span to fall. As the outer section fell, it caused a break in the cement pier that had been supporting it at the other end. As that pier tipped, the end of the second section dropped to the inlet.

It was not a construction error. The problem was traced to the drafting boards of the design engineers of Dominion Bridge Company. A small but fatal miscalculation had been made and missed in the many re-checks. Engineers John Bertram McKibbon and Murray McDonald had made and checked the fatal calculations. Both men died in the collapse.

The official report was released November 27. It showed beyond doubt that the collapse of the new Second Narrows Bridge had absolutely nothing to do with Gaglardi or the B.C. Department of Highways. Although the investigation absolved him, Gaglardi didn't believe the report. Workers had told him quite a different story. They said that with the delay caused by the steel shortage, somebody forgot to be sure temporary bracing tied together the I-beams resting on the piers. After work resumed, and the train was moving a beam into position, the crane's cable slipped on the drum. That caused a sudden jolt, enough to flip the I-beams and cause the collapse.

Whatever Lett's report had concluded, it would have been of little consolation to the families of the victims, nor to the highways minister who had seen and felt the catastrophe, and who had lived under a shadow of blame for more than five months. "There isn't any subject you could hit me with that hurts me more than that particular deal, and I'll never get over it, for someone that's as sensitive as I am about the feelings of other people. My God, man, it was devastating. It was something that I live with still to this day. You don't get over things like that."

Strait Talk

Make thee an ark.
GENESIS 6.14

Nothing to it.
PHIL GAGLARDI

For all the unwanted hassles dished out by fate to the Social Credit government during B.C.'s centennial, 1958 ended with a major political victory putting to rest a dark scandal that had hung over the W.A.C. Bennett regime for years. As well, the development of the new government–operated ferry system was about to accelerate in earnest, and it would become famous as the most comprehensive and efficient in the world. The next several months would see the completion of more major highways projects, and the province would be officially declared debt–free. In varying degrees, Phil Gaglardi played a role in all of it.

The scandal harkened back to the controversy over forest-management licences that had seemingly concluded with the 1955 Lillooet by–election and the defeat of Gordon Gibson. But it hadn't ended there, and kept bobbing to the surface like an obnoxious cork until another by–election in December 1958, this time to pick a successor to the disgraced Bob Sommers.

A few days after the vote in Lillooet, the bookkeeper for a company owned by Sommers' friend H. Wilson "Wick" Gray made an appointment with Vancouver lawyer David Sturdy. The bookkeeper was Charles W. Eversfield, who had worked for Pacific Coast Services Ltd. He showed Sturdy documents he'd copied while on the job. With a sworn deposition and 198 documents in hand, Sturdy and Eversfield met Attorney General Robert Bonner to demand a royal commission investigation into possible criminal conspiracy or activity in the forest industry. Bonner called the claims "far–fetched."

That set off a long and acrimonious battle in the courts and in the legislature, with the focus on Sommers and the question of whether or not he had used, or had tried to use, or had at least promised to use, his influence in cabinet to gain forest-management licences for the clients of Wick Gray. Sommers had received a lot of money from Gray, whom he'd known since before his election. Sommers and Gray maintained throughout that they were loans — not bribes — from one friend to another. On the other hand, Liberal MLA George Gregory insisted that loans were as bad as gifts if the purpose was corrupt. Gregory became Sturdy's lawyer when Sommers sued Sturdy — who was given $5,000 by Gordon Gibson to finance his investigation — for slander and libel Bonner said the lawsuit prevented him from discussing or taking criminal action against Sommers.

During the 1956 session, Bonner asked Gregory to turn over all his evidence to the RCMP, which he did. That started a five-month probe, but the opposition kept up a concerted attack on Sommers and Premier Bennett. On February 27, 1956, Sommers denied taking any bribes, but resigned his portfolio on instructions from Bennett, though he kept his seat. That didn't stop the opposition, either. Bennett expected the next attack to come during debate on vote 230, the salary of the minister of lands and forests, who was now Ray Williston. It was scheduled for an evening sitting, so Bennett stalled for several hours, calling for second reading of a mass of minor bills. At 1 a.m., with the public galleries, which had been packed when the sitting opened at 8:30, now almost emptied except for a clutch of groggy reporters, Bennett called for vote 230.

Gregory now attempted to bare details of the Sturdy charges to the House, but was refused permission, and there followed accusation after accusation by the Liberals and CCF as the Socreds maintained a stony silence. As the night sitting ground on, Gaglardi and Wicks napped in their chairs. At 3 a.m., all hell broke loose.

Gregory announced he had photocopies of tickets, itineraries and hotel bills suggesting that in October, 1953, Pacific Coast Services Ltd. had paid for a trip to eastern Canada for Gray, his partner Charles D. Schultz, and Sommers and his family.

For several more hours the bitter fight continued, with the opposition demanding that Sommers answer to conspiracy charges in the legislature. At 7:35 a.m., Saanich MLA John Tisdalle moved to block further debate. After eleven hours and five minutes, the sitting ended, breaking a record set eighty-one years before in 1875.

With the summer court dockets full, Sommers' suit against Sturdy was put off until November. The provincial election was called for September, and the Sommers case was a dominant issue. The RCMP investigation was completed, but Bonner did not release the report. Bennett said Sommers faced the "highest court in the land," the people. On September 19 the people acquitted him by returning the Socreds with their huge majority, and re-electing "Honest Bob" in Rossland-Trail.

But there was much more to come. The legal wrangling dragged on for another year until, in a bizarre turn, Sommers twice failed to appear for a pre-trial hearing into his lawsuit, which was dismissed October 28, 1957. It turned out Sommers had fled to California. Low on money, he drove up to Seattle and phoned Waldo Skillings in Victoria, telling him he needed help. Skillings, who later became a Socred MLA and cabinet minister, raised a quick stake from a man identified only as a prominent member of the Vancouver business community who wanted to help Social Credit by keeping Sommers out of the country. Skillings met with Sommers in a Seattle motel with an offer of $5,000 a year for five years if the former forests minister would stay in the U.S. Sommers hesitated. First it seemed he would accept the offer, but then he changed his mind and returned to B.C. after a few weeks of exile.

The government appointed Chief Justice Gordon Sloan as a one-man commission to investigate the whole affair. Sommers admitted publicly that he had received loans of several thousand dollars from Wick Gray, but the Sloan Commission adjourned under a challenge on behalf of Charles Schultz that the government had no right to set up such a commission to investigate criminal charges.

There was no alternative but for Attorney General Bonner to take Sommers to court. On November 21, 1957, Sommers was arrested at his Victoria home; Wick Gray and Charles Schultz were arrested the same day. The charges centred around gifts, as well as cash, money orders and bonds allegedly handed over to Sommers as loans to influence the issuing of forest-management licences on Vancouver Island. Specifically, B.C. Forest Products had supposedly put up money to "bucket-shop" lobby companies owned by Gray and his friends to influence Sommers.

Twelve bribery charges and one conspiracy charge were laid against the former minister. Five bribery charges were later thrown out of court. "Not guilty" verdicts were also ordered on two charges of bribery against Wick Gray and Pacific Coast Services Ltd., and one against B.C. Forest Products. In the end, there were sixty-six verdicts left to be delivered against all of those charged: Sommers, Gray, Pacific Coast Services, B.C. Forest Products, Gray's brother John, Gray's company Evergreen Lumber Sales Ltd., Charles Schultz, and C.D. Schultz and Co. Ltd.

During the 1958 legislative session, with the trial still waiting to get to court, forest-management licences became tree farm licences, and Sloan was hired to advise on applications.

The trial started May 1, 1958. Sommers' lawyer was the renowned Angelo Branca, retained by unknown benefactors. Branca himself didn't know who was paying his bills, but it wasn't the cash-poor Sommers.

Among the most damning evidence against the defendants was the trip to Toronto, during which Sommers and Wick Gray met with E.P. Taylor and Hector Munro of B.C. Forest Products. More than a thousand exhibits, a million words of testimony and eighty-two days in the courtroom were required to bring the case to conclusion. The jury retired October 30 and, after fifty-two and a half hours, came back with a verdict of guilty of conspiracy on Sommers. On November 5 he was found guilty on five of seven counts of bribery, involving receipt of $7,107 in cash, bonds and a rug. On November 14, he was sentenced to five years in prison. Gray also got five years, and his two companies were fined $19,250. B.C. Forest Products was found not guilty. Schultz and John Gray also went free.

It was a stunning decision. Defence and prosecution lawyers alike had believed the case against Sommers and the other defendants was marginal, and that any guilty verdict would bring a light penalty. Bennett predicted, "History will show that Sommers was an honest man — stupid and foolish perhaps, but honest." Sommers told the author in an interview for this book, "Common sense says that between the receiver and giver there has to be a link; in law there doesn't have to be . . . Nobody received a favour from me."

Gaglardi is one of those doubtful that Sommers was guilty of anything. Putting it bluntly, he says, "Bob Sommers was framed."

"Sommers was the last man in the world I wanted to go to jail," Gibson told the author. "Sommers was quite a nice man. Every cabinet minister at the time was knowledgeable of what was going on. If you all hold up the bank together you're really equally guilty. Sommers was just a scapegoat."

Sommers resigned his seat and appealed. So did the Crown. The Rossland-Trail by-election was set for December 15, 1958. There were rumours Sommers might get involved in the by-election in his old riding, against the government he felt had let him down. According to Sommers, Gaglardi phoned him to ask him not to betray the party. Sommers told Gaglardi he had no intention of betraying the party. Gaglardi wished him luck, promised to pray for him, and said, "See you again." Sommers never saw Gaglardi again.

There was another annoyance in store for the government. The economy had stalled, but Bennett pushed forward with his plan to get rid of the province's debt. In six years of power, he reduced the debt from $222 million to $95 million. He planned to pay off another $12 million by the end of 1958. The opposition was complaining that he was paying off debt at the cost of social services, but another critic suddenly appeared from an unexpected corner.

The same month Sommers was being sentenced to jail, H. Lee Briggs, the quiet, respected general manager of the B.C. Power Commission, accused Bennett of juggling books to give a phoney impression of debt cutting. Bennett, according to Briggs, wanted immediate payment of a $32-million bond issue with a loan to enable the government to accomplish its debt-free goal. The commission would have to reissue higher-interest-rate bonds, resulting in consumer-rate increases. Not surprisingly, Bennett fired him, then called a royal commission chaired by Dr. Gordon Shrum of the University of B.C. to study Briggs' charges. But Briggs, who proclaimed himself not politically motivated, dogged the Socreds into the Rossland-Trail by-election.

So it was against all of this background — a four-year scandal, the disgrace of a cabinet minister, the tragedy of Second Narrows and the defection of a respected civil servant — that the government prepared to fight a bellwether by-election.

Briggs took out a two-column ad in the *Trail Times* calling for a united front by Liberals, Conservatives and CCF to defeat the Socreds in the December 15 vote. He was ignored. The Liberals nominated Dr. H.E. Krause, a well-known local doctor, while the Tories went with former alderman Norman Brokenshire and the CCF with F.E. "Buddy" DeVito. Attempting to hold the riding for Social Credit was Donald Brothers, an uncharismatic local lawyer and Sommers' former campaign manager.

The Briggs controversy was of little concern to the constituents of Rossland-Trail. With Cominco's metallurgical and chemical plant in Trail as the centrepiece of its economy, the riding was wealthy. It had the money; it wanted more amenities. Gaglardi was first into the riding to speak for Brothers, and he spent much of the campaign there. The Socreds also went heavily into television and radio advertising to boost Brothers' fortunes. It looked like they would need considerable boosting. A lot of resentment had built up against Social Credit not only for Sommers' indiscretions, but over frustrations in getting what the riding felt it had coming. Though Sommers stayed away, the ugly spectre of his dishonour bided the campaign. The opposition parties saw it as a chance to dent the Socred armour, and Bob Strachan, Art Laing and Deane Finlayson (the latter two still clinging to their party leaderships two years after personal defeat at the polls) went into full tilt. They and their candidates wrestled uncomfortably with the Sommers dirt, not wanting to stir resentment against themselves for bringing it up, but not wanting the voters to forget it, either. Finlayson of the Tories briefly brought it out into the open. "Should a government that has failed to uphold the noblest, cherished traditions of government integrity be rewarded by the voters?" he asked in a radio broadcast.

But Gaglardi was going his hardest to sell the riding on the record of the government. He had to work hard, because he and Brothers were getting a rough ride. Even Gaglardi showed signs of weariness and impatience toward the end of a campaign marked by constant heckling. But he drew crowds. At a meeting attended by two hundred people in Trail's Colombo Hall, Gaglardi promised the city a new Columbia River Bridge by 1960.

The *Victoria Times* predicted the outcome: "Simple arithmetic is all on the side of the Social Credit candidate — the arithmetic of the government's huge campaign funds and, more important, the arithmetic of an opposition split three ways."

It was close. Brothers won, with 3,170 votes, followed by the CCF's DeVito with 2,807, Liberal Krause with 2,365 and Tory Brokenshire with 2,200. Sommers, noting the promises that had been heaped upon his riding to get Brothers elected, commented that his conviction was "the best thing that ever happened" to Rossland–Trail. "To think that for three years I was beating my gums for these things and never dreamed the way to get them was to go to jail."

Sommers' and the Crown's appeals of his sentence both failed. The following spring, he went to jail, the first minister of the Crown in the British Commonwealth to do so. He was paroled in 1961.

The labour strife that had hit the B.C. ferry system in 1958 continued in a broader way the following year. This time, the government battled labour to a draw. Although Bennett did not consider his government anti–labour, and could point to the atmosphere in B.C. that made it the most highly organized, labour–militant province in Canada as proof, there was increasing disagreement between the Socred cabinet and the union bosses. Bennett had brought in new labour laws in 1954, increasing the authority of the labour minister, but the influence of unions continued to grow, and the premier wanted new controls on labour–management confrontations. With a slump in the economy, and a rise in unemployment, Bennett tightened the string, cutting government spending and staff. The dip in the economic fortunes of the province coincided with a profusion of labour shutdowns in building trades, fishing and forest industries. In the 1959 session, Bennett introduced Bill 43, which would create a new Trade Union Act. The bill eliminated sympathy and information pickets, and pickets by raiding unions. Provision was made for union and management organizations to sue each other over violations of the act. The bill was supposed to make labour and management equally responsible for their actions, to avoid illegal lockouts by management without proper bargaining proceedings, and to restrict wild-cat walkouts by labour. The Canadian Labour Congress and the International Woodworkers of America condemned the new legislation as "restrictive" and "close to Fascism." The B.C. Federation of Labour, now officially aligned with the CCF, claimed it muzzled unions by making injunctions easier to obtain.

Gaglardi's own view of labour unions was that they had done a lot of good, but that they were capable of doing a great deal of harm. He was thoroughly opposed to the concept of closed shops, his opinion being that a worker should have the individual choice of whether or not to belong to a union. His job shouldn't be threatened if he didn't want to join. Unions, he believed, were religious in origin in that their objective was to improve people's condition. When they lost their sense of democracy — and closed shops were not, in his opinion, democratic — there was trouble.

Gaglardi was given the job, instead of Labour Minister Lyle Wicks, of publicly stating the government's concerns about big labour. On February 3, 1959, he made a speech in the House that touched on highways (a ten–year, billion–dollar program), the CCF's performance and other things, but his main job was to praise the spirit of Bill 43. The previous day, labour had staged a mass march on the legislative buildings, and a delegation had been received by cabinet. The public gallery was packed to await Gaglardi's turn to speak. The highways minister did nothing to soothe the troubled waters. Instead, he delivered a stinging broadside.

"Labour leaders, men with political ambitions, are using labour as a political football," he proclaimed. "We don't need gangsterism in labour. We don't want any Hoffas in this province!" Social Credit was not to blame. The blame for labour unrest should be laid on unscrupulous leaders who were "agitators" and who didn't give workers a fair shake.

Though debate continued after Gaglardi had spoken, the public galleries quickly emptied. "I wouldn't have missed him for anything. He's better than the movies," an elderly woman was heard to say as she made her way down the stairs with the aid of a cane. Others weren't so pleased with the performance. B.C. Federation of Labour secretary Pat O'Neal, for example, was enraged by the Hoffa remark.

"If Mr. Gaglardi has any specific evidence of dishonesty or crime in the B.C. labour movement, he should take it up with his colleague, the attorney general."

Public Works Minister William Chant joined Gaglardi in blasting the unions, saying gangsters were involving themselves in unions these days instead of in gambling and bootlegging. "We are now witnessing perhaps in greater measure than ever before the misuse of power which labour leaders have acquired."

Even some of their own party members couldn't support Chant and Gaglardi on this one. Comox member Dan Campbell called their remarks "improper."

The debate was renewed from time to time during the year, without being resolved, and the charges and insults became repetitive. The government had prevailed against one of its staunchest rivals.

Gaglardi spent most of May in Europe, travelling with forty-nine Vancouver Board of Trade members on a twenty-four-day trade junket. The delegation's airplane touched down at Vancouver International Airport at 3 p.m. on Sunday, May 24. Gaglardi made an immediate connection for Kamloops. As his plane circled over Vancouver and headed inland, he could see the Deas Island Tunnel site below. Hundreds of cars were backed up north toward Vancouver — it was one huge traffic jam down there.

The cars had started arriving early in the morning of the previous day, before daybreak. They wanted to be among the first to travel through the new tunnel. At exactly 7 a.m., guards had removed the barricades, and the vehicles started streaming under the lower arm of the Fraser. Since the freeway from Deas Island to the American border was not yet constructed, the tunnel led them instead into Ladner. There was really no place to go except back home. But for two days thousands of British Columbians made the trip without having to pay the fifty-cent toll charge. The official opening wouldn't come until the visit of Queen Elizabeth and Prince Philip in July, but the toll-free weekend was a popular prelude.

Bennett's dream of declaring the province debt-free was at hand that summer. He had wanted to do it in seven years and, with the help of healthy budgetary surpluses and by shifting direct debt to indirect debt through the Pacific Great Eastern Railway, Toll Authority and Power Commission, he claimed to have done it. These agencies now technically incurred their own debts. Some called it creative bookkeeping. Bob Strachan called it "propaganda," his fellow CCFer Gordon Dowding called it "undemocratic and irresponsible government." But in 1959, Bennett said the debt was down to $27 million, and he paid it off. Sinking funds of $96 million now matched the financial obligations of the government, he said, and it was time to party.

He made plans for a big celebration in Kelowna on August 1, at which $70 million in bonds would be burned. It was going to be an event worth writing home about, this giant party on the seventh birthday of his government, and reporters and magazine writers from across the country were invited. It would be sandwiched in a travelling cabinet road show. Such media and public-relations events proved to be popular. One mayor called the junkets "taking government to the people" and Bennett agreed. The format called for the cabinet to breeze into town for a meeting with local council or chamber officials and a dinner or luncheon with the townspeople. Bennett, Gaglardi and the local MLA, assuming he was a Socred, would announce some public works projects for the riding, and it always went over well. Bennett liked to travel in his special Pacific Great Eastern railcar, the *Northern Summit*, and this time he took sons Bill and R.J. with him.

After appearances in Kitimat, Dawson Creek and on Vancouver Island, the cabinet was ready for the Kelowna birthday party. Hotels and motels were booked solid. Skies were clear; the thermometer edged toward the ninety-degree mark as the cabinet arrived. Also heading for Kelowna was a Loomis armoured car, escorted by police and bearing the $70 million in bonds from Victoria. All arrived safely.

There was a tea-and-Ovaltine garden party at the premier's house, and an evening parade preceding the stage and water show and bond-burning. Gaglardi, among the local and provincial politicians, evoked the most enthusiasm as the parade passed. At the Aquatic Club, a youth adorned with a Bennett banner easily outswam three others labelled Strachan, Perrault (for Ray Perrault, who had taken over the Liberals from Art Laing), and Finlayson, though he needed a tow with a rope.

Then came the *coup de grace*. That afternoon, the voided bonds had been removed from the bank and trucked down to the lake, where they were loaded on a large log raft anchored near the ferry wharf. At the right minute, it was towed into view in front of Ogopogo Stadium. The bonds had been covered with old car tires, wood shavings and oil. The premier and cabinet boarded a boat and headed toward the raft. Standing beside Bennett were PR man Bill Clancey, Robert Bonner and Phil Gaglardi. At 9:27 p.m., exactly seven years to the day and minute since the first Bennett cabinet had been sworn in, the premier pulled back on a small bow and let fly with a flaming arrow. It bounced off some chicken wire holding down the bonds and fizzled out in the water, but an RCMP member waiting on the raft put a torch to the bonds. They burned admirably well.

"This is the greatest event in the history of British Columbia," Bennett expounded back on shore. "I am too full of emotion to express my feelings. It is the greatest thing that has ever happened since I entered politics and I wish to thank the tens of thousands who came out to help us celebrate."

It was a slight exaggeration, but there were about ten thousand people watching the spectacle, and the party was an unqualified success.

A few days later, H. Lee Briggs was appointed by Prime Minister John Diefenbaker to the National Energy Board. The Shrum Commission was ready with its report on the Briggs affair later that month. It found that Bennett had, indeed, wanted to refinance the power commission's debt in order to keep to his seven–year debt–free schedule, but that there was nothing improper about it. While praising the job Briggs had done in B.C., the report blamed much of his criticism of the government on misunderstanding. Bennett, who had an advance look at the report, publicly blasted Briggs for being a poor manager, but partially recanted when the full contents of the report were revealed.

Phil Gaglardi, busy with a dozen other projects and controversies, had been working all this time on the ferry assignment given him by Bennett as if it were the only thing on his plate. The contracts with the stubborn ferry unions had finally been signed January 30, 1959, but Gaglardi didn't wait for that to get going on the government ferry system. Gaglardi designed the new system, he says, after his own impatience — he wanted as short a trip on the water as possible, just enough time for a cup of coffee or a meal and to look at some scenery. The concept of downtown–to–downtown Vancouver-Victoria service was quickly abandoned because of the length of the trip. Better to drive a little further a lot faster and spend less time on the boats. Gaglardi's engineers started looking around for terminal sites on the island and the mainland and, as usual with anything Gaglardi did, it wasn't accomplished without controversy.

Instead of Sidney, regarded as a likely location for the island terminal, nearby Swartz Bay was chosen, though that site required extending and upgrading the Patricia Bay Highway to a new docking area. It was more sheltered, would shorten the run, and save fuel. The real debate, though, focused on the mainland terminal for the Vancouver–Victoria run. There were four possible sites: Steveston, Tsawwassen, Point Roberts and White Rock. Despite extra cost, Gaglardi and his engineers favoured Tsawwassen. It was the shortest and could shave as much as a half–hour off the time to Swartz Bay.

It took Gaglardi only six weeks to determine a design for the new ferries (based on blueprints of a new Washington ship) and to call the first contract. Eight engineers were hired, and there were soon two ferries being built, one in Victoria and one in Vancouver.

Even the choice of engines for the new ferries ruffled feathers. Lowest tender was submitted by Walken Machinery & Equipment Ltd., which said it could supply German Henschel engines for $721,000. Oredonda Industrial Ltd., a British firm, offered sixteen–cylinder Mirrlees engines for $30,000 more. Gaglardi flew to England for a look, and accepted the Oredonda bid.

The Mirrlees had never been used in ships, and they worried Spaulding, who favoured Cooper Bessmors. But Gaglardi was convinced the Mirrlees would hold up best. "Suppose I bought an engine and saved money on it, but later it broke down. Who'd take it on the chin? Me!"

The likelihood of the mainland terminal being located on the Tsawwassen Indian reserve was alarming the experts, armchair and otherwise. Noting Gaglardi's and the Socred government's total lack of know–how about any mode of transportation that didn't require pavement, they confidently predicted disaster. The Tsawwassen terminal would require construction of a mile–long causeway out to deep water in the Strait of Georgia, then a wharf and parking for about one hundred cars. Gaglardi went ahead with his tests, and Highways Department engineers' soundings found no problem with construction of the causeway, though the cost might reach $3 million or even $4 million, not the $2 million originally speculated. Critics of Tsawwassen, including the Nanaimo and White Rock boards of trade, claimed it would cost at least $5 million. Furthermore, they said, it was unsafe. Gaglardi asked for another, less scientific test. "I asked Fraser McLean to poll a bunch of sea captains. He polled twenty captains; ten of them said no and ten said yes. I decided that ten positives were stronger than ten negatives."

The controversy continued late into 1959, but Gaglardi got his way. "My men, in their wisdom, have looked at this situation from A to Z and I'll stand by it." He finally released the reports of his engineers, which showed that Tsawwassen was the best site from a traffic point of view despite the higher costs. An annual operating saving of $300,000 would be realized because of the shorter haul. While the dock and breakwater were difficult and expensive to construct, they would relieve safety fears.

The prospect of a government ferry service wasn't making Black Ball and Canadian Pacific very happy. "Black Ball and CP came to a cabinet meeting and demanded that I be stopped," says Gaglardi. "They said it was stupid, that I'd break the province. After they left, W.A.C. asked me if I was sure the thing would work. I said I was. He said, 'Phil, build the ferries.'"

Gaglardi was confident right from the start that the two new ferries and new terminals wouldn't be nearly enough. He was already thinking about two more ferries, and there would be many more after that, because his ferry system would be the most popular ferry system in the world. Vancouver Island would become a mecca for tourists from the United States and other parts of Canada. Indeed, the launchings of the $3-million *MV Sidney* in October 1959 and the *MV Tsawwassen* (the names were changed to *Queen of Sidney* and *Queen of Tsawwassen* when Bennett got the idea of upstaging the Canadian Pacific's *Princess* fleet) in November that year, though they didn't yet have permanent docking facilities, were only the beginning of the system now called the B.C. Ferry Authority. Service would be expanded from Tsawwassen–Swartz Bay to Horseshoe Bay–Departure Bay with the purchase of Black Ball's operations, and to northern B.C. Dozens of smaller ferries were purchased (the aging ships of the Gulf Islands Ferry Co. Ltd. included) and built for inter–island runs, making the service complete. From one route and two ships, the service would expand to more than a dozen routes and more than two dozen ships, from a couple of hundred employees to almost 3,000. Ferries would be lengthened and lifted, carrying not 100 cars and 500 passengers as did the *Sidney*, but more than 350 cars and 1,500 passengers. The new Tsawwassen terminal wasn't ready until 1960, but the new ferry service was an instant success long before its official startup June 15, 1960. Passenger cars were charged a mere five–dollar bill, $2 apiece for passengers. In its first year of operation, the service would make an $800,000 profit and, as Gaglardi puts it, "depopulate an airline," forcing Air Canada to cut its more than twenty flights a day to a half–dozen

At the helm, Captain Gaglardi takes new ferry for a spin.

between Vancouver and Victoria. It became known affectionately as "Bennett's Navy" and as the "Dogwood Fleet." Gaglardi was its admiral. As the ferry service came on stream according to schedule, and the public raved about the fast runs and comfortable ships, the sceptics became believers. The *Victoria Colonist*: "The provincial government's initiative launched a train of events with considerable consequences. The capital city as a result is opening its current tourist season with better tourist and shipping facilities than it has known at any comparable time before." These rave reviews were a marked turnaround from the early controversies when not even Gaglardi's fellow cabinet ministers wanted to be associated with the untried service, going so far as to avoid even the official acceptance run of the new ferries. "The premier wouldn't come on board, none of the cabinet ministers – except Les Peterson and Lyle Wicks – would come on board, because they'd been ridiculed so much. It was a rough day, raining, but the moment that I climbed on board that ship the clouds went away, the sun came out and the seas became calm."

Though the ferry system was launched under Gaglardi's department, it didn't stay there. It was first put under the B.C. Highways and Toll Bridges Authority, with a name change to the

" . . . thought so . . . Phil's drivin'. "

Ferry and Toll Bridges Authority. It eventually became the B.C. Ferry Authority, though in 1968, faced with a strike, Bennett abolished the ferry authority and handed the fleet back to the Highways Department. Gaglardi harboured a suspicion after it was initially taken away from him that Bennett didn't want to leave such a successful and popular enterprise under his control, but the premier acted on the recommendation of Captain Harry Terry, his adviser.

The government's purchase of Black Ball for $7.8 million in 1961 brought more controversy because of the price, but the terminals included in the deal were more important than Black Ball's decrepit ferries.

Even today, after more than three decades of service that have seen labour strife, a handful of tragic accidents, retrograde design changes, the system is one of the best.

Gaglardi: "The creation of the ferry system can never be taken away from me."

Flyin' Phil

He that is without sin among you, let him first cast a stone.
JOHN 8.7

Let any man in this House say he has never sinned. The only difference is that they haven't been caught.
PHIL GAGLARDI

One day, on one of his frequent on-site inspections, Gaglardi was being driven over a piece of highway near Blue River by an engineer. The road, still under construction, was a mudbog, and the engineer, to his great embarrassment, got their jeep stuck. Try as he might, he couldn't get it unglued.

Gaglardi waved the man out of the driver's seat and took over. It was just a matter of patience and knowing how to get those wheels moving slowly enough, back and forth, to work your way out, he explained. And a prayer never hurts. It was just like that day in the Fraser Valley near Mission in 1926, when a shrimp of a kid hopped into a car for the first time and got that inebriated driver and his old black Chevrolet unstuck. The only difference was that Phil Gaglardi had grown from a brash kid into a brash minister of highways, a man in a position of power and influence. He soon had the jeep and its red-faced engineer out of the mud and back on the way toward Blue River.

The love of automobiles, especially fast ones, stayed with Gaglardi for his lifetime. The big new cars supplied him by the Highways Department were really just modern versions of The Bug, that old Model T Ford chassis he had torn around the country roads of Silverdale in — the same one his mischievous brothers so methodically cut in half. No doubt, the young Gaglardi had appreciated that joke while at the same time thinking it a terrible thing to do to a piece of machinery. Gaglardi's mechanical abilities and his love of speed seem connected. Putting a car in top running condition was a challenge to him. And when it was as good as it could be, it naturally had to be put to use. It was like a light bulb being useless until you jolted it to life with electricity. It was like a life that came to naught until God breathed his love into it.

As he built a new highways system for Bennett, Gaglardi continued to personally check it out, to be sure everything was being done the way he wanted it. He had become widely known as Flyin' Phil, the fastest highways minister in the west. It was as much his driving as it was his airplane jaunts that earned him the nickname, for he flew over his new highways in his cars, too, touching down only long enough to make a colourful pronouncement on anything that struck his fancy. He was a political Pegasus, his love of fast planes and sleek cars fitting perfectly with the image he and an amused, bemused public had of him. "Being a freewheeling individual," he said, "I like to speed along without too many incumbrances."

Through the 1950s and into the 1960s he collected a drawer full of speeding tickets to go along with his press clippings about the airplanes. It seemed nothing — certainly not the controversy his love of speed generated — could slow him down.

His plane trips were frequently the subject of public discussion; the opposition parties loved to talk about his renovated supercharged Widgeon, known because of its call letters (CF–GPJ) as "Gaglardi's Pride and Joy." Gaglardi spent thousands of dollars fixing up the Widgeon to his liking, including installing new wallpaper. He liked to be comfortable when he flew. He often topped the list for cabinet travelling expenses. "And I put in many more hours on the job than any other minister," he would point out.

But when there was no airplane, he made due on the ground. Once, in a hurry to get from Vancouver to Kamloops for a speaking engagement and being without a plane, he took to the air in his government car instead, flying over the Fraser Canyon highway at seventy miles per hour. Gaglardi and the RCMP were bound to meet. They did, frequently.

"Fast cars and fast planes — that's something I love. If the truth be known, I have never driven a car fast just to drive fast. All my life I've been in a hurry. I talk fast, I work fast, I've never slowed down for anything, so it's a natural part of me to speed on a highway. There's nothing I like better than to travel fast.

"But even though I'm supposed to be a madman on the highway, I stay away from everybody else. I'm a very careful driver. I gamble a little bit, but I don't take unnecessary chances. I was pretty accident–free."

The first time he had to reach for his wallet to fix up a driving mistake was in November 1953, when he skidded into the rear end of a provincial–government vehicle in Victoria, slightly damaging its fender. A government interdepartmental safety committee found he'd been following too closely, and assessed him five dollars.

In March 1957, he was hustling to Vancouver International Airport from the courthouse, where his Buick had been ticketed for having last year's licence plates. Forced to stop at a service station to change the plates, Gaglardi was running late and fast when an off–duty policeman pulled him over. It cost Gaglardi $25. It was to be just another of many handshakes between the nimble highways minister and the long arm of the law.

Several months later, Gaglardi was piloting his Highways Department car along a new stretch of highway between Kamloops and Savona with highways safety inspector Harry Francis, former Pentecostal minister, former MLA and current member of Calvary Temple, in the passenger seat. They were discussing roadwork as they drove.

Gaglardi's foot pressed on the gas pedal and the speedometer nudged up past the sixty–miles–per–hour mark. The speed limit was fifty, but Gaglardi had been arguing for some time that the limit should be revised to sixty. His highways were getting so good, he said, that fifty was too slow. Safety advocates in the Lower Mainland were afraid of sixty because they didn't realize just how good the roads now were in the Interior. Modern engineering was creating highways that were perfectly safe at higher speeds. In fact, faster drivers were safer than slowpokes, because they paid more attention to what they were doing. Gaglardi, in fact, had the authority to change highway speeds any time and any place he wanted. In March 1955, a bill was passed amending the section of the Motor Vehicle Act that limited speeds to fifty miles per hour. The limit was now fifty "except where a greater speed limit is permitted and established by signs erected or placed on a highway by the minister of highways."

Gaglardi hadn't yet exercised that power, partly because insurance companies lobbied against it, claiming it would result in higher rates because auto accidents, though not necessarily more numerous, would be more serious. But he fully intended to convince the dawdlers to get with the twentieth century.

On this day, though, the speed limit was fifty and there was a red light flashing in his rear view mirror. Gaglardi eased off the gas pedal and steered the car onto the shoulder. One of the two cops in the ghost car that pulled up behind him got out and walked up to the highways minister as he rolled down the window. The constable was in street clothes. They had clocked him, said the young cop, at eighty-five miles per hour. Gaglardi hadn't thought he was driving that fast.

Gaglardi's Labour Day radio message that year carried a note of caution for the driving public: "This is P.A. Gaglardi, your minister of highways. I have a holiday message for you, Mr. Motorist. Wherever you're going this weekend take the time to enjoy beautiful British Columbia. . . . Honestly now, what's your hurry? Don't take chances. One miscalculation could be your last. Enjoy the day by making sure you arrive happy and alive."

Without having to go to court, Flyin' Phil paid a $10 fine for the second speeding incident. Since it was his second offence, the record — with no name attached — was forwarded to the education committee of the Motor Vehicles Branch for a decision on suspending the licence.

Asked about the ticket, Gaglardi called the claim that he was flying low at more than eighty-five miles per hour a "pack of trash." He had simply been testing the curves. "I build them. Somebody has to test them." And the two policemen who had apprehended him "looked like a couple of punks."

Gaglardi decided not to wait for the Motor Vehicles Branch to act on a possible licence suspension. He would turn in his licence himself. "I'm going to give up my licence for at least a month, whatever the MVB decides," he announced. "I'm doing this to guard against any accusations of favouritism. . . . I have broken the law, and I am ready to be punished."

And he renewed his assurance that he was testing curves. He had not intended to call the two constables who pinched him punks. "What I said was that in their disguise as casual travellers speeding along the highway, they looked like a couple of fellows whom we often refer to as punks."

At 7 a.m. Sunday, November 23, 1958, Gaglardi was on his way to Vancouver International Airport again to catch a plane. There was little traffic. In the forty-miles-per-hour zone approaching the airport, he was stopped by a Richmond RCMP member for travelling fifty miles per hour. The officer presented the highways minister with a ticket, his third in twenty months.

When Magistrate A.I. Thomas heard the case two weeks later in Victoria police court, Gaglardi was fined another $25, but this time his licence was yanked for three months. Gaglardi appealed the suspension, and the Motor Vehicles Branch cut it to a month.

Gaglardi kept pressing for his sixty–miles–per–hour limit. When Attorney General Bob Bonner got a ticket, Gaglardi saw it as justification for legalizing higher speeds.

"We are really building highways in this province," he told a conference of the B.C. Associated Transport Association in Kelowna. "When the roads are so good the attorney general moves fast enough to be picked up by the RCMP, it really is something unusual. There's hardly a man in this room or in this city who does not drive over fifty miles per hour."

For months Gaglardi encouraged the doubters to throw caution to the winds and support "at least" a sixty–miles–per–hour limit. "When you want to get out and go, you should be able to get out and go," said Flyin' Phil. To pacify the safety nuts who persisted in their opposition, he reached back to his Pentecostal roots for another villain in highway deaths. The big killer, he insisted, was not speed, but alcohol. Speed caused less than half as many accidents as liquor did. People who wanted to drive slowly could feel free to do so. That's why he was building four–lane highways, so slow drivers could pull over to the slow lanes. If they didn't pull over, of course, he'd fly over them. "I should have wings and a joystick fitted in my car so I can fly over some of those slow trucks."

Those weren't the words of a man bitter about a couple of speeding tickets, or afraid he would suffer political backlash from them. Flyin' Phil had quickly learned to enjoy the extra attention he was getting courtesy of the RCMP. As much as anything, Gaglardi's speeding tickets were making him known nationally and internationally. When he attended conferences outside the province, he was the toast of the local media, who announced him as B.C's colourful little politician who built highways and then got speeding tickets on them.

But while Gaglardi enjoyed his notoriety as the continent's best–known driver, he was absolutely serious about boosting the limit. He finally announced that "good, long stretches" of highway would go to sixty miles per hour in three pilot locations on Vancouver Island, the Fraser Valley and the Okanagan–Thompson–Cariboo. In addition, the new Deas Island highway from the Oak Street Bridge to the U.S. border would be sixty. Other pieces of highway would soon follow.

Gaglardi, having taken the plunge to sixty, was already thinking about sixty–five. He had read in an American magazine that, on good roads, sixty–five miles per hour was the safest speed. "The safest speed anywhere on properly designed highways is sixty–five miles per hour," he concluded. "The most dangerous

Hoofing it, a man without a driver's licence, Gaglardi checks out bus schedule in 1961.

speed is thirty–five miles per hour. At thirty–five miles per hour, most people are cotton–picking, yakking and dillydallying. People behind nibble their fingernails, then try to bolt. Sometimes they don't get away with it."

He soon announced more sixty–miles–per–hour zones. The Vancouver and Victoria papers grumbled that engineers, not Gaglardi, should decide speed limits, but the province of B.C. moved easily into the era of sixty miles per hour. Some people moved too easily. Eighteen–year–old Bob Gaglardi was clocked at seventy near Spences Bridge, and was fined $15 in Kamloops court.

Twenty–two stretches of highway were eventually brought under the sixty–miles–per–hour limit. Despite continuing controversy, the sixty zones stayed, though they didn't prove to be enough for poor Gaglardi's personal driving needs. He was soon in trouble again, guilty of making an illegal turn in Vancouver in 1960. An incident in July 1961 involved another wrong turn of sorts. He veered onto a shoulder to pass a slow car on his way into Victoria, and was tagged with a $25 fine for passing on the right.

That September, only ten days after paying this latest fine, off–duty Lytton RCMP constable David McLay was driving the Trans–Canada Highway near Savona with fiancée Shirley Friend in his private car when another auto came up behind him. At a curve in the road, the car swung out to pass, cutting in sharply ahead of him as an oncoming vehicle drew near. McLay sped up to tail the car, keeping an eye on the driver. The man at the wheel appeared to be driving with his left hand and speaking into a radio microphone with his right. At one point, it looked like he slid across the front seat to peer out the passenger-side window at a sawmill, the car nudging the edge of the highway as he did so. At Savona, about eight miles later, McLay pulled the car over and told the driver he had been speeding and driving carelessly. The name on the driver's licence was that of Philip Arthur Gaglardi, who was on his way to "The Shack," the family cabin on Kamloops Lake.

"Forget it," Gaglardi told him. "It won't happen again. I've got enough problems trying to do my job without worrying about another driving charge."

McLay laid the charges: speeding, and driving without due care and attention.

Kamloops subdivision RCMP weren't sure how to handle the situation. The case was referred to the General Investigations Section, which started a follow-up probe. They didn't know whether or not to press the constable's charge or let it drop. When the press got hold of it, they tried to stall. Finally, it was decided to go ahead. The trial was set for Kamloops on December 12.

Meanwhile, the always obsequious women's auxiliary of the Social Credit League approved a resolution calling upon the government to provide Phil Gaglardi with both a chauffeur and a helicopter. "Please make it a jet helicopter," Gaglardi requested at the Socred convention that followed the women's meeting the next day in Vancouver.

McLay and his girlfriend were not to be shaken from their impressions of what had happened on the highway. Gaglardi, they said, had hit eighty-five and ninety miles per hour. Gaglardi, appearing himself in court, said he had seldom gone over the sixty-miles-per-hour limit. McLay and Friend said Gaglardi had passed on a blind corner with a solid line. Gaglardi said it was a "leisurely" corner with a dotted line. Furthermore, the highways minister said, he wasn't talking into the radiophone mike, just listening. And he didn't actually slide across the seat.

Magistrate D.M. McDonald found him guilty as charged of driving without due care and attention. "If the young RCMP officer and his lady friend had been stranded on the highway, Mr. Gaglardi would have been the first motorist to stop to aid them.

What do you do with a man like that?" asked McDonald. Answering his own question, McDonald levied a $75 fine plus $6.50 costs and recommended to Motor Vehicles that the licence be lifted for three months.

The conviction, said Gaglardi, was "a pile of crap." He said photographs presented by police in court had been taken "a thousand feet" from where he'd supposedly crossed a solid line. Getting traffic tickets wasn't fun anymore. Gaglardi, some of the *joie de vivre* gone, was convinced he was a marked man every time he got behind the wheel. Kamloops RCMP, he believed, were on the lookout for him, hoping he'd make some small mistake they could nail him for. There was some sort of conspiracy to tarnish his reputation, to disrupt his family, to hurt the government. He believed it so strongly he began to talk about quitting if the cotton-picking police didn't lay off.

The suspension, in the meantime, took effect the following January 2. On January 3, Gaglardi landed at Patricia Bay airport and was driven into Victoria by a Highways Department employee. The public purse would pay the price of chauffeuring Gaglardi for three months.

When Gaglardi was in Kamloops, Highways Department employee Sam Perry was assigned to drive him around. Perry recalled being at home one evening when Bob Gaglardi drove in with his father. Phil knocked on the door and retrieved the keys to the government car from Perry. Perry could only assume Gaglardi wasn't borrowing the government car for Bob to drive. "He was just asking for trouble."

The subject of Gaglardi's driving record was bound to come up during the 1962 session of the legislature. The CCF, sporting a new name — now the New Democratic Party — but as fastidious as ever, decided to go after him. NDPer Cedric Cox of Burnaby charged that Gaglardi had "no regard for the courts and the laws of this province" and that his driving endangered the lives of B.C. residents.

But Gaglardi, as usual, was a moving target, and later in the session he decided his fellow MLAs needed a lecture in safe driving. "For every ten thousand people who are killed by accidents attributable to alcohol only one person dies from the bite of a mad dog. Yet we shoot the dog and licence alcohol."

He listed ten rules of the road, including: "If I do not wish to drive the posted safe speed limits, may I never in any way restrict those who do."

NDPer Camille Mather of Delta, herself twice convicted for speed-ing, came back later with two more commandments for Gaglardi:

"Thou shalt obey the law of the road, neither speeding in thy chariot, nor passing others on the wrong side of the highway.

"If thou breakest the law, then thou shalt submit thyself to the officers of the law, neither bewailing thy fate, rending thy garments, tearing thy hair, nor claiming that an injustice has been done thee."

Gaglardi lost an appeal on the McLay conviction, and became uncharacteristically quiet for the rest of the legislative session. On a fine early spring's afternoon on March 29, 1962, Provincial Secretary Wesley Black spoke the traditional words: "Mr. Speaker, and members of the legislative assembly. It is His Honour the lieutenant-governor's will and pleasure that the legislative assembly be prorogued until it shall please His Honour to summon the same for dispatch of business, and this provincial legislative assembly is hereby prorogued accordingly."

Phil Gaglardi wasn't around to hear Black. He had slipped out early to be taken for a spin in a brand-new Jaguar sports car. He had to settle for the passenger's seat, but he enjoyed the sleekly styled, spoke-wheeled little convertible. It had dual overhead camshafts, triple carburation, and was capable of accelerating from zero to one hundred in eleven seconds. Top speed, 150 miles per hour. Price, a hefty $6,100.

It was highly unlikely Gaglardi could get the government to supply him with a Jaguar, but there were certain, well, necessities on an automobile that behoved a minister of highways. Other cabinet ministers could make do with the ordinary; not Gaglardi.

The cars driven by most members of the Bennett cabinet weren't exactly car show material. While Bennett had a chauffeur-driven limousine at his disposal for highly official functions, he normally drove a two-year-old Rambler. Cabinet ministers had good reason for economy. Most of their ministry cars were old, barebones transportation. And the mileage allowance for ministers was tight. They couldn't afford the jazzy stuff. Besides, Bennett preferred his ministers not to be showy. He liked the appearance of him and his cabinet members driving common cars. Common cars, for grass-roots ministers in touch with the common people. Plain folks.

Gaglardi never was one to abide plain old beaters. He needed speed and convenience. In 1954, the Highways Department bought him a brand new Buick Century, just about the hottest thing on four wheels. His current Vancouver-based car was a new Olds. But his Victoria car was now an ordinary 1958 Chevrolet. "One of my men said, 'You need a new car.' So I said, 'OK.' The department bought the cars, not me. The boys in the department treated me like King Tut."

So his purchasing officials began looking around for something better, asking prices of several car dealers. What they wanted was something in the way of a new Chevrolet Impala, with six-way power-adjustable bucket seats, two-tone paint, four-barrel carburettor, deluxe radio, dual exhausts, power steering, four-speed transmission, power windows and a 409-cubic-inch engine. And a special buzzer that would sound when the driver exceeded the speed limit, like the one Gaglardi had on his own car.

This particular model could do around 110 miles per hour, zero to sixty in ten seconds or less. No Jaguar, but no clunker, either.

To Gaglardi, these features were not options; they were standard equipment. Considering all the hassles he'd gone through, he didn't enjoy driving the way he once did, and if he was going to drive, his car needed these things. "I don't want anything posh," he ordered. "I have no grandiose ideas." It was one thing to price a car and another to buy it!

Big cars with big engines weren't just for fun, as far as Gaglardi was concerned. He was constantly being threatened, more so than any other cabinet minister including Bennett. "There were maybe half a dozen times in Vancouver alone I would be driving up Granville Street and there would be a car crowding me, and then suddenly come up alongside of me and try to run me into a pole. I knew immediately what was going on, I'd hit that old throttle and get out of there. That's why I had the extra power in those automobiles. I couldn't tell anybody that at the time."

He also had extra security. The doors, trunk and hood were wired to set off an alarm if anyone should try to tamper with the car. Gaglardi wasn't worried about theft; he was worried about bombs. "I think there were times when the hood was lifted. There were times when there were indications that someone tried."

Threats and bomb scares were with Gaglardi everywhere. "The Vancouver Hotel used to empty out the seventeenth floor every month or two, because of me being on that floor, because of threats. If I went to a radio station to do an open-line show there were always four policemen there, two in uniform and two in plain clothes. They'd walk or drive me back to the hotel afterward." In Kamloops, his wife and children were often awakened in the middle of the night by police, who would take them outside while the house was checked for bombs. A male mannequin still stands in a downstairs living room, a leftover

from the days when it served as a decoy to would–be intruders.
"Many times I'd go down to Calvary Temple in the morning, and
the RCMP would be there, searching for bombs." At the height of
one of the patronage controversies, department secretary Edith
Scarff was working her way through the day's mail when she came
to a poorly wrapped parcel addressed to Gaglardi. She tore the
paper from the box and opened it up. In front of her was a
homemade bomb. It failed to detonate.

On one occasion, Gaglardi was offered assistance from an
unusual source.

> *One day a great big moose of a guy came up to my room in the*
> *Hotel Vancouver. This fellow stood about six feet six inches and*
> *must have weighed 275 pounds. It was about eleven o'clock at*
> *night. He asked to come in, and he sat down and said, "I don't*
> *like the way a lot of people are treating you. Is there anybody*
> *you know I could break a couple of legs and a couple of arms?" I*
> *said, "No, I don't think I need that." He said, "Who looks after*
> *you?" I said, "The Boss Upstairs looks after me. There isn't a*
> *bullet made that'll blow away Phil Gaglardi before it's time."*

The estimates on the new Impala came back. To the average
Joe, the cost would be about $5,000. To the government, tax free,
it would be about $3,000. A car without all that special equipment
would be around $1,500.

Bennett heard about the car when he returned from a
vacation in California with his wife. Gaglardi was on a trip to
Japan, officially on a trade mission for the B.C. government and
to look at some "revolutionary" front–end loaders in Tokyo.
Some cabinet members were quietly cheesed off about the hot
rod. Ray Williston, never a complainer, wondered to himself how
he scraped by with one old car while Gaglardi zipped around in
several cars and a fleet of airplanes.

When Gaglardi got back, Bennett suggested to his highways
minister that he didn't really need such a car. Since Bennett was
both premier and finance minister, and had final say on any such
purchase, Gaglardi took his advice. The plain–Jane 1958 Chev
would have to do.

"What do they want me to ride on, a bicycle?" Gaglardi grumbled. "There was a day when I used to enjoy driving. That day's gone."

It's tough to teach an old speedster new tricks. Gaglardi
continued to run afoul of the law, even getting a ticket in Alberta
when he hung a left turn into an Edmonton Transit System bus.
("I didn't run into the bus, the bus ran into me. If he'd been a
good bus driver he'd have stopped in time.")

He continued to be bitter about law enforcement on speeding. He hated the use of radar against violators. "I think policemen should come out from behind the bushes and travel on the highway like everyone else. Make men out of them, not sneaks."

He was down on safety programs, and said so in Los Angeles or wherever else he travelled to talk about highways. Safety campaigns "are not only a bore, they are a menace." He has stayed with that belief over the years. Now, he says, "If I were the minister today I would take the speed limit completely off the Coquihalla. I would put up signs about every five miles saying the next five miles are safe at ninety or 110 or whatever. This business about speed killing people is completely out of context. If you have an accident at high speed more people are killed, but the rate of accidents at high speed in my day was very, very low."

Gaglardi managed to retain his sense of humour despite his frustrations with police. All an RCMP constable needed to do to get a promotion to sergeant, he said, was to give Phil Gaglardi a speeding ticket.

"He must be joking," RCMP superintendent C.B. Macdonell said. "As far as I know all our men who caught him were constables then and are still constables."

Macdonell was right about Gaglardi joking. "Some people thought I was serious, but I got stopped lots of times after I said that by the RCMP when I wasn't speeding, and they'd say, 'Phil, I was just trying to get to be a sergeant.' But they wouldn't give me a ticket. They'd stop me just for fun."

And deep down inside, he didn't really believe the RCMP were out to get him. "I've never bought that about the RCMP. Within tolerances, some of the speeding tickets weren't justified, but I would say more were justified than weren't."

The Greatest Roman Roadbuilder

And my highways shall be exalted.
ISAIAH 49.11

Building highways is as easy as ABC.
PHIL GAGLARDI

British Columbia has never been an easy place to build roads. Since Governor James Douglas battled in vain with his House of Assembly in the 1850s to get money for road construction, provincial governments have been caught between the high political cost of not building roads, and the high financial cost of building them. The importance of a good road system to the province has always been recognized, but the will to create it has been fickle. The problem is mainly one of geography. B.C.'s mountains, rivers and lakes make it a splendid, but obstinate, piece of real estate on which to construct roads. Highways Department PR man Ray Baines described the challenge in a booklet he wrote for the government a few years after Phil Gaglardi left the portfolio: "For the highway engineer (B.C.) offers within its borders almost every engineering problem found in other parts of the world — and a few found nowhere else. Dense rain forests on the Pacific coast, arid hills in the southern Interior dry–belt regions, high mountains, deep canyons, swift rivers, innumerable lakes and coastal inlets, an endless variety of soil and rock conditions, 150–inch annual rainfalls and 600–inch snowfalls — all these features and many others can be found somewhere in British Columbia's 365,000 square miles. Road building here is a challenging, arduous and formidable task."

The province stumbled into the twentieth century with a road system that reflected the sporadic nature of commitment to it. A highway following a trail originally cut by surveyor Edgar Dewdney in 1861 between Hope and Princeton was talked about well before the First World War, but talk was all it amounted to. The Hope–Princeton became known as The Great Procrastination.

The Southern Trans-Provincial, of which the Hope-Princeton was to be part, edged painfully in bits and pieces toward the Alberta border. During the 1930s and early 1940s, roadbuilding in B.C. virtually stopped, with the opening of the Pattullo Bridge between Vancouver and New Westminster in 1937, and some occasional paving along the Fraser Canyon route among the few significant projects that were completed. It wasn't until the end of World War II that the provincial government, looking for ways to create jobs for returning soldiers, renewed its enthusiasm for roads. Herbert Anscomb, the minister of public works at the time, attempted to design a comprehensive system of roads for the province. Contracts were finally awarded for the eighty-three-mile Hope-Princeton in 1945 but, even then, the Great Procrastination suffered delay after delay, finally opening for traffic in late 1949, by which time Ernie Carson was the public works minister. Carson, determined to finish what Anscomb had begun, built 206 miles of John Hart Highway north of Prince George, started patching up roads in the Okanagan and elsewhere, and began replacing obsolete equipment. But building a modern road system in B.C. was such a massive and daunting prospect that the few millions of dollars cast its way each year could barely dent it. Not until the election of Social Credit in 1952 was the job accepted as a priority, and, once accepted, it took not a generation, nor even the lifetime of a single government, to do it. It took the leadership and intuitive know-how of one man — Phil Gaglardi — together with the support of his premier and the entrepreneurial spirit that pervaded B.C. at the time. Between 1952 and 1958, Gaglardi built 825 miles of new highway under contract, surfaced or resurfaced 2,800 miles and rebuilt or improved another 2,900 miles with his own crews. By that year, half a million automobiles were on the road in B.C., and the work was really just beginning. In 1946, when the bespectacled Carson became public works minister, the entire provincial budget was $37 million. When Gaglardi came into office, roadwork still accounted for well under ten percent of the provincial budget, and Bennett had to scrounge from other departments to get him that. By the late 1950s Gaglardi was spending about $80 million a year, more than twenty percent of the total provincial budget and second only to education expenditures.

The network of asphalt and concrete binding this diverse province is all the more impressive when you consider that most of the major construction and engineering achievements were brought to completion within a few short years, between 1958 and 1964. And that, during the last two years of that time period, the pace had slowed dramatically and really represented a few finishing touches. Most of B.C.'s overland transportation system, therefore, came into existence during a period of four years of such hyper–intensive activity that it is almost impossible to imagine.

Some perspective is provided by the fact that, with the exception of the Coquihalla Highway built in the late 1980s (and even that route was planned during Gaglardi's tenure), not a single major highways project of any significance has been completed in B.C. since Phil Gaglardi left office. Yet, in the late 1950s and early 1960s, Gaglardi finished the Rogers Pass, the Vancouver–to–Washington and Vancouver–to–Hope freeways, the Upper Levels highway and Burnaby's famous sawdust highway. When he wasn't building brand–new highways, he was rebuilding old ones — the Hope–Princeton, the Fraser Canyon, the Southern Trans–Provincial, Highway 97 through the Okanagan and Cariboo. They were tied together with spectacular bridges like the Second Narrows, the Port Mann, the Alexandra, the Agassiz–Rosedale and the Princess Margaret. His construction crews blasted and bulldozed links north to south and east to west, up and down Vancouver Island, into the Kootenays, through the Okanagan heartland and across the north country.

Little wonder Bennett affectionately called Gaglardi "the greatest Roman roadbuilder of them all." A press that had sometimes mocked him as the "Paul Bunyan" of the Socred government — a man who built "sand castles in the air" — and an opposition that complained about the government's pay–as–you–go construction policy were silenced as, year after year, Gaglardi created his highways system. His plan, though it sometimes seemed haphazard, was uncomplicated. He intended to bisect the province with major highways from top to bottom, and from one side to another. On paper, his plan resembled the lines of an Xs and Os game. From these major highways would run the spurs that would develop the province.

While the Gaglardi years in the highways portfolio are typically written off by political historians as populist blacktop government, a kind of crass and materialistic politics, there was considerable method in what often seemed at the time to be madness. It was, of course, partly designed as a visible reminder to voters of the prosperity parented by Social Credit. Every time a British Columbian drove down one of those fine new highways, or marvelled at the natural wonder of a big new bridge spanning a seemingly impassable gorge, he couldn't help but think that this was the good life. And, usually, there was one of Phil Gaglardi's "Sorry For Any Inconvenience" signs to be sure the motorist knew who was responsible for it. "Road Under Construction," they said. "Sorry For Any Inconvenience. P.A. Gaglardi, Minister of Highways." They were just common courtesy, Gaglardi said. People liked them. They reminded them there was good reason for waiting in their cars collecting dust in front of bored flagmen. (The signs, a bit of public–relations genius, were dreamed up by Gaglardi himself, who rejected several other slogans suggested by his engineers. "Sorry For Any Inconvenience" quickly became famous not only in B.C. but around the world, widely copied everywhere from the United States to Africa. The slogan also earned him his first nickname, Sorry Phil.)

There was, however, much more to building highways than good propaganda. The mute pact between Gaglardi and Bennett to make British Columbia more than the sum of its parts, the recognition that the vast resources of the Interior could only be tapped by installing a three–part economic driver — transportation, communications and utilities — was the cornerstone of the province's economic development. It brought B.C. into the modern age of industrialization and trade, and provided its people with the essential means for a prosperous lifestyle.

> *Transportation means highways, and that means you can jump in your car any place in British Columbia and travel on a major route to anywhere in the province. Communication: nobody likes to be isolated. Once you put in a highway the immediate result is electricity and telephone. If you have utilities it does away with outhouses and gives you civilization – the iron, the washing machine, the flush toilet, the bathtub; it gives you the complete home. If you were to take your wife away from a populated area and put her in a place where these facilities weren't available, she'd feel out of touch. That's why, when I set out the policy, which the premier neither dictated nor stopped, it really developed the province. Before we were in power the statement was common that the province ended at the Pattullo Bridge. People used to ask me why in common sense was I building a road that didn't seem to go anywhere. I built roads to places nobody even knew existed. It's the old question of which comes first, the chicken, or the egg.*

Besides opening up new areas for development, the construction of highways provided an immediate stimulus because it pushed money through the economy so quickly. The hardhats who sweated their way through the dust and rocks to build roads were fast spenders. They bought mobile homes and houses, television sets and record players, clothing, cars and all the other trappings of the good life. Equipment manufacturers, retail merchants, advertising media, wholesalers — all made money. For every million dollars spent by Gaglardi on a few miles of highway, $5 million more made its trip through the economy. Quick spending, quick return.

> *The highways budget created a boom all on its own, on the simple basis that when you're building a highway you're paying a contractor, who's employing people, and everybody who's employed is spending money for others to live on. The building of homes is one of the most contributing forces to a boom. When you build a house because a highway is there you're buying lumber, you're employing people, you're buying cement, you're using equipment, using utilities, and buying things to put into a home. And then the premier comes along and builds hydro dams to provide the electricity and it starts all over again. All of that is brought about when a contractor builds a highway; it opened up areas to these extra activities, it brought about the boom that lasted for the twenty years that we were in there. The premier could see that and I could see that. Very few people knew what I was doing. But that's what really made the province of British Columbia.*

A relatively simple economic philosophy, perhaps, but one that took great drive, courage, ability and, yes, ego. And Phil Gaglardi had all of those. He needed them, since he seemed constantly beset by controversies and problems that would have driven a less self-confident man into political retirement. There was, for example, the tragedy of the Second Narrows Bridge, and the naysaying over the ferry system. Though his integrity was vindicated on the first, and his judgment on the second, they provided trying moments.

Not all of the political angst generated by his mission was so visible. The Deas Island Tunnel beneath the Fraser River (soil conditions made a bridge too expensive because the river bottom made it difficult to support piers) was constructed over the well-publicized objections of the likes of chief highways engineer Neil McCallum. But there was more to worry about than protests about its timing and location. Not that construction of the $35-million tunnel — the first of its kind in North America and only the second in the world — didn't go well. It was a unique project that drew thousands of spectators every day. With approaches 2,900 feet long and another 2,100 feet under the Fraser River, the tunnel connected Lulu and Deas Islands with the north and south shores of the waterway. The tunnel was built in segments, each 344 feet long and weighing 18,500 tons, constructed next to the site. Due to freshets and shifting underwater sand dunes, there was only a five-month window of opportunity to put the segments in place. Each one was dropped into a trench under the river and the sections joined up by a special sealing device — resembling a huge inner tube — developed especially for the project by a Canadian company. The placing of the tunnel sections required Gaglardi's characteristic decisiveness. The tides and freshets made the operation risky, and nobody would take the contract because of high insurance and the possibility of disastrous cost overruns. Gaglardi, without consulting cabinet or the premier, authorized the job on a cost–plus basis. "The Deas Island Tunnel would never have been built if I'd left it up to the engineers. I took the full responsibility. I took a chance, I said, 'Go ahead,' and we won." It wasn't a decision that anyone knew about, let alone one that gained him any headlines, but it was crucial to the project and an example of Gaglardi's leadership in the highways portfolio.

After the sections were sealed, sand was blown under them for support. Then further sand and ballast were added to protect and stabilize them. Fans ventilated the tunnel, and carbon–monoxide monitors controlled the fans. Television screens were connected to an observation room, and there were public–address systems inside the tunnel as well as a fire–sprinkler system. It was completely safe, a feat not simply of imagination over engineering, as Gaglardi had once been quoted wrongly as saying, but of imaginative engineering, and leadership. Or, as Gaglardi now said, "This was not a feat of imagination over engineering . . . It was sound, sensible, sane." The completed tunnel was more than forty feet under the surface at low water, deep enough to handle the Queen Mary should that large a ship ever need to get into the river.

At the completion of every major project, ceremonies marking its "official opening" were obligatory. Usually, invited guests would have a fancy lunch, there would be speeches, and then a ribbon would be cut, a button would be pushed, or a piece of machinery would perform some symbolic task. Gaglardi collected an entire basement full of gold–plated scissors, ceremonial hardhats, certificates and plaques. It was preferable to have on hand some special dignitary for these ceremonies, but when one wasn't available, Gaglardi and Bennett happily took the spotlight themselves. Gaglardi loved such occasions, for they provided him with a reason to use his well–known oratorical skills. He usually stole the show, beginning with a thanks to the Big Builder Upstairs for providing the invariably perfect weather, and then bragging a bit about whichever feat of engineering and foresight was being marked that day. The opening of the Deas Island Tunnel was typical fare for a project-opening ceremony, but featured the added attraction of royalty. On opening day, July 15, 1958, three thousand spectators were gathered as Gaglardi noted the criticism he and his department had received over the location of the tunnel, while Bennett told the crowd they "hadn't seen anything yet" because there would be a billion dollars' worth of highways projects in the next ten years.

Queen Elizabeth herself snipped the ribbon with a pair of silver scissors and the tunnel was officially open. After the unveiling of a couple of plaques, everyone took the ceremonial ride through the tunnel, the Queen riding in the premier's car and Prince Philip in Gaglardi's.

"Now we'll see if it leaks or not," the prince quipped as they entered the tunnel.

It took another three years to complete the new highway between Vancouver and the American border. All was ready for another official opening May 30, 1962, and with Washington state visitors present, Bennett proclaimed it a "great day." It was also, he said, a great freeway, great province, a great state and a great Seattle world's fair.

But there was a lot of other activity going on in all parts of the province between the time of the Deas Island Tunnel completion and construction of its freeway. Much of it had to do with the Trans–Canada Highway, a federal–provincial project formalized as a national goal in 1949, when "An Act to Encourage and Assist the Construction of a Trans–Canada Highway" was signed. It was supposed to be the greatest nation–builder since construction of the CPR. By rebuilding old sections of existing highways and connecting them with brand new ones, the country would create a 4,900–mile paved highway from sea to sea. It was designed to take seven years and $150 million. When it became obvious that those projections were overly optimistic, an amendment to the act in 1956 boosted the federal share to half of all construction costs, plus ninety percent of the cost of the toughest ten percent in each province.

British Columbia presented some of the toughest and most expensive parts of the Trans–Canada — almost six hundred miles of the total. From Mile 0 in Victoria the highway headed north to Nanaimo, where motorists hopped one of Gaglardi's new ferries for the short ride to Horseshoe Bay north of Vancouver. Back on land, the new four-lane Upper Levels — completed in 1961 — took them through North Vancouver and onto the Second Narrows Bridge. It was on the other side of the Second Narrows, in Burnaby, that one of the more intriguing challenges was presented to

At Deas Island Tunnel opening, Gaglardi walks beside the Queen. Jennie Gaglardi is visible between and behind them, with Premier W.A.C. Bennett on her left. Prince Philip is at the right of the picture.

Gaglardi's roadbuilding plans. While his job was to build the B.C. leg of the Trans-Canada, the many different sections of it had to serve local needs. And, despite the avowed importance of extending the province past the Pattullo Bridge, there was still much work to do in Vancouver. Gaglardi's department looked at the traffic situation in the province's largest city and decided it needed a $340-million freeway and rapid-transit system. The plan was never carried through to completion, mostly because public opinion was against the city being cut up by turnpikes the way so many American cities had. Not until the first leg of Skytrain was finished in time for Expo 86 did the concept of rapid transit become reality. But in the late 1950s, Gaglardi could see the future, and he knew that the existing roadways couldn't support the growth of such a city. Though he might not be able to drive his bulldozers through it, he could certainly take them to its doorstep. So while the Deas freeway was being built, he also worked on the eastern approach, the bottleneck at the infamous Pattullo Bridge. Determined to turn that entrance from a roadblock to a gateway, he had his engineers map out an eight-lane route from Vancouver through Surrey connecting up with a freeway all the way to Hope. He could see the entire Lower Mainland metropolitan area eventually extending out past Chilliwack. Without a throughway, traffic would become impossible. He wanted to give drivers an easy two-hour trip between Hope and Vancouver.

Key to the plan was the Burnaby section, which didn't present any particular difficulties except for one thing. Real estate in the suburbs was becoming more and more valuable, and the municipality was reluctant to give any of it up to pavement. Gaglardi was asked to build his highway over a peat bog that extended for several miles. Huge peat bogs were common in the Lower Mainland, and the normal construction technique was to mine out the peat and replace it with stable fill. But in Burnaby, the peat was a hundred feet deep in some places, and so soft that a locomotive had once disappeared in it, never to be found.

Gaglardi called in Norm Lea, a young Harvard-educated transportation engineer who worked for Foundation of Canada Engineering Corporation, the same company that had worked on the Deas Island Tunnel. Lea and his associates tested out the swamps, and then went looking for precedents. But every other engineering firm they talked to, from eastern Canada to California, told them the same thing: building a highway over such unstable ground had never been done. They were on their own.

Lea theorized that if they dumped sawdust on top of the peat, then loaded gravel on top of that to squeeze it into the bog, the whole mess would consolidate enough to hold up a highway. Where there was soft clay, holes could be drilled and filled with sand to act as wicks and dry it up. But the secret was to keep the sawdust moist and airtight in the peat so that it wouldn't rot or become combustible, so the sawdust had to be pushed down into the water table. Some engineers were sceptical about the chances, but Lea was relatively confident.

"I said, 'Norm, will it work?'" recalls Gaglardi. "He said, 'I think so.' I said, 'Will you guarantee it?' He said, 'No.' I said, 'Well, who's going to take responsibility for it?' He said, 'You are.'"

Lea remembered that conversation. "There was a bit of tension, but we knew that the safety factor would increase with time."

Gaglardi took responsibility again and ordered the sawdust highway built. Total cost was $22 million, considered cheap, thanks to inexpensive land and materials. Had the highway failed, says Gaglardi, he would have had a multi-million-dollar scandal on his hands. "It was a horrendous gamble. I did some tall praying."

The sawdust and the sand went down, and after a year of

settling it was ready for the highway, six miles of it, virtually floating on a bed of sawdust. Though four lanes were built, there's room for four more. The highway has stood up remarkably well for close to thirty years.

Work on the Trans–Canada system also continued well out into the province's interior. Past the flat agricultural area of the lower Fraser Valley where Gaglardi grew up, and in which he had to buy up $7 million worth of rich farmland to build his freeway to Hope, lies the Fraser Canyon. No other natural phenomenon can compare with "The Canyon" for sheer scenic fascination. There was no way to build a straight highway through the canyon, but with a series of spectacular bridges and tunnels this challenging route was transformed into a modern transportation link — bridges like the Nine Mile Canyon connecting Lytton with Boston Bar, and the $4.8–million Alexandra, with the second largest arch span in the world, and tunnels like the 2,094–foot–long China Bar, opened May 1, 1962. The China Bar Tunnel, one of seven in The Canyon, was the most expensive piece of highway in B.C. — $5 million — and cut off a dangerous stretch.

But Gaglardi's greatest highway–building challenge, and the one he believes to be his greatest triumph, was the Rogers Pass, a ninety–two–mile section of highway that was more than ten years in the planning and construction. He wanted the Trans–Canada to aim east from Cache Creek through Kamloops and on to Revelstoke, and then through the Rockies into Alberta. As had been the case with the Canadian Pacific Railway, B.C. awaited the final section of the Trans–Canada to give it a modern–day link with the rest of Canada. Even before Gaglardi's entry into the government, provincial engineers had been putting their money on the Rogers, which runs through the Selkirk mountains between Revelstoke and Golden. When the Socreds came into office, the only way between those two communities was to drive 193 miles of gravel road on a north–south detour via the Big Bend along the Columbia River. In the elbow of the Big Bend lay Glacier National Park, a green patch on the map with no roads leading to it. And in the heart of the park was Rogers Pass, discovered by Major A.B. Rogers in the late nineteenth century for the CPR. The railway eventually gave up trying to combat the avalanches that kept collapsing its wooden snowsheds, ripping out its above-ground tracks and killing its workers, and constructed the world–famous spiralled Connaught Tunnel through Mount Macdonald. The pass itself was a short but spectacularly dangerous five miles, its ten–thousand–foot peaks buried in up to six hundred inches of snowfall each year. Dozens of glaciers retreated inexorably through its trenches. A highway version of the Connaught Tunnel was financially out of the question, but Gaglardi had at his disposal the latest in engineering technology with which to conquer almost any obstacle Mother Nature cared to put in his way. A highway could be blasted through the pass, and modern concrete–and–steel snowsheds, avalanche troughs and snow–control methods could keep it open.

> *I had talked about building through the Rockies, because we had to get away from this blasted business of going through the United States to get from one part of British Columbia to another part. The only place that we had to go was over the Cascade Pass and you couldn't continue it; the other was the Big Bend. None of those was acceptable. That had been going on for fifty years. But winter conditions were a problem in the Rogers. It wasn't my idea to build concrete tunnels. I suggested building suspension bridges over the slide areas, but then one of my men said, why not build concrete sheds and let the snow go right over top? Simple, but why hadn't anybody thought of it? In the final analysis I was the guy who started it all.*

The Trans–Canada, wherever it went, would carry with it all of those considerable economic benefits that accrue to communities in the path of a new highway. The shortest, cheapest or easiest routes aren't always the best in the politics of highways construction. Down in the Kootenays, hungry for its share of the prosperity, the prospect of the rival Rogers Pass getting the nod didn't sit well. Though the Kootenays were getting millions of dollars' worth of highways improvements, such as the thirty–five–mile Salmo–Creston cutoff bypassing the Kootenay Lake ferry, a new bridge across the Columbia at Trail, the Southern Trans–Provincial between Grand Forks and Castlegar, reconstruction of the eighty–three–mile Kimberley–Radium highway and general upgrading, they wanted the Trans–Canada. Led by the Nelson Chamber of Commerce, the Associated Boards of Trade and Chambers of Commerce of Southeastern B.C. was waging a fight on behalf of the Jumbo Pass, forty miles north of Nelson. The Rogers was prettier, shorter and probably more economical to construct, but Gaglardi promised to consider the Jumbo.

Although incomplete engineering reports appeared to be confirming the Rogers as the best route, Gaglardi did take his engineers with him for a look at the Jumbo in May 1956, finding the route "not impossible," but "heavy and hazardous."

During the wait, the Nelson chamber lobbied and complained,

and the issue was debated in the House of Commons. It was July of that year before the announcement finally came.

"I have now reached a final decision. I have chosen the Rogers Pass on the recommendation of my engineers and after the most careful consideration. The main reason is that only eighty-eight miles of construction is necessary on the Rogers Pass route; the alternative Jumbo Pass route would require 234 miles of construction." The Jumbo would cost double what the Rogers would.

The route through the Rogers Pass cost $50 million to build, a third as much as the original estimate for the entire Trans-Canada from coast to coast. It was done on the 50-50 cost-sharing basis with Ottawa, except for the section through Glacier and Mount Revelstoke National Parks, where the federal government paid the entire $14-million shot. A single mile at the 4,400-foot summit below Mount Macdonald cost more than a million dollars. One snowshed alone, the Lanark, was more than a thousand feet long. Avalanches would be controlled by using howitzers to prevent dangerous snow buildup on the mountainsides, and radio-equipped Highways Department vehicles would patrol the highway in winter to watch for slides. By 1962, the entire Trans-Canada project had cost almost $1 billion (it would reach close to $1.5 billion by the time the agreement expired in 1971), $209 million of it in B.C.

The federal government had some big plans for an official opening of the pass September 3, since it marked completion of the Trans-Canada. Gaglardi, however, planned his own opening for July 30 near Revelstoke. He resisted the idea that he was trying to upstage the feds. "I'm simply opening a provincial highway and they're opening a national highway and a section of highway through a national park. There's no conflict at all. This highway belongs to the province of British Columbia and I'm the fellow who made the decision where it was going to go."

It was simply, he said, a recognition of the "contributions" of Revelstoke to the project. "I felt I owed Revelstoke something. We didn't want to leave Revelstoke out." It would be "a partial opening."

He went ahead with his plans for the usual luncheon — actually, a huge public barbecue — and ribbon-cutting, and the embossed invitations went out.

Gaglardi had to fight off suggestions that he had leaned heavily on contractors to pay for the ceremonies. A report was circulating in Ottawa that contractors were hopping mad about having to put up $17,000. "That stuff is all poppycock. We have not asked the contractors for a five-cent piece."

Not asked, but they did pay.

In all the openings that I ever had, the contractors used to pay for their own. The government never paid for the dinner, it was always the contractor – it was the standard procedure because the contractors took a tremendous interest in the amount of construction that was going on, and it was a proud thing for them. Everything that we opened we used to have a very big opening so that it was advertised and the contractors always paid for a banquet. It wasn't me who suggested they pay. I think the contractors volunteered.

On July 30, it was ninety–five degrees at the site as 150 reporters joined three thousand other people to watch Bennett and Alberta Highways Minister Gordon Taylor unveil a cairn and snip a ribbon. Gaglardi was, as usual, master of ceremonies. A plaque says, in part: "To commemorate the official opening of the Rogers Pass route of the Trans–Canada Highway between Revelstoke and Golden, completed July 30, 1962, by the Province of British Columbia and the Government of Canada. An achievement by men of ingenuity, skill and determination . . . Let all who use this highway look with awe and reverence upon the majesty and the God–given beauty of these mountains. Hon. W.A.C. Bennett, Premier; Hon. P.A. Gaglardi, Minister of Highways."

Then the highway was opened to traffic. Which left the federal opening at the east entrance to Glacier Park not really an opening at all. But Gaglardi was at that one, too, watching as Prime Minister John Diefenbaker cut another ribbon and unveiled another ceremonial plaque, this one with the coats of arms of all the provinces. Gaglardi even got to thank God for the fine weather.

Diefenbaker came over to me after it was over and said, "Phil, I've never driven over a finer scenic highway in my life. Why wasn't this done seventy years ago?" So I said, "Dief, that's simple. Phil Gaglardi wasn't born seventy years ago."

One final link in the Trans–Canada was officially opened at another ceremony two years later back at that eastern–approach bottleneck in the Lower Mainland. The location chosen for a new bridge over the Fraser to replace the Pattullo was a little south of the old bridge, and a spectacular new span was designed. The Port Mann Bridge is, with the possible exception of the Lions Gate, the most beautiful in the province. Crossing between Coquitlam and Surrey, its brilliant orange arches and yellow girders tie the freeway from the Second Narrows to the four–lane stretch to Chilliwack. But it, too, was a challenge.

Gaglardi himself played a part in the design, pushing for a special kind of expansion joint – called an orthotropic deck –

that he admired in bridges he'd seen in Germany. His design engineers built it into the Port Mann. Formed of two–inch–thick, curved slabs moving under a fixed plate, it allowed the bridge to expand or contract as much as three and a half feet according to the season. The weight was reduced to a fraction of what it would have been using cement.

Still, the bridge had its problems. It was supposed to have been in operation by 1961, at a cost of $25 million. In 1964, the cost climbed to $27 million. The extra $2 million had been caused by problems with the river bottom. A strike lasting thirty–seven days interrupted work. But those difficulties were forgotten on the sunny afternoon of June 12, 1964, when public and dignitaries gathered 145 feet above the Fraser to officially open the bridge. True to form, Gaglardi and God held the rain at bay for the opening.

Gaglardi announced that the speed limit on the freeway would be raised from sixty–five to seventy miles per hour, on the advice of others in his department and of the RCMP. "They twisted my arm, but I agreed," joked the tiny perfect speedster. He pointed out the engineering wonders of the bridge, and also reminded everyone about the sawdust highway. As was standard practice when the two of them got on a platform together, the Phil–and–Cecil show turned into a mutual admiration society.

"He is the genius of the purse strings that made all this possible," Gaglardi said of Bennett.

"But he got $2 worth for every dollar spent and that's worthwhile," the premier joined in. Then he repeated the ultimate compliment: "Next to him, the Roman roadbuilders were pikers. He is the world's greatest highway builder." The moniker stuck. During a trip to Hollywood, Gaglardi was introduced to a gathering of movie stars by Canadian actor Raymond Massey as "the greatest Roman roadbuilder in the world."

Opportunity Knocks

Ask, and it shall be given you; seek, and ye shall find; knock, and it shall be opened unto you.
MATTHEW 7.7

I think this a free country and one of the advantages God gives to you and me is the opportunity to make a million dollars or go broke.
PHIL GAGLARDI

When Social Credit came to power in 1952 and W.A.C. Bennett handed Phil Gaglardi the chore of building a new highways system, part of the assignment was to do it with the least possible money. B.C.'s new highways were not to be constructed by throwing money around whenever get–rich–quick entrepreneurs tipped their itchy palms toward Victoria. That had been made perfectly clear. Gaglardi must operate with economy, moving dirt and laying down pavement cheaper than the Coalition had done.

The province's major contractors had had it pretty good under the Coalition. Gaglardi had no evidence there was collusion in trading off bids, but would–be interlopers were kept out of the competition as surely as though there was. Gaglardi was aware of that situation when he got into office:

> *The only thing I can say is that five major contractors always seemed to get the work. Now whether there was something sinister about that or not, I've got no proof. There was, oh, some talk that there could be some extracurricular situations going on in regards to how the contractors always seemed to be able to get a bid in sort of rotation. It was suggested to me that contractors had to have a certain financial structure about them so that when they got into a job they would be able to complete that particular job regardless of whether they ran into difficulties or not; what they bid they would have to stick by. I never inquired as to rumours about this kickback business. All I'm saying is that when I was made the minister there were five contractors doing all the work. After that, in a very short time there were as many as twenty–six contractors doing the work.*

Social Credit's shocking ascendency to power seemed like it shouldn't be cause for concern to the cartel. After all, Bennett and Gaglardi were going to go ahead with the massive roadbuilding program the Coalitionists had planned and talked about, but never really got around to doing. Times should be better than ever under Social Credit. But they didn't reckon with Bennett, Gaglardi and an impudent young construction man by the name of Ben Ginter. Together, he and Gaglardi, almost unwittingly, would break the cushy cartel and hang an "open for business" sign over B.C.'s highways projects.

Benjamin George Ginter grew up on a farm in Swan River, Manitoba, with six sisters and a brother. His father died when young Ben was in the eighth grade, and he left school to help support the family. He wasn't a good student anyway. "I was off in a daze while I should have been doing my work." The cocky fourteen-year-old put a quarter in his pocket and hopped a boxcar west to look for employment. He hauled logs, picked sugar beets and sweated on dairy farms to earn money to send home. During the war he worked in a tire factory; after the war, he got on as a construction labourer. He decided the way to make real money was to work for himself instead of others, so he went home to Swan River, borrowed $1,500 from his mother, and put it down on a $12,000 war-surplus bulldozer he'd seen for sale in Lethbridge, Alberta.

He did well clearing land for Alberta farmers, but decided to try subcontracting in general construction. Ginter took his pickup truck, a trailer home and his wife, Grace, and headed for north-central B.C. That's where he stayed, buying out a partner and forming Ginter Construction in 1951. He continued to get subcontracting jobs and, shortly after Social Credit came to power, he decided to bid on government roadwork.

In 1954, he was running into a stone wall with Gaglardi's deputies, who were worried about the new boy's inexperience and possible inability to muster the necessary equipment for highways contracts. As any angry constituent would do, Ginter vented his spleen on his MLA, who was Ray Williston. With his gravel-crusher voice, barely thirty years of age, Ginter demanded a chance to prove himself. Williston called Phil Gaglardi.

> *Ray phoned me and asked me if I could see Ben and I said, "Sure, send him over." So Ben came over and he told me what his predicament was. This was the first time I met him and I asked him a few questions in regards to his ability, what equipment he had, and then his ability to meet the financial*

requirements. He said he could handle any job he got. I said, "As long as you can prove that to my controller there's no reason in the world why you can't bid on a contract and if you're the low bidder, get a contract." And so I called the deputy, Evan Jones, and he came in and I said, "Evan, I want you to meet Ben Ginter," and I said, "Evan, anybody who's qualified has to have the right to be able to bid on any job in the province of British Columbia if he meets the requirements," so I said, "Give Ben a set of plans and let him see what he can do." And, amazingly, he came up with the next contract that was let by the department. Immediately that started the trend that set the pattern for the future because the moment it was voiced abroad by the newspapers and by ourselves that anybody who had the qualifications and the equipment to do a job of the size we were asking them to bid on, they were invited to do so, and that opened the gate and I want to tell you the province of British Columbia saved not millions but hundreds of millions of dollars by that particular change.

Ginter came through for the highways minister, completing that job and millions of dollars' worth of others, consistently underbidding the competition, and making himself rich. He didn't sound very bright when he talked, and though a sense of humour occasionally revealed itself, he generally had the personal charm of a bear with sore haemorrhoids. A lawyer once complained under oath that Ginter was "a hypocrite and a scoundrel." But he was street–smart and he was dependable. Gaglardi on Ginter: "He was the kind of man who couldn't say fifteen words without messing up the English language, but he was a smart businessman." He got his jobs done, and when the particular problems or need for haste of a project demanded no–bid, day–labour construction, Gaglardi's engineers often called on Ginter to do it. Ginter started picking up other construction companies, and eventually branched out into breweries, pulp mills and other businesses, building a fourteen–company empire holding $25 million in contracts. He extended his construction activities into Alaska, and his other interests into eastern Canada. It seemed this born–again Baptist bulldozer operator couldn't stop. It was said a triumvirate controlled the Interior of the province: Gaglardi, Ginter and God.

Like Bennett and Gaglardi, Ginter was a workaholic. He started early in the morning with a cup of coffee and might not stop to eat until late at night when he was ready for bed. Then, he'd make up for the day's abstinence by cramming anything he could find into his mouth. His formerly solid body became 245 pounds of jelly, much of it located in his huge gut. Though he liked to say he needed little money for his own needs, his personal fortune was estimated at anywhere between $30 million and $40 million at its zenith. Among his interests were prize Arabian stallions. He sold one to Gaglardi for $300, and Gaglardi quickly developed a love of good horseflesh.

Others soon came to the conclusion that any uneducated, bumptious country boy who could make that much money wasn't doing it all on his own. Suspicion of patronage hung over every Ginter contract like bad breath. It worried Bennett more than it did Gaglardi. It was the premier's job to care about public opinion; all the highways minister cared about was building highways. To Phil Gaglardi, it was good enough to say there was nothing to the rumours, that everything was one thousand percent aboveboard. "Those kinds of stories were manufactured by the carload. I never accepted a bribe in my life, never even was offered one because I think the contractors had more respect for me than to try. Ben Ginter never gave me a dime." For Ginter's part, he felt insulted by suggestions of special deals. He found it easy enough to make money by working hard and being smart, without having to be corrupt. "Sure, I made money, but that has nothing to do with Gaglardi. It's because I knew how to bid."

The secret to bidding under the new order was to pare to the bone, and to do that a contractor had to know what he was doing. Although all contractors were encouraged to go after government work, qualifications weren't thrown out the window. They still had to be bondable, and had to be Canadian or have a Canadian partner. "I made it a rule I would accept the lowest bidder, and if that figure was only in difference to the next bidder by one cent, he's the fella that got the contract." One of the major differences in procedure under Gaglardi was in flexibility once contracts were underway. If a contractor ran into problems that hadn't been predicted when the bids were let, says Gaglardi, he would be dealt with fairly.

> *In any bid there are an awful lot of things that you cannot include in a contract because it would take far too much time to get the specifications together. If there were certain things that were not written up in the contract that imposed a considerable amount of extra cost to the contractor, heretofore he had no place to go nor anyone he could talk to, but when I was there they learned they could come and talk to me and I would listen. Suppose we called a contract and there was no rock price on that contract, and after starting and going down thirty feet he found a huge amount of rock in that cut. Well, you couldn't expect a*

*contractor to take out that rock without there being a price. If the
entire engineering staff and the deputy agreed, then I would say
OK, we have to be fair. So the contractors always had confidence
that they could appeal to me. And so their bidding could be tight
and it could be close.*

The intensity of the competition among contractors, though it
saved the province money and created successes, also was bound to
cause some jealousies and disappointments. Government jobs had
attracted a new strain of entrepreneur, the small–timer who, as long
as he could meet the conditions, got his chance. That worked in
Ginter's favour for awhile, because he started as one of the little
guys, but the cutthroat competition for roadwork it encouraged
started to slow him down. He started losing a lot of bids, and by the
early 1960s the Ginter–Socred alliance, not to mention the
Ginter–Gaglardi friendship, began to pale.

Ginter became convinced that Bennett, ever worried about
public opinion, decided to put the hammer down and squeeze
Ginter out by keeping government work out of his hands. He
claimed the government owed him $2 million from previous
highways contracts in which unexpected costs had arisen. He
believed he was resented for refusing Socred requests for generous
campaign contributions. He became bitter, and changed his opinion
of Gaglardi from "friend" to "jackass."

Eventually, Ginter's magnificent empire crumbled. With the
slowdown in roadwork, he started selling off some of his
construction companies and concentrated on beer and wine, but
run–ins with liquor authorities, legal hassles, labour problems and
intense competition from major breweries spelled doom. His
breweries went into receivership, his fortune was whittled away, and
his family split up. When Ginter died of a heart attack in 1982 at the
age of fifty–nine, Gaglardi eulogized him at his funeral as "the
epitome and the amplification of the Canadian dream. . . . Our great
nation and this province were built by men of his type."

Kind words for a solemn occasion, perhaps. Today, Gaglardi
looks back on Ginter with respect but not affection. "Ben Ginter was
one of the most greedy individuals that God ever gave breath to. He
and I were never the close friends that the public seemed to think."

Gaglardi was justifiably proud of having opened up contract
bidding. Naturally there were risks; that was free enterprise. Some
contractors had, indeed, claimed to have lost money on highways
jobs. The opposition, lobbied by the construction–industry
establishment, demanded time after time a pre–qualification system
of awarding contracts, but Gaglardi insisted that would result in a

return to a preferred list of contractors. As far as Gaglardi could see, construction companies were always supposedly going broke, but he noticed they were still able to buy big machines, pay higher wages, build new homes, buy Cadillacs and holiday in Miami. Maybe "going" was the key word. They were always going. But they never seemed to get there.

For the most part, the system worked very well, with reputable contractors like Ginter, Perini Pacific, Dawson, Emil Anderson, and Jamieson Construction proving themselves time after time. A very few weren't as smart or as lucky as the others and took advantage of God's gift of the opportunity to go broke. And, while the government and public benefitted for the most part whichever way it went, there were rare occasions of near disaster.

Project 819 covered 12.8 miles of Trans–Canada Highway work between Craigellachie — the historic CPR "last spike" site near which the federal government eventually held its official "opening" of the highway — and Twin Bridges near Revelstoke. It was a tough $1.6–million job destined to become the source of much pain to Phil Gaglardi as the contract turned into a complicated network of financial wheeling and dealing.

The contract had been let June 28, 1957, to L and M Logging Co. of Kamloops, a small outfit with shaky finances. L and M was controlled by Burton Lymburner, who had formed the company in 1954 with his former employee, Syd Marriott. They had survived well enough on small jobs — including non–bid government day–labour work — for Lymburner to pilot a Beechcraft Bonanza around the province. One acquaintance who worked for a competing contractor described Lymburner for the author as "a likeable rogue." A business acquaintance of Lymburner's said he was "a real smooth kind of a guy." Gaglardi got to know Lymburner fairly well.

> *He'd be broke one day and he'd be a millionaire the next. He was quite a clever fellow in many ways. One time when he came up from Vancouver he said, "Phil, I'm going to Kamloops, I'm flying up in my own plane." I said, "Fine, I'll go with you," and we were flying and talking and all of a sudden the motor stopped. So Burt looked around and noticed that the gas gauge was at empty. Luckily there were two tanks on the plane, so without batting an eye, never said a word, he reached over and shut the tap off from the empty tank and turned the one on for the full tank. Well, the propeller was still going around so the moment that the gas went through the carburettor, bang, it started, so we didn't lose much altitude nor worry about anything. He seemed to know what he was*

*doing. But, really, I think he might have been a little bit out of
his field as a contractor.*

L and M wasn't a builder of highways; its only previous
experience had been in constructing bush roads. Project 819 was its
first major job of any kind. By summer, the underfunded, poorly
equipped company was in financial trouble. While Lymburner was
conscientious about meeting payrolls, he had to borrow heavily to
do it. Meanwhile, the company couldn't pay for materials and was
behind on equipment leases — while it had a couple of good
bulldozers of its own, beat-up rentals made up the rest. The road
project proceeded in fits and starts as L and M moved from one
easy part to the next. Lymburner needed help. Burton Glazer, a
Seattle metal dealer, listened to his problems. Glazer, in turn, talked
to Portland businessman Rodney Rosencrantz, who agreed to a loan
on the strength of progress payments expected from the
government by L and M. After repaying the first loans, Lymburner
talked Glazer and Rosencrantz into another $25,000 each.

Then he went looking for new blood. He gathered together a
group of potential investors, and they sat down in a room of the
Placer Hotel in Helena, Montana, to talk deals. There was Clyde
Thornton, a Troy, Montana mine developer, and a long-time Seattle
acquaintance of his, Glen Geery, who had helped Lymburner set up
the meeting. Also present was Dick Holzworth, a gritty middle-aged
contractor who already owned a construction company in Miles
City, Montana. Lymburner's proposal was to share the stock of L
and M with those who put money into it to keep it afloat.
Lymburner would be president, Geery operations manager,
Holzworth treasurer, and Thornton vice-president. They set up an L
and M bank account at Bonner's Ferry, Idaho, Thornton and
Holzworth kicked in $35,000 apiece, and the deal was clinched
without so much as an audited statement.

With the company came the company's debts. By this time,
the three-month deadline on the loans had come and gone (so
had a ninety-day extension), the injection of new money went to
other necessities, and repeated reminders from creditors Glazer
and Rosencrantz brought no action. L and M had more
immediate concerns than repaying loans.

Thornton, whose knowledge of roads went no further than
the fact that you drove on them, decided to go up to British
Columbia and take a look at where his money was going. He'd
left the roadbuilding to those who were supposed to know
something about it, but his inexperienced eye told him things
weren't going well at all. For one thing, the one-eyed Geery, who

was supposed to be managing the project, didn't seem to be spending much time there. At one point, he was away for ten days, and Thornton heard horror stories about bank overdrafts and Geery supposedly taking off to Phoenix on company money with some woman. Thornton eventually tracked him down in Vancouver, fired him and charged him with theft over $50 in connection with some worthless secondhand wire Geery had taken from a job site. During an argument as Geery was getting into his car, Thornton took a swing at him. Geery responded by kicking at Thornton.

A change was clearly called for. L and M was transformed into Union Contractors. Holzworth was named president, and Thornton took over effective control. Lymburner remained as a salaried employee of Union because of the inexperience of Holzworth and Thornton in building Canadian roads or dealing with the B.C. government.

But trouble seemed to breed trouble; the jinx of Project 819 infected others. Lymburner had a friend named Vince Gresty who worked as mechanical superintendent at the Kamloops regional office of the Highways Department. In fact, Lymburner's plane was registered in Gresty's name for awhile. Gresty attended Calvary Temple, had known Phil Gaglardi for twenty years, and was active in the Kamloops Socreds with Gaglardi and Walter Smith.

Gresty had a long–dormant company called Gresty Bros., which he handed over to a friend, Harvey "Slim" Campbell, who wanted an existing company to bid on road construction jobs.

Campbell renamed the company Mid–City Construction. Although Gresty wasn't supposed to go near private road work because of his Highways Department job, and had no official capacity with Mid–City, he helped arrange sales and backed Mid–City's notes on its equipment purchases. Mid–City got its first share of government money by obtaining a subcontract on Project 819 from Gresty's friend and former business partner, Burt Lymburner, about the same time Dick Holzworth and Clyde Thornton were enticed into the picture. But Mid–City's slim pocketbook was made even slimmer when the equally troubled Union Construction started missing on payments, putting Mid–City in arrears on its own debts. Word filtered up to Gaglardi about Gresty's involvement, but when the highways minister asked his employee if he had any direct or indirect involvement with any company engaged in Highways Department work, Gresty assured him he didn't. The situation deteriorated into the summer of 1958, with Union finally coming through and paying some of Mid–City's bills directly. But it wasn't enough; Mid–City folded its tent. As Gaglardi might put it, God's opportunity to go broke had knocked.

The RCMP, wondering why a Highways Department employee seemed to be financially involved in a failing company doing government work by subcontract, launched a secret investigation. But before their report came to any action, Gresty quit the Highways Department under pressure. A joint investigating committee of provincial and federal government engineers looked at Project 819 for possible irregularities, concluding that the problems experienced by Union weren't affecting the project adversely enough to recall the contract. Project 819 stumbled to completion. Finally, in the summer of 1959, its problems were becoming rather general knowledge.

Bob Strachan, who had taken over as CCF leader in 1956, ever ready to demand investigations of Gaglardi's department, noted "suggestions of possible patronage in the granting of contracts," and called for "a full independent investigation into the whole operation of the Highways Department."

Strachan alleged that a director of a company on Project 819 was an elder in Gaglardi's church (he was talking about Gresty, who was still listed as a director of Mid–City due to a foul–up in communications between Slim Campbell and the Registrar of Companies); that the director of a second was a defeated Social Credit candidate in Kaslo-Slocan (Mickey Moran, lawyer, developer, who had unsuccessfully taken on Randolph Harding in the 1956 election); and that the director of a third was a defeated Social Credit candidate in Kamloops and was now administrator of the government extension of Woodlands school at Tranquille Sanitorium in Kamloops (Roy Merrick, a longtime Gaglardi acquaintance, Socred worker, unsuccessful candidate in the 1958 federal election, appointed to the Tranquille job only in March 1959). The CCF leader appended a long list of companies and their directorships.

"It is obvious from an examination of the factors outlined that Mr. Gaglardi is using his office for political patronage. . . . Many of the road contracts are given to companies that are sympathetic to, or have directors connected with, Mr. Gaglardi, Social Credit, or Mr. Gaglardi's church."

At the least, Strachan was misinformed. At worst, he was being irresponsible, making giant leaps of cynicism for political gain. It would have been very difficult for Gaglardi to fix the awarding of contracts. They went to the lowest bidder, and he didn't handle the bidding personally; others in his department did that. There were stories about Gaglardi being handed a $35,000 cheque by a contractor, and about him supposedly being slipped a wad of bills wrapped in a newspaper at the Victoria airport, even about equipment suppliers paying travel expenses in return for favourable consideration. But never did anyone prove any of it. In fact, says Gaglardi, there were only ever two occasions when anything inappropriate was suggested to him. One was when Dawson Construction was working on two major jobs in the Fraser Canyon, and won a third. A contractor Dawson had underbid by $900 asked Gaglardi to reconsider. Dawson didn't need the third contract, the man said, and since the difference was so small, why not give it to him instead?

> *I said, "Harry, I'm sorry, but if it was only nine cents' difference, I couldn't do anything for you." I may have felt that maybe he was about to suggest something but in my recollection I remember that little doubt that I had, but I would have to say in all fairness that if he had any intention I didn't receive it. And at no time, not one contractor in the province of British Columbia ever came to me suggesting that if I would do this they would do that. But an equipment supplier contacted Bob, who was just a boy going to school, and suggested that if his dad would buy equipment from a certain company he would be able to get certain privileges. And I said to Bob, "You just don't pay any attention to anybody who says something like that because your dad is not about to do something like that."*

Nevertheless, the entire province was abuzz with the blossoming scandal. As British Columbians prattled about it over their coffee and their cocktails, fed by the excited headlines of each new edition, Gaglardi bristled. His department was "an open book to anyone who is authorized to look into it."

Gaglardi refuted a claim by Strachan that he was spending $20 million a year on day–labour contracts. It was only $3 million, or about three or four percent of his total budget. The day–labour situation had been the subject of a lot of gossip in itself, because it was used for small jobs that didn't go to tender. The potential for abuse was, therefore, greater. Ginter was supposedly getting more than his fair share. Not so, says Gaglardi.

> *Day–labour work is where you haven't got any contractual specifications for a short job, say of a half a mile. The contractor would be able to rent his machines on an hourly basis to the department. Supposing a contractor didn't have a job and he had millions of dollars' worth of equipment that he had to be making payments on. Sometimes he would come to me and say, "Mr. Gaglardi, have you got any day–labour work?" If there was*

*I would say, "Well, here's a month's work for you." It always
went through Fraser McLean and (controller) Al Rhodes.*

But the *Vancouver Sun* had some new questions. In 1957, said
the paper, two men who worked on Calvary Temple construction
for several months had their wages paid by Bonanza
Construction, Lymburner's L and M spinoff, from Project 819
funds. It said statements for the men's wages were made out by
Tony Gaglardi and sent directly to Bonanza. The men, Dominic
Donatelli and Larry Jontz, were paid a total of $4,171.91 by
Bonanza. Donatelli was paid a little under $3,000 between July
and December 1957, and Jontz about $1,300 between September
and December.

The *Sun*'s revelations were absolutely true, as far as they
went (the RCMP had confiscated the cheques during their Project
819 investigation), but Gaglardi couldn't see what they had to do
with anything. If Burt Lymburner wanted to give something
toward the building of Calvary Temple, it was up to him. ("I
never received one cent from Calvary Temple.") Tony Gaglardi
had been hired to look after the job, and had stayed with Phil and
Jennie. He'd brought up a couple of the boys from Mission to
help him out, and Lymburner obviously had figured a good way
to contribute would be to pay their wages. Bert Gaglardi was
there, too, and some volunteers for awhile. It was a big job and a
lot of people wanted to help out. Phil Gaglardi's position was that
he didn't know from Adam's off-ox what was being paid to
anybody by anybody. So he denied knowing anything about
Bonanza paying the wages of Donatelli and Jontz.

The fact remained, of course, that cheques *had* gone to Jontz
and Donatelli, some from L and M, some from Bonanza, sent to
Tony at Phil and Jennie Gaglardi's St. Paul Street home in
Kamloops. The payments had stopped, on Lymburner's orders, in
December 1957 as winter forced a wind-down in work on Project
819. Though none of it necessarily meant anything devious was
going on, it again raised suspicions. Despite the protests of the
highways minister, the media coverage and opposition sniping
were again raising the question: did people who contributed to
Phil Gaglardi's church expect to do so gratis, or did they expect
to be listed in some book of political debts neatly ledgered in Phil
Gaglardi's mind?

Throughout all this, Burt Glazer was getting impatient. Union
still owed him his $25,000. So he stepped things up, hiring
Vancouver lawyer Ken Meredith, who got wind of the fact that
Union Contractors was being phased out (a new Holzworth–Thornton

company, Continental Contractors, had won Project 1023 near
Creston) and worried that Glazer was going to get cheated out of his
money by the switch in companies. Glazer sent Meredith to court
and, finally, in October 1959, received a judgment from Mr. Justice
Tom Norris restraining Union Contractors or its officers from
receiving payments from the Highways Department, and appointing
Montreal Trust as receiver for any payments forthcoming.

Meredith immediately wired Gaglardi in Victoria telling him of
Norris' order, and mailed a copy for good measure. But Gaglardi
was in Kamloops, so Edith Scarff gave the telegram to Tom Miard,
who turned it over to Rhodes. The controller called Attorney
General's Department solicitor Neil McDiarmid and read him the
telegram. It was McDiarmid's opinion that Norris' decision didn't
bind the Highways Department and that the normal procedure for
making payments should be followed. That normal procedure was
to make payments only to the contractor. But McDiarmid told
Rhodes to draw Thornton's attention to Norris' injunction.

On November 13, 1959, a cheque for $75,696 was sent off to
Thornton's bank in Bonner's Ferry, with an admonition from
Rhodes to "govern yourself accordingly." Thornton didn't. He
discussed the injunction with his bank manager but neglected to
do anything about consigning the money back to Montreal Trust.

On January 6, 1960, Meredith launched a suit on behalf of
Glazer in Supreme Court in Vancouver, giving notice that he
would apply to have Phil Gaglardi jailed for contempt of court for
disobeying Norris' order of October 29. He alleged that Gaglardi
aided and abetted Union Contractors to receive the payment in
spite of the injunction. M.M. McFarlane, QC, argued for Gaglardi
in front of Norris. "My client would not wilfully do anything to
the detriment in any way of the authority and dignity of this
court. . . . I submit that no case for contempt exists."

Norris was a big, gruff fellow with a starch–like shrub of hair
setting off his black judicial robes. He had been named to the
B.C. Supreme Court only the previous year, but he dominated his
courtroom. His sympathies hardly lay with Social Credit or
anybody who had anything to do with it. For years he'd practised
law in Kelowna. Back in 1936, he'd defeated W.A.C. Bennett for
the provincial Conservative nomination in South Okanagan
riding. Norris was beaten in the election by a Liberal, and
charged his defeat to lack of help from Bennett.

Glazer's lawyer now was Jay Gould, who produced affidavits
from Glazer and Meredith that insisted Gaglardi had helped
Union in getting the loans via a letter written for Lymburner to

Rosencrantz. Gould argued that the claim that Gaglardi, as highways minister, simply relied on a legal opinion from Bonner's lawyer showed a magnificently closed set of eyes to the facts of the Norris injunction.

Norris reserved judgment (in the meantime, he would have to hear a similar application on contempt of court against Clyde Thornton), guaranteeing that Project 819 wouldn't be forgotten for awhile. It was taking on the appearance of much more than a missed opportunity. It was a golden egg that had turned to stone. And Phil Gaglardi was the goose.

A Helping Hand

Woe to him that is alone when he falleth, for he hath not another to help him up.
ECCLESIASTES 4.10

The day I stop helping people is the day I'll be buried, because I don't want to be around. . . . If I'm doing wrong by helping people out, then I'll continue to do that kind of wrong.
PHIL GAGLARDI

Gaglardi, said Bob Strachan, had always refused to answer allegations about his department, but this time he would have to come up with some facts. Strachan listed twenty–two companies and individuals he alleged were involved in patronage. He was a bulldog, his teeth clenched on the pantleg of his elfin adversary. His jaw set, he refused to let go.

"I think contracts are being given and handled in a manner that does damage to the public purse of B.C.," the socialist leader's brogue echoed resolutely through the public debate. "Contracts are being awarded to companies by the minister without regard to the financial stability or engineering experience of the companies concerned . . . I find it difficult to believe there has been no political interference."

Strachan claimed there were three major groups linked with the highways minister via interlocking directorships and shareholders. One included the L and M Logging–Union Contractors–Gresty bunch, while a second comprised several Ben Ginter companies. The third group allegedly consisted of several companies connected to Fritz and Lloyd Jordan and Mickey Moran. The first two groups had already received attention. So had Moran, the high–profile Castlegar lawyer, one–time Socred candidate, and Gaglardi acquaintance. But while the Jordans, who hailed from Edgewood, were well–known in the West Kootenays, they were a new entry on Strachan's growing list.

Strachan demanded Gaglardi open his department's files for scrutiny, and that the RCMP report on Project 819 be released.

Gaglardi expanded his not inconsiderable chest, filled his ample lungs, and pleaded innocence. "You can go through the public accounts with a fine–tooth comb," he said. "I live in a glass house and you may take a look any time you please."

Only one or two percent of contractors who had ever done jobs for the Highways Department had got into financial difficulties, Gaglardi said.

It was a dramatic battle. A night sitting of the legislature was forced to get approval of the $85.4–million Highways Department estimates. After five hours of debate, they were passed.

The 1960 session was loaded with election talk, but Bennett waited for fall, finally calling it for September 12. That year's vote was interesting both from a provincial and from a parochial point of view. Its results were contradictory to the apparent public clamour for Socred blood, and Gaglardi blood. The Socreds were facing their first general election since the Sommers scandal. Bennett was having trouble establishing financing for his Peace River power plan. The party machinery was not in good shape. On the plus side, B.C. had a new ferry system, a host of impressive new highways edifices, and had officially torched its debt. "Vote for the government that gets things done," Bennett exhorted the voters. But the CCF was unusually strong and well–prepared for the campaign. Its coffers, thanks in part to the new alliance developing with labour, were bulging. The Horde was confident. Bennett, rather than fretting over the complicity between the CCF and unions, decided to use it to turn the campaign into a battle between his Little Government and Big Labour.

Labour wasn't happy at being cast in the role of heavy, and took a predictably defensive and indignant posture. Gaglardi, often complaining about "wild statements" from the opponents of Social Credit, was accused of making a few wild statements himself. "Gaglardi's wild harangues against labour are nothing new," concluded B.C. Federation of Labour secretary Pat O'Neal. "The little fellow, as he refers to himself, likes to wind up periodically and attack labour with wild and irresponsible statements."

In Dewdney, Lyle Wicks was worried about a challenge from CCFer Dave Barrett, a staff-training officer fired from Haney Correction Institute by Bonner ten months earlier, allegedly for trying to organize prison workers, so Gaglardi went to Haney to campaign for Wicks.

The highways minister spent a few days in the Kootenays, too, handing out promises and warning against the CCF and the unions. B.C. workers didn't go for unification of labour with the socialists, he said. "Instead of being unified, labour is being broken up. This is not good for labour."

Gaglardi even made it home to Silverdale, where two hundred people turned out to hear him. "You people know all about me and I'm just the same as the boy who grew up here," he told them. The only difference was that now he had millions of dollars a year to spend. He spoke for two hours, spending much of his time joyfully CCF-bashing.

Gaglardi ran into a lot of heckling, especially in his own riding. He arrived late for one all-candidates forum in Kamloops and was booed and insulted for the entire evening. Nevertheless, a week and a half later, he was voted in for another term with a solid majority. It wasn't the hecklers, the disillusioned reformists, nor the professional confrontationists who decided who would represent Kamloops and who would rule in Victoria. It was the vast, silent majority that never made headlines, never stood up in a meeting to harass, never led a march or carried a banner. They voted Gaglardi in because, in spite of his airplanes and speeding tickets, the controversy over contractors and so-called patronage, they still believed in him. He was the unpolitician, the cutter of red tape, the nemesis of bureaucracy. He was their rebel.

As Kamloops was re-electing Gaglardi, British Columbia as a whole was re-electing Social Credit, handing it another mandate to govern. They reduced Bennett's majority from thirty-nine to thirty-two seats. And though Strachan's prophecy of a Socred sepulchre proved false, the CCF did gain significantly, jumping from ten to sixteen seats, and the Liberals doubled to four seats, one of them thanks to the retirement of Tom Uphill in Fernie. George Gregory, Gaglardi's ace Liberal antagonist, was defeated, but Ray Perrault, in his first campaign as Liberal leader after taking over from Art Laing, gained election. Once again, Deane Finlayson, so confident of his party's prospects, was thrashed. This time, he quit as leader of the Tories.

In Dewdney riding, Lyle Wicks, labour minister, the man who created Social Credit as a viable political entity in B.C., went down to defeat at the hands of Dave Barrett. Now, only one fellow cabinet minister came by to express disappointment and to wish him luck — Phil Gaglardi on his way through from a visit to Silverdale. For all his misgivings about Gaglardi, Wicks remembered that gesture, and appreciated it.

Though Gaglardi was upheld by the people's court, he still had to face the law courts, and there he was not so popular. In a Vancouver courtroom a little more than a month after the election, Gaglardi stood alongside Clyde Thornton, listening to the condemning words of Mr. Justice Tom Norris as the decision was handed down in the contempt charges brought by Burt Glazer.

"His actions throughout show a lack of a proper sense of responsibility in the observance of the law. . . . He permitted his subordinates to ignore the order of the court in favour of carrying out the 'practice and policy' of his department."

Norris said he had given the evidence careful consideration during the months since the trial. He found that Thornton and his company, Union Contractors Ltd., had "stood to gain" as a result of the contempt that had seen Gaglardi's department send a cheque to Thornton instead of the trust company as stipulated in Norris' October 1959 court ruling.

"As to you, Gaglardi" — he spat out the words as if trying to rid his tongue of a disagreeable taste — "your offense was an extremely serious one but it may be said in mitigation that there is no evidence that you gained in any way from your failure to obey the order of the court."

The judge's words stung Gaglardi deeply. Gaglardi felt a mixture of anger, shame and disbelief. But Norris was even tougher on Thornton.

Thornton "totally disregarded the duty on him to observe the order implicitly and to the letter."

"Clyde Wilbur Thornton, I have found you in wilful contempt of the order of this court made by me in this action on October 29, 1959, and I commit you to prison for your contempt.

"Philip Arthur Gaglardi, I have found that you aided and abetted the defendant Union Contractors Ltd. in its contempt of the order of this court and thereby obstructed and caused the course of justice to be obstructed. I fine you the sum of $1,000. . . . " Thornton would stay in jail until he had "purged himself" of the debt to Glazer. Gaglardi would be held in custody until his fine was paid.

Gaglardi wanted to tell this judge exactly what he thought of his stupid judgment. McFarlane, his lawyer, was worried he might do just that. "I moved close to Gaglardi and he started to jump up and I said, 'Don't say anything.' He could have said something foolish."

Gaglardi was led to the sheriff's office with McFarlane. There, he wrote a personal cheque for $1,000 and was released. He told McFarlane to file an immediate appeal.

Thornton appealed, too. He had to wait in Oakalla prison until December before his lawyer could get him back in court, but the three Court of Appeal judges didn't budge. Thornton would have to stay in jail until he paid the $25,000 owed to Glazer.

That was a foreboding of what was in store for Gaglardi's appeal. It, too, was rejected.

As it happened, McFarlane and Norris had served in the army together and were good friends. Later, they would serve together again, this time as fellow benchers. On at least one social occasion after Gaglardi's contempt conviction, McFarlane took advantage of their friendship to give Norris hell for what the lawyer was convinced was a bad decision. "I never had the slightest difficulty at all about telling him the decision was wrong. I often told Norris I thought he was wrong. I still think he was wrong."

Several aspects of the case troubled him. The mistake had been in the legal advice given the Attorney General's Department. "It was for that error that Gaglardi was found personally guilty of contempt of court." The error in Norris' judgment, as McFarlane saw it, was in the consequences. Gaglardi, as minister, was responsible for the errors made by the civil servants involved in the payment of money to Thornton. The fact he was following legal advice didn't excuse him from that. But, said McFarlane, Gaglardi should have been required to repay Glazer the money out of Highways Department funds, or to get the money back from Thornton, but not face a contempt conviction.

The politics bothered McFarlane as well. "In the whole case there were political overtones. Norris was a real Tory and he was absolutely opposed to W.A.C. Bennett and the Social Credit party, and Norris was the kind of man who would feel that kind of thing keenly. I don't think it could be said he was out to get Gaglardi, but he would be predisposed against him."

Jay Gould, the opposing lawyer, was also involved in politics, with the Liberal party. Gould's political activities, in fact, stretched back to the old Coalition government. He was a Liberal MLA for the dual–member Vancouver–Burrard riding in Boss Johnson's government from 1948 to 1952. He was beaten in the 1952 and 1953 elections. There was, in Gould's opinion, no hint of political bias or indication anyone was trying to get Gaglardi. "We were not interested in doing anything to Gaglardi. We were interested in getting (Glazer's) money." He felt Gaglardi got off lightly with a $1,000 fine. "He could have gone to jail, and he could have lost his seat (in the legislature)." Gould would be named to the Supreme Court bench in 1965.

Result of the appeals left Thornton in bad straits. He couldn't put his hands on the $25,000 needed to get himself out of Oakalla. Two days before Christmas, Norris gave Thornton his freedom, after another tongue–lashing.

Gaglardi considered taking the appeal of his own contempt conviction to the Supreme Court of Canada, but dropped the idea, convinced he couldn't get it overturned.

Phil Gaglardi's personal pride — if he would admit to such an attribute — was based on helping people:

> *I feel that if you can help somebody you should do it. I've always been that way. I think I get that basically from Scripture because the Apostle Paul said, "I am a debtor." And my feeling is that every individual that God gave breath to has certain talents. I think the most selfish thing you can do in life is to think in terms of what can I gain. I am an individual that has always had a feeling that the greatest achievement is in lending a hand to somebody in need. I would think the greatest motivator that I've ever had is need.*

The love–thy–neighbour approach to life had, of course, been part of Gaglardi's upbringing in Silverdale. He carried that with him into the ministry and had, he believed, practised it anywhere he and Jennie pastored. There are those who remember how, in 1937, he drove twenty miles a day to milk the cows, and split and stack wood for a woman whose husband was too sick to do it himself. And how he harvested an entire potato crop for an injured farmer. Many a motorist stranded with a flat tire or stalled engine had Phil Gaglardi to thank for getting a car rolling again. One night he became a stretcher–bearer at a highway accident near Kamloops. At Calvary Temple he had counselled criminals, fed the hungry, and handed out money from his own pocket to those who were broke.

A friend who knew Gaglardi well both as a minister of highways and a minister of the gospel acknowledges his achievements in government but always liked him better as a preacher. "Phil Gaglardi is one of the outstanding men of this century — the credits far outweigh the debits. He knew how to build roads; he could be ruthless as a highways minister. He had two personalities, and I liked him better as a minister of the church. He was genuinely concerned about children having good shoes to wear. His real strength was his concern for the gospel, for people, and his knowledge and ability in religion. His weakness was in coming on too strong according to what Phil Gaglardi thought. If you agreed with him, fine; if you didn't, well, he didn't appreciate having anybody stand up to him."

By helping, it had always been Gaglardi's belief, you were in return helped. God saw to it. To a large extent, this self–image of the boss–servant was true; he genuinely wanted to do the right thing by those he cared about. Gaglardi didn't always stop to consider the consequences of his own generosity. If somebody was hungry, you fed him. If he was out of work, you gave him a job. Though it angered him when anyone suggested otherwise, he sometimes had trouble distinguishing between his job as a minister of the church and of government, and appreciating the potential problems of this melding of roles. He thought he knew the dividing line, yet if a friend or a member of his church needed help, and Gaglardi could give him that help as a member of government, he gave it. He didn't stop to change hats.

This inevitably displeased some people. Like the time an old friend, a teacher named Donald Backman, moved to Kamloops from Saskatchewan and Gaglardi wrote the school board on government stationery asking them to give the friend a job. People didn't accept that in a positive light. They talked about interference, about patronage.

Ideally, patronage is simply the use of one's position to bene-fit, unselfishly, another. In the corridors of power, patronage takes quite another form, one that's regarded by many not only as acceptable, but necessary. You appoint political "friends" to jobs, offer them preferred treatment, or give them government contracts as rewards for loyalty. As Jeffrey Simpson points out in his *Spoils of Power: The Politics of Patronage*, it often has nothing to do with breaking the law, much more to do with ethical conduct. And that depends on the eye of the beholder, conditioned by political culture.

Historically, the building of highways in British Columbia has offered ample opportunity to engage in various forms of patronage, especially pork–barrelling. In virtually every election in this century, voters have been promised new and better road systems by all parties vying for public support. So when W.A.C. Bennett and Social Credit asked for the confidence of the people in 1952, the anti–patronage rhetoric, not to mention the call for a better provincial highways system, was not exactly new.

Neither should it be surprising, then, that Phil Gaglardi was plagued by charges of patronage throughout his years as public works and highways minister. Far more remarkable, perhaps, is that so little of it was true. In fact, the elimination of the construction cartel and the opening up of bidding on highways work was one of the first and most dramatic acts of the new Social Credit administration against what had been an entrenchment of patronage for decades. By awarding contracts according to the ability of the contractor to do the job, instead of depending on more subjective criteria, and by keeping himself at arm's length from bidding, Gaglardi guarded against the dispensing of highways work as patronage. Though he was accused of using discretionary day labour to reward contractor friends, there was never any proof of that, and he would have required the unlikely collusion of an entire department full of engineers, in any case. Often, he was accused of pork-barrelling by building roads in Socred ridings while ignoring constituencies that had elected opposition MLAs. It was expected practice for opposition members to harangue Gaglardi in the legislature about the condition of roads in their ridings, claiming they would have had better treatment if they belonged to the right party. CCF caucus chairman Randolph Harding was one of the most effective in trying to bait Gaglardi. Harding had first been elected in the West Kootenay riding of Kaslo–Slocan in 1945, and he was a respected and able member, serving as his party's caucus chairman. He claimed the ridings of Bennett, Gaglardi and Wesley Black got more than their share of highways work. During the 1961 session, for example, he complained especially about Black's riding, adjacent to Kaslo–Slocan. Gaglardi hotly disputed Harding's charges. "Everywhere in the province we are trying to treat fairly. We are doing everything we can to keep away from discrimination. I will give you all the work I can next year," he told Harding. But Harding didn't back off. "Special privileges, you bet your life some cabinet ministers get special privileges as far as highways. Any minister who can pussyfoot into your office can get work done."

Practice indicated differently — Gaglardi built his highways through NDP-rich Vancouver Island and the Kootenays, as well as other parts of the province. A classic example was the famous sawdust highway in Burnaby: it was constructed over peat bogs because the civic government asked him to spare more valuable residential land. The mayor of Burnaby at the time was a New Democrat. "I want to tell you absolutely that anybody who came to me and showed work needing to be done in his riding got it done," says Gaglardi. He and Bennett weren't shy about promising new highways during election campaigns, however. It was often said that survey stakes littered the land like pegs on a cribbage board during elections, and disappeared just as quickly the day after. Yet Gaglardi built more highways through every part of the province than anyone has before or since. In the Rossland–Trail by-election of 1958, for example, Gaglardi promised voters a new bridge in Trail if they elected Don Brothers. They did; he built their bridge.

Some of the allegations against Gaglardi were of the criminal type: accepting bribes from contractors, "fixing" contracts so that friends could win them. As has already been discussed, and will be discussed further, none of these charges was ever proven, and most of them simply afforded the opposition a few fleeting newspaper headlines. Nepotism would also be charged, and he did indulge in it to a limited and mostly harmless extent. The really serious claims of using his office to help family, like so many other of the patronage allegations, were thrown about like so much mud by his political enemies, who then quickly retreated to let Gaglardi fend for himself. Although the highways minister's cries of "smear" and "wild charges" often sounded like a panicked defense, they usually accurately reflected the situation. The politicians, mostly Liberals and NDPers, who went after Gaglardi didn't necessarily do so insincerely. In their political zeal and cynicism, they usually genuinely believed the highways minister was guilty without the requirement of proof. If Gaglardi was guilty of patronage of any kind, it was of a less serious variety in which a number of his friends and acquaintances found their way into government appointments and civil-service jobs. Though distasteful, cronyism is neither criminal nor corrupt, since the jobs exist and must be filled. And always, Gaglardi's defense was that the people he helped into those jobs were qualified. However, while the Project 819 and "The Three G's" type of scenarios could be denied and explained away, the dispensation of jobs was not easily shrugged off.

Gaglardi never did fully understand the importance of justice not only being done, but of being seen to be done, and never got the hang of discretionary patronage when it came to helping people out. He cared only that, in his eyes, justice was being done, not whether others would see it the same way. To Gaglardi, it boiled down to this: being a Socred or a Pentecostal surely didn't disqualify you from getting a job! There were examples, Gaglardi admits now, of "hundred-percent patronage" on his part. But he sees none of it as unjustified. When a Calvary Temple member named Wally Broening asked him for a job because his railroad work was keeping him from his family, Gaglardi recommended him for an opening as a government building inspector. Broening got the job. "I would say it was in the line of patronage but yet it wasn't patronage, it was a necessary thing in regards to their family." Another church member, Fred Renk, was technically ineligible for government employment because he was a German citizen. "He kept pressing me so eventually I suggested he ask the department for a job and he did and they gave him a job. I did that because he had children and so on."

Ironically, both men later turned against him. Broening sided against Gaglardi in a dispute with the Pentecostal Assemblies of Canada, and Renk tried to ruin him politically by swearing Gaglardi had taken Highways Department materials for use on the Silver Sage Ranch.

It doesn't really matter, says Gaglardi, that his friends and church members got jobs, because they were always qualified. "I would never stick a square peg in a round hole."

Yet, the qualifications of the people finding employment with or through Gaglardi were quite often untraditional. When Jake Krushnisky, Socred and member of Calvary Temple, needed a job, he became an engineer in the Highways Department, even though he wasn't qualified to be an engineer. When Vince Gresty, a friend and member of Calvary Temple, came down with heart trouble and had to give up his business, he became mechanical superintendent in the Highways Department, even though his previous experience was in contracting. When Roy Merrick, president of the first federal Socred group in Kamloops, and unsuccessful federal Socred candidate, needed a job, he became superintendent of Tranquille School for the mentally handicapped, though, like Gresty, his previous experience was mainly in private contracting, with some accounting. When Beverley Kriese, a twenty–one–year–old member of Calvary Temple, wanted a job, she was hired as a rehabilitation officer and caseworker for the government, without civil–service competition, though her only experience was as a stenographer. And, when Walter Smith, Gaglardi's former campaign manager, the man who had enticed him into politics, needed a job, he became superintendent of public works for the government in Kamloops, even though he had placed sixth out of six in a civil–service competition for the job.

"Certainly, some of these people were friends of mine, no two ways about that. When you're talking patronage, certainly I had a lot of say about what happened in my department, but only on the basis of my personnel department making a recommendation."

Sometimes Gaglardi's generosity didn't matter. Such as in the case of his teacher friend, Backman. The school board, independent of outside influence, ignored Gaglardi's request, treating Backman's application as it would any other. The only damage done was to the dignity of school trustees who found it highly inappropriate for a minister of the Crown to suggest to the board who it should hire. In Krushnisky's case, the Highways Department got an employee who performed his job competently for many years. In Gresty, Gaglardi and his department got a large headache when the mechanical superintendent dabbled in places he should have stayed clear of.

In some cases, people got jobs in spite of Gaglardi's help, not because of it. Roy Merrick was highly recommended by Gaglardi for the job at Tranquille School. But although Merrick's immediate past experience had been in the unrelated field of construction, his appointment to an administrative position at a provincial health facility wasn't as simple a case of patronage as it appeared. More justice was being done than appeared to be done. Merrick had grown up in Alberta, cut his teeth adding A plus B and talking about the national credit. He was one of those Douglas disciples who believed in the economic philosophy of Social Credit, not simply its moralistic emphasis or political potential. In other words, Merrick and Social Credit were to each other everything Gaglardi and Social Credit weren't. But the movement brought them together in Kamloops nevertheless, and Merrick deeply respected Gaglardi's community work and political ability. When Merrick applied for the job at Tranquille, he was shortlisted with two other applicants. After five and a half hours of tests by a private consultant, he was given the job.

Yet, although Merrick was confident he'd got the job on his own credentials, Gaglardi remained just as convinced he had done much to help. A few years later, Gaglardi was miffed when Merrick refused to hire a man at Tranquille because of inadequate qualifications. The man needed a job and Gaglardi thought Merrick should repay past favours by giving him one.

The fact Gaglardi may have thought he was doing more to help people get jobs than was actually the case may reveal another contradiction about him. While it was an inherent part of his nature and upbringing to assist people in that way, and damn what anybody might think, he rejected any notion he was abusing patronage. Each time he was accused of it, he strenuously, indignantly protested. Should a man be denied a job just because he belonged to Social Credit? Or to Phil Gaglardi's church?

Walter Smith was another appointee who believed he got his job strictly on his own merits and nobody else's. Smith, three times Gaglardi's campaign manager, like Merrick, once a contractor, and a federal Socred candidate against Davie Fulton, was well respected in the community. And, like Merrick, he preceded Gaglardi in Social Credit, becoming interested in the party's monetary reform policies in his late twenties in eastern Canada. Long before meeting Gaglardi, he would sit around with other Socreds philosophizing A-plus-B and dreaming of, and planning, the day when the movement would come to power. His religion was not Gaglardi's religion, his politics were not Gaglardi's politics, but a common sense of the need for a new morality in political life brought them together. That, and Gaglardi's obvious vote-getting potential.

When Smith applied for the job as superintendent of public works for Kamloops in November 1960, the Civil Service Commission recommended another applicant who had been working in the Public Works Department at Essondale. Smith wasn't even close, but Public Works Minister William Chant, an old friend of Smith's from those early Socred days, got him the job via order in council.

Alex Cassidy, like Merrick and Smith, had a solid-citizen reputation. A former bus driver, contractor, gift-shop operator and tire-company owner for twenty years before retiring, he was active in Social Credit and was a deacon of Calvary Temple. It was with considerable interest that rookie Vancouver East MLA Alex Macdonald discovered a couple of years after the Smith controversy that Cassidy was a "tire consultant" with the Highways Department in Kamloops. For $20 a day plus expenses, his job was to inspect tires on government vehicles.

Cassidy explained that he knew all phases of tire servicing. His current job was province-wide, giving advice on recapping and replacement of tires and casings and types of tires to be used. He made policy recommendations and reports to the superintendent of maintenance. He also trained other inspectors, and gave safety instruction.

Gaglardi defended Cassidy's hiring at the time, and still defends it. "Cassidy was an awful nice guy. We were completely out of line in the department as far as tires went. Perfectly good tires were being thrown away until I got in there. Tires went to Cassidy for repair, so the regional director in Kamloops said, 'Cassidy should give us advice on tires,' so I said, 'OK, you hire him.' It saved us thousands and thousands of dollars. That wasn't patronage at all. The men in the department asked me for it."

During the public controversy over the hiring, Gaglardi asked again, "Just because a man belongs to the party, does it mean he can't get a government job?"

The answer, as a general rule, was a qualified 'yes' — at least in the sense that party affiliation or friendship not be valued more than job qualifications — but though Phil Gaglardi agreed with that caveat, he never did grasp the absolute political importance of proving the distinction.

The Hand of the Philistine

And David said, 'The Lord, who delivered me from the paw of the lion and from the paw of the bear, will deliver me from the hand of this Philistine.' And Saul said to David, 'Go, and the Lord be with you.'
I SAMUEL 17.37

I may be a little fella but I'm not scared of any big fella and I'm not going to be intimidated by any big fella!
PHIL GAGLARDI

Early in the new year, there was talk about lawsuits and political action to boot Phil Gaglardi out of the legislature. The Constitution Act said a member of the legislature must forfeit his seat if he was convicted of a "felony or any infamous crime," while the Provincial Elections Act disqualified anyone convicted of "treason or any indictable offence."

The idea of getting Gaglardi thrown out based on the statutes never amounted to anything, but an old political foe was preparing in January 1961 to mount a more serious challenge.

Gordon Gibson had a six-year grievance to take up with Gaglardi and the Socreds. After his 1955 defeat at the hands of the Gaglardi–Bonner machine, the crag-faced bullhorn spent three years out of politics. But in 1958 he was elected again, this time representing North Vancouver. He was as loud and brash as ever, and still drinking hard (he gave it up a few years later when a doctor convinced him it was killing him). Despite Bob Sommers' conviction, Gibson remained appalled at what he saw as the government's failure to stop the patronage train that ran for a privileged few.

Gaglardi and Gibson, in private, got along very well. Gibson relished their vociferous exchanges in the House:

> *Sometimes the House would get very dull, and to be truthful with you, not more than a maximum of ten percent had much wit, humour or acting ability, or to hold an audience. You know, if you sat in those galleries and heard some of them talk you'd*

almost fall asleep. So when Phil and I got up – and we were both known for throwing away our microphones and speaking loudly and trying to be dramatic – we'd try to put on a show. You have to have a little fun when you're getting $5,000 a year and wasting a hell of a lot of time at it. Phil and I never said an unkind word to each other, but I remember one time he said, "I've been spending my time working for the people in Kamloops and for the Sunday school children while you've been out trying to make money in those lumber camps, and you've made it!" And I said, "You're a liar. You tried to make money logging and you went broke. You can run a bulldozer and that's as far as you got!"

For all the "fun" he and Gaglardi had with each other, Gibson convinced himself that the problems surrounding Clyde Thornton were worse than the Sommers case, if not legally, then morally. It took Gibson an hour to get it all off his chest when it came his turn to speak in the House. He started fast and never slowed down, paying particular attention to Gaglardi. "This government is riddled with moral dishonesty and moral corruption! Physical corruption has already been proven once!" he barked, referring to Sommers.

He slammed the cabinet: "The ministers have banded together to protect a minister whose offence is far more serious than that which sent his former colleague to jail for five years. If it had a shred of decency it would have resigned in a body long ago."

He ripped into the new power structure created by Gaglardi: "The heavy construction industry in B.C. has been mesmerized by what are called the three G's: Ginter, Gaglardi and God!" Ginter had received "millions and millions of dollars" from the Highways Department in eight years. Gaglardi, said millionaire ex–logger Gibson, was known as "the man who makes millionaires."

It was the most derisive speech of the session so far, and this time Gibson's good friend Gaglardi was ruffled. But he didn't respond that day. He would wait until that Thursday, when he was scheduled to conclude the debate on the throne speech in an evening sitting. Gaglardi was pondering, during the wait, what to do about some potentially devastating evidence that had come into his possession. He held two affidavits alleging that bribe attempts had been aimed at getting some dirt on him. One was from Clyde Thornton, claiming he'd got numerous phone calls in the fall of 1958 asking if he had received any favours from Gaglardi. In June 1959, he said, a man who leased equipment to contractors for highways jobs invited Thornton to lunch at the snooty Vancouver Club. The man had leased to Thornton, Geery,

Holzworth et al on the infamous Project 819. At the club, he introduced Thornton to Gordon Gibson and two other men. Afterward, he returned to Thornton's room in the Devonshire Hotel with him and told him, "The fellows want to nail Gaglardi to the cross" and would pay "any price" to do it. The offer of money was later repeated several times, said Thornton, who claimed the equipment leaser visited him in Oakalla in November 1960 and offered him a down payment of $10,000, plus another $50,000, to implicate the Highways Department. He said he also received a message in jail asking, "How foolish are you going to be and how long are you going to hold out? Why don't you let these boys put up this bond and get out and get some relief for yourself?" And Thornton said he replied: "I would stay in Oakalla 100,000 years before I would resort to any blackmail." The other affidavit was from Burt Lymburner, who said he had been approached by the same man on behalf of people "who would pay a fancy price for information that would discredit the minister of highways Mr. P.A. Gaglardi and the Social Credit government of British Columbia." Lymburner said another man had offered him a bribe on April 2, 1959, to falsify information, and when Lymburner refused he'd been told, "If you don't take this money, the world isn't big enough for you to hide in, and they will find you floating down the river." The threats and bribe offers had continued into mid–January 1961. Thornton and Lymburner swore out the affidavits, they said, for their protection and for Gaglardi's. They believed the bribe attempts were made in an attempt to get information that could be given to Gordon Gibson.

Gaglardi found this information disturbing, and didn't quite know what to do about it. Despite their tongue–wrestling in public, he felt much the same way as Gibson; he harboured no animosity towards him — Gibson was a good friend of his — and found it difficult to believe he could be responsible for such a thing.

The House and the public galleries were wedged tight when Gaglardi delivered what was to become known as his "confessions" speech, one of his best. In this Colosseum he was the Christian facing the lions; he was once again David going out to do combat with only God at his side and the sling of truth as he saw it. The Philistines sat there waiting for him, and he was there to take up the challenge, a stripling, a little fellow, there alone to do the job. So he clattered and banged around, and threw off his armour, his convictions and faith the only weapons he needed. Voice clamouring, arms flailing a phantom sling, he denied there was anything wrong in his department. But he was, he admitted, guilty of certain things.

"I am guilty of refusing to stoop to unscrupulous means that spokesmen of certain parties have stooped to. I have listened to the statement 'money talks.' " (Gibson had made his money–talks speech in 1954.) Looking straight at Gibson, he fulminated, "I would like to ask of the man who made the statement, whose money talks? Who is behind the approaches that have been made to certain individuals in B.C. of offers of $10,000 to $50,000, if they would make any statement that would incriminate the minister of highways? Whose money is behind these things? . . . What money talks? And whose money talks? And how loud does it talk?"

Years later, Gibson told the author he didn't have a clue what Gaglardi was talking about that day, partly because Gaglardi wasn't coming right out and charging him with wrongdoing, and because he had nothing to do with any bribe attempts. "The only part I took in that was in debate on the floor. I knew nothing about that part of it." The rest of the House didn't understand, either. And reporters, there to record the bloodshed, to scratch down every word, passed off the talk of bribery as Gaglardi's vivid imagination working overtime. None of them knew about the affidavits. It is a clue to Gaglardi's personality that he didn't simply march into the legislature and throw down the affidavits for all to see. Certainly, his political adversaries would have done it had the tables been turned — they would demonstrate that very soon. Gaglardi, on the other hand, tried only to make his point without direct accusation of wrongdoing. He couldn't bring himself to play the innuendo game, and there were times when it would hurt him badly. His reluctance to go for the throat left him on several occasions with little ammunition but to stand on his tiptoes and shout "smear" and "conspiracy," which he did often enough, but with little effect. On this occasion, it was a lost opportunity to push his political enemies into a corner and put them on the defensive. He relied instead on his own oratorical skills.

As Gaglardi rolled along, his cabinet colleagues, his appreciative fellow Israelites, thumped their desks in support. Bennett, Gaglardi's Saul, sat, eyes aglint with tears of emotion, looking up approvingly at his champion.

The grand finale: "I don't know what my future holds, but I would like to make a confession to this House. I am guilty of certain things." Like working too hard, not taking holidays, being too dedicated to his job, helping people, taking flack without fighting back. "I am guilty of being determined, tenacious, bull–headed, if you wish. I have come up the hard way and everything I have I fought for!"

Gaglardi was shouting so loudly he could be heard outside in the hallways. "I want people to know I have fought a clean fight, and if necessary I will go down fighting!"

And Gaglardi retired from the field of battle, having smote the Philistines, especially the Goliath from North Vancouver.

Around Victoria, Gordon Dowding was regarded as something of a radical even for one of The Godless Socialists. The CCF's — now the New Democratic Party's — expert on parliamentary procedure, the lawyer/MLA was always coming up with new ideas about how the legislature should be run. A pretty fair debater, he generally chose not to use the parliamentary privilege accorded MLAs in the House to harangue opposing sides with sly innuendo or crude insults. If he had a question about something, he asked it without inference.

In February 1963 Dick Holzworth came to talk to him in his Victoria office. Opinions of Holzworth ranged from rough diamond to plain rough, but he possessed a certain boisterous charm. Smarting from his financially disastrous experience with roadbuilding in B.C., he had been making the rounds with stories about graft and corruption in the B.C. Highways Department. "I wasn't out to get Gaglardi. I just wanted my money back." Nevertheless, while Holzworth's suspicions would be disproven, Gaglardi would first be put through several weeks of hell.

Part of his story was based on what he claimed Thornton told him: that Gaglardi had asked Thornton to pay off a $6,700 mortgage for his buddy, church member and one-time highways employee Vince Gresty in November 1958, and that Union would then be "well taken care of" with lucrative highways contracts.

Holzworth also said that, one day at a meeting in the farmhouse office on Project 819, as the switch was being made from L and M to Union, Burt Lymburner brought up the subject of the organist at Gaglardi's church, whom he said he'd been paying $350 a month from L and M funds. Would Union Contractors continue this policy, since that had been part of the deal for L and M getting the 819 job? It was decided, claimed Holzworth, that Thornton would look after paying the money out of the Union Contractors budget. Then, later on, during breakfast at the Strawberry Inn restaurant in Creston, Slim Campbell of Mid-City Construction told him the organist at the church was Flo Gresty, Vince's wife.

Intriguing as these charges were, potentially the most damaging was one about tinkering with project estimates. Highways jobs were broken down into components, with estimates being made for various parts of the job, and payments being made upon completion. Holzworth had copies of worksheets for Estimate No. 5 on Project 819, dated October 31, 1957, that showed figures for rock and "other material" had been altered by $35,000 to the benefit of L and M Logging.

Another estimate, No. 4, had been raised by $100,000. According to Holzworth, there was no way L and M had the equipment or capability to move that much material for the month covered by the estimate. Besides which, the payroll for the period in Estimate No. 4 didn't reflect the change. According to Holzworth, the payments were made to L and M before Union Contractors took over, but Union got stuck cleaning up L and M's mess.

Since Project 819 hadn't gone well, he said, Union was supposed to be taken care of with a "get–well" contract on Project 1023 in Creston. Holzworth said they were instructed on what to bid in order to win the contract. But instead of making a killing, the job was another disaster, primarily because of errors in estimates on moving earth and rock, and Thornton and Holzworth had to bail out, letting another company take over.

When Dowding began speaking on February 26, 1963, only fourteen Social Credit members were in their seats in the House. Bennett was in Chilliwack for a speaking engagement; Gaglardi was at an equipment show in Chicago.

"Recently," said Dowding, "a body of evidence was laid before me in the form of an affidavit and some exhibits. It concerns the public welfare." Within eleven minutes there were twenty–two government members listening carefully to Dowding's quiet, matter–of–fact delivery. He was saying he possessed evidence suggesting Phil Gaglardi's department was guilty of graft. The Socreds sat in stunned silence.

Presenting Holzworth's affidavit, the estimates, cheques, correspondence and other material, Dowding asked the government to launch an inquiry.

Oak Bay Liberal Alan Macfarlane immediately demanded that the RCMP be asked to investigate, but Bob Bonner filed notice of motion to refer the issue to the public accounts committee, the "court of the legislature."

The news got to Gaglardi quickly at his equipment show in Chicago. He called Bennett, who asked him if there was any reason for concern. "Cec," said Gaglardi, "you've got nothing to worry about."

The issue of who was playing the organ at Gaglardi's church

was quickly straightened out, and the truth was nowhere near Holzworth's story. The organist at Calvary Temple was not Florence Gresty, but her eighteen-year-old daughter, Gloria, who received no pay.

If the public accounts committee could have added two more rings when it began its hearings a few days later, it would have had a circus. As it was, it opened to a packed house, with Dick Holzworth called as the first witness (committee chairman Irvine Corbett, Socred MLA for Yale, went along with consensus on who to call).

Holzworth was a belligerent schoolboy in his testimony, obviously unimpressed with the proceedings and with committee counsel Lloyd McKenzie's efforts to keep him under control. Throughout there were chaotic arguments between Socred and opposition committee members about procedure, but they managed to get out of Holzworth a lot of background on Project 819, though the validity of much of it was in question. L and M, he said, had "gutted" Project 819. "They just took out a chunk here and there, and moved around like a bunch of kids . . . never completed one thing, just moved a little bit here and a little bit there, and shot out some of the easy rock."

Angelo Branca, acting for the Highways Department, asked him, "Did you receive any favour insofar as bidding?"

Holzworth: "As far as figures, no. All I can say is that Thornton said Gaglardi said, 'Bid this figure at such and such a price and, in order to get it, you have got to bid it for us to help you.'"

Holzworth caused a stir when he yanked a letter from his pocket and started reading it. It was addressed to "Friend Dick" in Montana from Clyde Thornton in Kamloops. The letter said Gaglardi's department had promised Union Contractors "every break in the world" and "liberal treatment" on new contracts that would make them at least two million dollars, maybe three.

After Holzworth finished testifying, he packed up and went home to Montana broke, unrepentant, and convinced the hearing was "the most crooked setup the government ever pulled." When he left his motel, he handed over to Dowding a huge box of papers and documents from L and M Logging and Union Contractors. Dowding passed them on to the NDP caucus researcher and executive assistant to Bob Strachan, a man named John Wood. He was the same John Wood, the former civil servant, who tangled with Gaglardi a few years before at a campaign meeting in Nakusp, when Gaglardi left the impression of a threat to fire him for his political opinions. Wood could find nothing in Holzworth's box of mementos to help in the graft case.

Holzworth had made it clear to the committee his joint business venture with Thornton didn't result in a lasting friendship. Now Thornton told the committee his "Friend Dick" letter was being misinterpreted. He had simply meant that, if they conducted themselves well, they could recoup the 819 losses on Project 1023, not that any favours were being done for anybody. The statement about making two or three million dollars was absurd; it was just a phrase. The Highways Department was fair, had made no concessions, no commitments whatsoever.

"The only comment I want to make is this, that I erred by not fully explaining to Mr. Holzworth the full contents of the meaning of that letter. I didn't know at the time that I was dealing with a degenerate."

Then the committee brought on a parade of contractors and Highways Department personnel to talk about how Project 819 had managed to turn into a disaster, and to try to explain the altered estimates.

Between and during witnesses, the committee members argued and yelled at each other about procedure while the patient McKenzie attempted to maintain a modicum of dignity and decorum about the proceedings, and the press had a heyday. McKenzie tried to talk Lymburner into appearing at the inquiry, but Lymburner wasn't about to leave the pleasant warmth of California in favour of a grilling in front of some "mudslinging committee" in B.C.

One afternoon following a session of the committee, Gaglardi sent a note to Ray Perrault in the legislature to meet him outside in the hallway. Perrault and Gaglardi had always got along, although, much like Gaglardi and Gibson, you'd never know it by their public feuds. Perrault had his suspicions about Gaglardi, yet he admired the little man's style and energy, and they were on friendly terms most of the time. And Gaglardi liked Perrault. Perrault later recalled that corridor conversation with the embattled highways minister:

> *"Ray," he said, "I've got something very serious that I've got to tell you. I've been informed that one of your highly placed Liberals has offered thousands of dollars to a certain individual if he'll testify falsely against me and try to hurt me." He said, "I've never done anything to warrant that kind of abuse. I can't give you any names, but I have a letter on my desk about it." I said, "Make it public, call the press in." "No," he said, "I don't want to do that. But Ray," he said, "let's leave that part. You know this investigation is terrible the way they're persecuting me. Look, I've*

got great respect for you. If at the meeting this afternoon you should make a motion that no evidence has been found against Phil Gaglardi and these charges should be withdrawn, it will find a seconder and our people on the committee would provide the necessary votes. Coming from you, that would be helpful. Meanwhile, I won't let that letter out. It'll stay on my desk."

At which Perrault stormed back into the legislature, pulled his members out for a caucus, told them of the conversation and said he was going to write Gaglardi a letter demanding release of the contents of the affidavits.

"So I wrote him a letter. I said, 'I want all of the facts on the table.' And I sent the letter to Gaglardi, and he wrote across it, 'Forget I ever talked to you,' and sent it back to me. I still have the letter."

So the inquiry staggered on past the end of the legislative session, and the committee continued calling its witnesses and fighting within itself. But despite the committee members' own reluctance to work together, solid information did begin to emerge. From the testimony of chief engineer Fred Brown, the now-retired deputy minister Evan Jones and other department personnel, it became evident that while the department had been guilty of a big error in judgment in letting projects to Lymburner et al, it was a case of twenty-twenty hindsight being superior to foresight. The paper work was so complicated, the cross-checking so thorough, it would have taken a gigantic conspiracy on the part of Gaglardi and his entire engineering and administrative staff to have indulged in blatant graft on Project 819 or related jobs currently under scrutiny. At the end of each month, the resident engineer had to sign work sheets with copies to the construction engineer and federal engineer. By the time they got to the controller's department for processing and payment, ten different engineers might have been involved. But Gaglardi, as the minister of highways, wasn't aware of any particular estimate or payment because his signature wasn't required.

The changes in the estimates, alleged by Holzworth to have been done in order to pay for work not carried out, were found to be legitimate adjustments. The increases had come as a result of double shifts and the need to put more equipment on the job, and final estimates on the project were within two percent of the actual earth and rock moved. Federal engineers found the project, by the time it was completed, a good job. Ted Webster, the director of construction, had been fully aware of the changes, and had signed the new estimate sheet in place of resident engineer Eric Barclay, but that wasn't unusual.

As titillating as the idea of Gaglardi ordering a contractor to pay off a friend's mortgage had been, that too was explained. Vince Gresty had personally backed a loan taken by Mid–City Construction on equipment, not a house. When Union Contractors ran into trouble, and the Highways Department was being besieged with creditors, controller Rhodes had ordered Union to start paying the bills of some of the creditors directly. One of them was Mid–City Construction. Gresty was being threatened with legal action on the equipment mortgage, so Rhodes — not Gaglardi — called Thornton and asked him to pay it off out of the $13,000 owed Mid–City by Union for subcontract work on Project 819. So Thornton went to Kamloops and paid the bill.

Fred Bell, Lymburner's bookkeeper, testified, and so did Rhodes and Florence and Vince Gresty, Syd Marriott, Tom Miard and several others. It was April 16 before Gaglardi appeared in front of the public accounts committee to give his testimony. By now, Branca was claiming to have disproven all allegations against the highways minister, but Bob Strachan had asked Corbett to summon Gaglardi, so he was there. (There's no doubt Branca did a fine job on Gaglardi's behalf, and they became very good friends. For Branca, it was his last major case as a lawyer before being called to the bench.)

Standing, hands in his pockets, Gaglardi told the committee that "as far as I know" there had been no preferential treatment in the awarding of Project 819 to L and M Logging, nor had he done favours for any of the contractors who eventually worked on the project.

Gaglardi was on the stand the entire day, and when he was finished, the inquiry was finished. Jennie had flown to Victoria to offer what support she could. When her husband appeared at her suite in the Empress Hotel, only then did she realize how trying the experience had been for him. She'd never seen him so pallid, so tired-looking. They got down on their knees beside the bed, and prayed.

Branca was blunt in his summation to the committee the following day. Dick Holzworth, he said, was a soldier of fortune.

"It is, indeed, regrettable that an irresponsible man who lives in another country can come here and swear irresponsible statements, as Holzworth did, and cause men to be held up before the public when the evidence discloses they have done nothing wrong at all."

The committee agreed with Branca's assessment. At least, most of it did. After two days of work, a majority report was approved with the help of chairman Corbett, who had to break a

Testifying at 1963 inquiry into highways contracts, Gaglardi listens to question about alleged patronage. Second from left is committee chairman Irvine Corbett, next is court stenographer and at right is Lloyd McKenzie, counsel for the committee.

tie vote when fellow Socred Don Smith of Victoria dissented along with the opposition. The majority view cleared Gaglardi of all fault. Corbett took the report to Bennett at his Victoria home about 6 p.m., Friday, April 18.

The report commended Gaglardi, his engineers and administrators "for their conduct during the course of Project 819 and for their devotion to duty and their tireless efforts on behalf of the people of B.C., and their conduct during this inquiry." The report was signed only by Corbett, but those concurring included Socreds Waldo Skillings, Dan Campbell, Don Brothers, Jacob Huhn, Tom Bate and Eric Martin.

As Bennett released the report to the press, Smith, Perrault and NDP committee members Randolph Harding, Leo Nimsick, James Rhodes and leader Bob Strachan worked late to complete a minority report. Its conclusion: "After studying the evidence provided, we agree there is no impropriety or wrongdoing on the part of the Department of Highways officials in respect to Contract 819 and no misuse of public funds." But the report criticized Gaglardi's department for giving the under-financed L and M Logging a contract, and described the situation surrounding the estimate sheets as "unusual."

That, of course, wasn't the immediate end of it. The corridor and coffee talk continued. Perrault, though the opposition committee members had no choice but to clear Gaglardi, remained suspicious. He didn't stir up a big outcry over it, but he privately just wasn't convinced of Gaglardi's innocence. Other opposition members on the committee had similar doubts. Harding felt the failure of Geery and Lymburner to appear at the inquiry hurt its effectiveness. Leo Nimsick remained suspicious about the changing estimates, feeling there was more information somewhere. Gordon Dowding, who had started the whole thing, called the majority report a farce.

But on the government side, all was satisfaction. Skillings, for example, had decided long before the conclusion of the hearings there was nothing to the charges. Dowding and the NDP had gone through bushels of Holzworth's documents with a fine-tooth comb and come up with one cheque for a mortgage, and that had been easily explained. Clearly, there had been no misuse of public funds.

Gaglardi wasn't in a forgiving mood. If Dowding had any guts, he would resign. "They just put me on the torture rack for seven weeks, you know. What did they come up with? A big goose egg."

Like the opposition members who were sure there must be something to the accusations, even if they hadn't found what, there was a part of the general public that now viewed Gaglardi with suspicion. It was a milestone in his career, though he contends the public accepted his vindication by the committee and that the damage to his career shouldn't be overplayed.

While there seemed a paradox between the hard-working, caring pastor and the tough politician, it didn't really exist. Gaglardi operated very much on a straight line drawn for him in his family and religious upbringing, a combination of philosophies and perceptions that resulted in a unique faith not only in God but in his own judgment. He could no more deviate from it than a man could fly (unless he had an airplane, of course). As he told the legislature during the early stages of the Project 819 controversy, "I work only one way and that is the proper and fair way." Gaglardi's way had to be proper and fair. Any other way must not be. So when Gaglardi did something, he looked neither right nor left to check out the traffic, to consider the political and personal consequences, because he knew he was right. He went straight ahead. Because of that characteristic, he accomplished much good. But this attitude also created a double standard, for Gaglardi believed that if somebody wanted to help Gaglardi the pastor, it didn't commit Gaglardi the cabinet minister to anything, and this should be obvious to all. But when Gaglardi wanted to help someone, he didn't necessarily find it imperative to waste time sorting out whether he was doing it as a minister of the Gospel or of the Crown.

Despite the six–year scandal of Project 819, the faith the voters still had in him was to be quickly illustrated. It was a surprise when Bennett called an election for September 30, 1963, because a by-election had been held only in July to fill the Columbia seat left vacant by the death of Orr Newton. But by now, Bennett was well settled into his preference for elections every three years. He was forging ahead with his Two River Policy of developing hydro power on both the Columbia and Peace rivers, had introduced a record $372-million budget that year, raised the homeowner grant again, and set in motion plans for two new universities and a system of regional community colleges. The economy was booming and the government felt secure. But legislation to expropriate B.C. Electric and create the B.C. Hydro and Power Authority was ruled unconstitutional that summer by Chief Justice Sherwood Lett, who said the amount offered by Bennett wasn't enough. That was a major factor in Bennett's election call, because the takeover was key to his plans for hydro–electric development.

Strachan's enthusiasm for the NDP leadership was waning, and he was facing growing discontent within the party. Ray Perrault of the Liberals was honeymooning in Hawaii when Bennett called the election, and wasn't at all pleased about the timing. The Tories were in the middle of a major rebuilding program that had not had a chance to set. It was based on a new commitment from within federal Tory ranks to the B.C. party, and the hope was in E. Davie Fulton, a Rhodes scholar, federal cabinet minister and true native son of Kamloops.

In the years following the collapse of the Coalition, the federal Tories had drifted toward acceptance of Social Credit as the conservative presence in B.C. That resignation would become more firmly entrenched than ever in later years, but Fulton was convinced he could effect a change. When Fulton was demoted from justice to public works minister by Prime Minister John Diefenbaker after a narrow Tory election win in June 1962, he started thinking about a change of political scenery. He formally assumed control of the B.C. party early in 1963, hoping for at least a year to build. "British Columbia is my province, my place, the province of my destiny," he said.

Speculation about where Fulton would run began immediately, but he hedged for several months, passing up a golden opportunity in Columbia, where an unknown Tory candidate came second to the

Socred. He was advised not to consider taking on Gaglardi in Kamloops, but all the logic and advice in the world couldn't change one thing for Fulton. If he didn't run in Kamloops, he would be a political coward. Kamloops was his home; he must run there. In May 1963, at a Conservative meeting in Kamloops, he announced he would challenge Gaglardi in the next election. "This is the place I claim. To run anywhere else would show a lack of conviction."

Gaglardi wasn't worried. "As far as I am concerned, I am happy to welcome any contest with anyone." On the trail, Gaglardi faced heckling and questions about the Dowding inquiry from those who refused to believe the outcome. At home, he insisted that his strongest competition came from the NDP. But Fulton was the real competition, and Gaglardi knew it. Their battle was the star attraction in the election. The press and public loved the contrast: the brash human whirlwind versus the sophisticated, dour statesman. They challenged each other for domination of the media, placing page after page of advertising in local newspapers, and taking to the airwaves on radio and television with advertising and open–line shows. Fulton's red, white and blue signs and posters competed with Gaglardi's green and white for space on lawns and highway rights–of–way.

The premier himself climaxed the Gaglardi campaign with a rally, packing the house at a downtown movie theatre. "Gaglardi could never be paid in filthy lucre," Bennett assured the crowd. "Only public appreciation can properly reward him. I don't want to be premier after September 30 if Gaglardi's not there, too."

Bennett was able to announce, thanks to a phone call from Robert Bonner earlier that day, that the B.C. Electric issue was settled. Negotiations had set a price of $197 million for the takeover. "Rise above the party, raise Gaglardi to office with a victory that will ring across the nation!" Bennett urged.

On Sunday, September 29, Calvary Temple quietly celebrated the eighteenth anniversary of the Gaglardi family's arrival in Kamloops in September 1945. Associate pastor Reverend A. Kalamen and Alex Cassidy offered a tribute on behalf of the congregation: "We cannot forget the days of our 'small beginnings' and can only hope for God's continued blessing on Calvary Temple. In so doing we pay tribute to Pastor and Mrs. Phil Gaglardi." It had also been eighteen years ago that Kamloops elected Davie Fulton to the first of his six federal terms.

On election day the race started out close as the early returns came in with Gaglardi ahead by a only few — sometimes fifty —

Victory hug from wife Jennie after Gaglardi beat Conservative leader E. Davie Fulton to retain the Kamloops riding in 1963.

votes. But when the big polls started reporting, Davie Fulton's future in British Columbia politics quickly died. Final count was Gaglardi 5,658, Fulton 4,473, with the NDP and Liberal candidates trailing far behind.

Provincially, it was a huge sweep for Social Credit. The party took thirty-four seats, cutting the NDP to thirteen, while the Liberals clung to their five. The Tories were wiped out.

Fulton tried to sound undaunted by the disaster. "My appeal didn't go over with the electors. It is a temporary setback."

"Tomorrow morning, I'll head for my office and let a whole bunch more highway contracts," Gaglardi promised. Which he did, ordering that tenders be called on eight jobs worth about $5 million, mainly replacement bridges and new road construction in the northern half of the province. "How about a government that does this after an election?" asked Gaglardi.

The election seemed the second great exoneration for that year. They had called him a crook, and he had proven them wrong. At his most vulnerable, he had turned aside the most formidable political opponent of his career. Those who had judged Phil Gaglardi had themselves been judged.

And David, the little fellow, had prevailed.

King Lear

Oh that I had wings like a dove! For then I would fly away and be at rest.
PSALM 55.6

You can't run the Department of Highways from a swivel chair.
PHIL GAGLARDI

Somewhere in the bowels of the Coast Range of British Columbia, Mother Nature was having a tantrum. It spread rather gently through the length of the province, a minor hiccup of an earthquake registering only three on the Richter scale. At 3:56 a.m. Saturday morning, January 9, 1965, it rumbled through a narrow valley eleven miles east of Hope. A small slide hit the valley bottom in the darkness and tumbled across the Southern Trans–Provincial, better known on that stretch as the Hope–Princeton Highway.

As forty–two–year–old Norman Stephanishin of Kamloops jockeyed his Kenworth tanker truck over the pass, running empty from Kelowna, he was getting an undeniable feeling that something bad was going to happen. Once before, in Italy during the war, he'd had a premonition that came true. Interviewed twenty–five years to the day after that night on the Hope–Princeton, Stephanishin remembered well the eeriness of it. "It was a feeling I had, I suppose, that particular night. It was a weekend and the traffic was extremely light, and usually on a weekend there were a lot of people travelling to the Interior. It was a strange evening." It came into his mind that there was going to be an accident involving a girl. "I don't have these things regularly. It was only the second one." That premonition saved his life, for when he came upon the slide, he parked his rig and caught a ride back down the highway with a Greyhound bus.

Up on the mountain, a massive pressure was building. The carboniferous wall of rock, ridden with cracks, began to falter. A few minutes before 6 a.m., the mountain collapsed. A hundred and twenty–five million tons of rock roared down into the little valley. Rocks the size of houses plummeted for a mile toward the

Looking up, Gaglardi and other department officials hear a rumble from mountain as they survey Hope Slide in January 1965. Left to right are chief engineer D.R. Godfrey, director of location Norm Zapf, director of construction Ted Webster, deputy minister Tom Miard and Phil Gaglardi.

highway, smothering a five–acre lake and rolling toward the trees beside which Norm Stephanishin had parked his truck for protection. Four people, including a woman, were buried in the slide.

Phil Gaglardi's Highways Department radio system proved its worth that night and into the next day as word was relayed quickly around the department and on to Gaglardi. As soon as he got the phone call in Kamloops, he was on a helicopter heading for the scene. From Victoria, Tom Miard, Ted Webster (director of construction), Norm Zapf (director of locations) and Bert Wilkins (director of research and development) were flying to Abbotsford Airport, where they, too, would transfer to a helicopter.

Gaglardi and his engineers immediately began planning a new road to cut through the slide area and reattach the severed Southern Trans–Provincial Highway. They estimated that in four days they could carve out a passable road. Good progress could be made in some parts of the slide where it consisted mostly of mud and snow. But for at least half of it, the giant rocks would have to be skirted or blasted. It would take almost four miles of road to cross the one–and–a–half–mile slide.

On Sunday, an RCMP dog led searchers to the bodies of two victims. The search continued for the others. Instead of four days, it took two weeks to reconnect the highway, three more to turn it from muck to gravel. The searchers gave up; the mountain ceased its complaining, and the public moved in for its first look at the disaster. By the hundreds, they parked their cars at the viewpoint constructed on the temporary road by Phil Gaglardi's department, ate their lunches and looked in awe at the spectacle. The merchants of Hope noticed a big upswing in business on the first day the road was opened, and happily predicted the slide would become a major tourist attraction. A cairn was planned at the site in memory of the dead. Meanwhile, more employment would be created. The temporary road cost $100,000. The permanent replacement would cost a million.

Gaglardi's quick action on the disaster was typical of his style, which now more than ever was have–plane, will–travel. Air travel was viewed by the minister of highways as an absolute necessity for doing the job right. The Gaglardi air force had multiplied in 1961 with the purchase of four more twin–engined Beechcraft Expediters. Two of them were converted for aerial photography work. The Highways and Lands and Forests Departments went in together on the deal, which Gaglardi said was sealed for a ridiculously low price.

Gaglardi began thinking of replacing his department's Anson, which would leave him with at least two (including the Widgeon) planes for his own use, if lands and forests used three. The Expediters were light transport planes that could handle five to seven people.

As his airline grew, Gaglardi set up the necessary support services: engineers, maintenance crews, pilots. Jack McNeill and Bert Toye, both Pacific Western Airlines pilots, joined Gaglardi in 1963, flying out of Victoria. Lou Iverson, another PWA man, was already on board, piloting the department's Beaver in Kamloops. Other pilots and co–pilots came and went, or rotated part–time duty as required. Gaglardi was a highly popular boss. "He was Number One, just the best," said Iverson. "He treated us like his own boys. He was just fantastic." McNeill concurred: "I found him a delight. There's not one bad thing I can say about him."

As with every other phase of his department, Gaglardi had his finger on everything that happened with the aircraft. His private pilot's training helped him understand the problems of his pilots, and they appreciated the way he backed them up. "If there was any problem, he liked to get firsthand information," Iverson recalled. "He was a pretty dedicated person that way. He was aware of everything going on. He was one of the sharpest men I've ever met. I really love that man." Again, McNeill agreed. "It used to amaze me because he kept his finger on everything. He always supported you. He had a way of smoothing everything out."

Gaglardi was a fearless flier. His pilots had trouble talking him out of flying if conditions were bad, which they frequently were. McNeill: "Nothing scared him. He was absolutely fearless. His attitude was if the weather was bad let's take a look at it anyway." Flight over The Rockpile, as pilots called the Coast Range, could be a hairy experience even in the Beechcraft, which weren't pressurized and weren't meant for high-level flying. Over the rocks, cold and warm, moist air collided to create dangerous icing conditions at lower levels. One night as McNeill was taking Gaglardi into Kamloops, the propellers were shedding ice like rocks from a slingshot, throwing the chunks into the side of the plane with a terrible crashing noise. McNeill looked back at Gaglardi; the highways minister was praying, talking to "The Big Man." On a flight near Lillooet, the Widgeon was battered with huge hailstones that dented the metal. Disaster was averted by climbing into the storm so the hail bounced off at an angle. Once, in a Beech, Toye and a co-pilot were flying over the Rockies when they hit some dense, damp air that iced the carburettors and slowed the plane to near-stall speed. Gaglardi went into the cockpit for an assessment from Toye. "I said, 'What's our chances?' He said, 'Fifty-fifty,' so I went back and sat down and breathed a prayer and fell asleep." A short time later the weather cleared and so did the carburettors. But when they landed in Kamloops the co-pilot quit on the spot. "I said, 'What're you quitting for;' and he said, 'Who's going to take those kinds of chances in this crappy equipment?' " Gaglardi remembers having to take over the controls from Toye on occasion when the heavy-smoking chief pilot would run short of oxygen at high altitudes. And there were frequent instrument failures, making for tense moments while tower officials tried to figure out if landing gear was properly set. But the Anson provided the most thrills. "Anybody that had guts enough to fly around in an Anson the way I did should have had a gold medal, not criticism," says Gaglardi. "I remember once getting into a hail storm with that crazy thing and it filled the wings full of holes because they were covered with fabric."

The potential for danger in all that flying was underscored in May 1962 when deputy minister Roy McLeod, who flew the Anson himself, took the Bamboo Bomber up with district engineer A.F.

Provenzano to inspect a highway near Esquimalt. On takeoff, the Anson stalled and crashed in flames in front of the Patricia Bay control tower. McLeod and Provenzano were killed.

Gaglardi figured jet engines shouldn't be limited to the air, so United Aircraft sent him a Pratt and Whitney prototype for installation in a plough–snowblower truck to be used on the Hope–Princeton or Rogers Pass. That in itself was an engineering challenge, since there was nobody around who could supply a truck capable of taking the jet engine. It needed a special transmission and several alterations, so the department started altering one of its own trucks.

A jet-powered snowblower may seem like just another executive toy for a highways minister, but keeping B.C.'s roads in service year–round was part of the challenge of blacktopping the province. Gaglardi and his department were proud of their snow–removal capabilities. Keeping roads open during winter wasn't something motorists had been used to before Gaglardi's day, according to the highways minister.

> *There was no such a thing as winter maintenance before I was elected. People would just put their cars up on blocks. After I became minister I called (deputy minister) Evan Jones in one day and I said, "Evan, when an automobile owner puts a licence on his car, is that for nine months or twelve months?" He said, "Well, twelve months, of course." I said, "But there are no highways for three months. At the first snowfall, I want the crews to use the graders and all our equipment to clear those highways." So I brought in a winter plan so that people could travel twelve months out of the year. The Americans weren't doing winter maintenance, either, and they'd send people up to see how we did it. One time I went to Japan to look at some equipment plants, and I got a call at my hotel from whoever it was who was in charge of highways in Japan. I agreed to meet with him and he asked an awful lot of questions about winter maintenance, because they get a lot of snow in some parts of Japan. I told him he should send some engineers to B.C. to see how it was done, and that's what he did a few months later, and my engineers trained them. So that's how I brought snow maintenance to the roads in Japan.*

B.C., he insisted, had the best winter road–maintenance system in the world. Gaglardi spent $3 million a season keeping his highways cleared of snow. Three thousand men and two thousand pieces of equipment got the job done. The new radio system, which Gaglardi estimated at having cost $4 million, allowed the department to move equipment around in a hurry "and keep our boys on the job twenty–four hours a day."

"Groundcrew or aircrew?"

The new jet–powered plough went into operation on the Salmo–Creston summit in January 1966 and sped along at forty miles per hour up a six–percent grade tossing snow two hundred feet into the bush. Gaglardi said it could hit zero to thirty in ten seconds with its turbojet.

Highways Department use for jet engines, though, would become much more important in the air than on the ground. A new love affair was about to begin. The object of Gaglardi's affections was a bit used, but she was sleek and, Jumpin' Jupiter, she was fast. She could cruise at better than five hundred miles an hour; in twenty minutes, she could take him from Victoria to Kamloops, compared to an hour and a half in the 160–miles–per–hour Expediter. "She" was a Lear executive jet, and she came with a price tag of $645,000, but Gaglardi had to have one for himself. He had spent seven hundred hours in the air in 1965, and doctors told him he shouldn't really fly in unpressurized aircraft. He was no kid of twenty–four or twenty–five anymore. More importantly, he liked to get places in a hurry. If a man's time was worth anything, then he should fly in the fastest aircraft available.

"Bennett never appreciated the Lear jet. How I got it was what you might call a bit unorthodox. I told Cec I thought I deserved to be flying around in a bit better than a Widgeon that didn't even have pressurization. I was getting over the fifty mark and I needed it from the safety point of view and everything else. He agreed, but he didn't know I was going to get a Lear."

Chuck Lyford, vice-president of Jetair Corporation of Everett, Washington, personally flew a Lear like the one Gaglardi was interested in up to Vancouver so Phil could try it out. Gaglardi and a couple of his men got in for the test flight and found a plush interior done in brown and gold leather and wood with white trim. A similar Lear owned by Frank Sinatra was done in baby blue and gold. It had weather radar, automatic pilot, power brakes and, as Lyford put it, "everything the big babies have." This particular plane had just set a speed record, circling the globe in fifty hours, twenty minutes flying time.

If Gaglardi was going to get himself a jet, he would have to convince the public, the cabinet and W.A.C. Bennett of its absolute necessity. There were many reasons he could find that the public should support his getting a jet: it would save him time on his busy schedule, improve efficiency by allowing him to visit highway projects and yards throughout the province, and other cabinet ministers could use the plane. Jetair was willing to let the Lear go on a lease-to-purchase plan for the bargain-basement price of only $480,000. That was a saving of almost $200,000 to B.C. taxpayers.

He worked on his fellow cabinet ministers for a month. The premier was the last to get the sales pitch, after Gaglardi had lined up enough other support to help get him Treasury Board approval. Under the deal with Jetair, the province would pay $5,915 a month on the lease-purchase plan. All that was needed was the signature of W.A.C. Bennett. The timing had to be right.

Gaglardi waited until a government function in Prince Rupert provided just the right opportunity. Gaglardi flew, Bennett went by ferry. After a day of ceremony and speeches, the premier was in a good mood. When Bennett was ready to leave, Gaglardi whipped out the contract and asked if Bennett might jot his name on it before he left. Bennett hurriedly scribbled his signature. And Gaglardi had his jet. "I planned the whole thing. He didn't even notice what he was signing. I don't know if he ever woke up to it or not. He never mentioned anything about it."

King Lear, heading for a test flight in the Highways Department's Lear jet in 1966.

Toye and McNeill were sent south to learn how to fly a Lear. When the plane being prepared for Gaglardi was ready, McNeill would fly her back. Just before he left, the question came up of whether to paint American or Canadian registration numbers on it. A call to Gaglardi resulted in the decision to use four-inch-wide tape for temporary letters. That done, McNeill was in the air approaching the congested Chicago traffic area when the Lear began to shudder violently. When he got it down in Chicago, it was found the tape had peeled off, and wedged in the ailerons. Another call to Gaglardi, who told his man to leave the plane in Chicago and fly home by commercial airline rather than keep fooling around with peeling tape and sticky ailerons. Next day, Lyford delivered instead the famous record-breaking Lear he had been piloting himself, handing it over at a bargain price on condition Gaglardi not erase a map painted on the side of the plane commemorating the global flight.

The reaction, once Gaglardi had jet in hand, was not positive. Oak Bay Liberal Alan Macfarlane angrily told a Rotary Club meeting the jet was the "worst extravagance yet in this free-spending Bennett government. It is extraordinary to observe that the government cannot relieve the burden which the hospitals and the public are forced to carry, but can afford to spend over $450,000 on the purchase of a luxury airplane . . . Whose health is more important — Gaglardi's or that of Joe Public?"

The editorial pages were filled with the opinions of readers. "If Mr. Gaglardi's parishioners wish him to be with them each and every Sunday, let them provide the money for the plane he so urgently needs," wrote one. "So far I have just been stunned by the monumental self–importance and egotism shown by this action of Mr. Gaglardi," wrote another.

But he had his supporters: "As a teenager, I find it increasingly tiresome to hear complaints from persons whose only fun in life seems to be criticizing our illustrious minister of highways."

Bennett, having signed for the darn thing, felt behoved to defend it. He never flew, himself, preferring to go by car or train. When he did fly, he took commercial flights. "A great airplane," Bennett said as he was about to enter a cabinet meeting from which Gaglardi was absent (he'd flown to Calgary in the jet). Using a file folder to demonstrate, Bennett showed how easily the plane could land on any landing strip in B.C.

Gaglardi was back the next day, stopping over in Vancouver. "You find yourself a nice large lake where you can put a fifty–pound anchor around your neck and jump in!" he advised one Victoria reporter who gave him an early morning call. But he soon cooled down, rejecting the rumour that he'd gone to Calgary to attend the famous Stampede. He was there on business, he said, and attended only a few chuckwagon races. He also denied another rumour that he was going to spend $1 million to convert all the Beechcrafts to turbo–props. "That's just speculation of the worst type. That's just propaganda."

Gaglardi did love his jet plane. Sometimes, he would order his pilots to rocket over a new section of highway, a hundred feet above the asphalt, to get the feel of the road. Sometimes he would take the controls himself, under the watchful eye of the pilot. "Once near Revelstoke, we had to do a bypass when opening up some deal. I took the controls and went over. I was the only one brave enough to go close to the ground. We had lots of fun."

He flew from Vancouver to Kelowna for the annual regatta, to see the unlimited–class hydroplane races on Okanagan Lake, posing for pictures in the cockpit of a two–thousand–horsepower boat. Then it was back for one of the twice–weekly cabinet meetings in Victoria, where he encountered a mob of reporters at the door. He patiently listed the government's air force as currently containing the jet, five Beechcraft Expediters — including a new turbo–prop conversion, and two used almost exclusively for photographic work — an Otter float plane, a Beaver float plane in Kamloops, and the twin–engined amphibious Super Widgeon at Pat Bay. He said he

At work in his Victoria office, beside model of famous Lear jet.

didn't list them in public accounts or his annual report because "they're just a small part, a very minor part" of the $35 million worth of equipment owned by his department.

The press began referring to Gaglardi as Jetman.

W.A.C. Bennett never was one to wait five years for an election. He liked to call them every three years, and the three were up, so he called it for September 12, 1966. He didn't have a real good issue, so he made one up. Redistribution of electoral districts in March, which had increased the number of ridings from fifty–two to fifty–five, marked a turning point, he said, and when a turning point was reached a government should hold an election.

Health Minister Eric Martin would not be a candidate, due to ill health. "It was a terrible shock to me," said Bennett.

What about the premier, at sixty–six? Would this be his last campaign?

"Certainly not. It isn't a man's age in years that counts, it's the way he feels."

Gaglardi garnered 5,542 votes, compared to Lance Randle of the NDP with 3,132, and Liberal Nick Kalyk with 1,921. The Socreds were returned handily to office, keeping their thirty–three seats, while the NDP raised its total by two to sixteen. The Liberals fared well, electing six, while the dispirited Tories, who ran only three candidates, were shut out. Several new Socreds joined the caucus, including teacher Bob Wenman, business investor Herb Capozzi (the son of Bennett's old friend Cap) and florist Grace McCarthy. But Robert Bonner lost in Point Grey, where Liberals Pat McGeer and Garde Gardom were elected. Bonner regained his seat two months later in a by-election in the Cariboo riding.

Gaglardi's use of the Lear grew, and so did the static directed his way. Rumours abounded that it had been flying all over western Canada. In fact, it was flying further than that. From the time Gaglardi leased it in June 1966 to the end of that year, the plane flew about 89,000 miles. Among the trips taken outside B.C. was a flight to New Orleans. Other destinations for the Lear in 1966 included Edmonton, Calgary, Regina, Seattle, Portland and Wichita, Kansas. The trip to Wichita was for repairs at the Lear factory. Others were taken by various government members for conferences and speaking engagements, although names of passengers and reasons for the trips were not recorded.

For all his flying around, though, Gaglardi was forced to watch as the importance of his department continued to decline. The Deas Tunnel was almost a decade old. The province had the best highways-maintenance program on the continent. The Port Mann Bridge, the Rogers Pass, the Deas freeway to the border, the Hudson's Hope bridge, Burnaby's sawdust highway, the ferry system — all were fine accomplishments, representing the fulfilment of the mission Gaglardi had been given by Bennett fifteen years before. He'd even got Beautiful B.C. magazine established for Bennett, who turned it over to the Tourism Department. It seemed all the worlds, as far as highways were concerned, had been about conquered.

"I'm low man on the totem pole and I'm getting lower all the time," Gaglardi complained as he looked at his roadbuilding program for 1967. The highways budget for that year was up $8 million to almost $104 million, but it now accounted for only fourteen percent of the provincial budget, and was considerably lower than either education or health and welfare. Gaglardi considered his problems "up $50 million." His budget money was already spoken for; he was over-committed by several million dollars.

"Within fifteen years I had wiped out everything that had been longed for for a hundred years," he says today, "and so that's when I really felt that my job had been done, and that I had accomplished everything that I should, and I was ready to take any other challenge."

He and Bennett had, during the past two years, engaged in one of their most serious disagreements, and it had to do with a Highways Department project. In discussions with consultants, Gaglardi had been looking at a $109-million scheme for either an eight-lane bridge or a tunnel to link Vancouver's North Shore to a new downtown waterfront freeway. Either way, he wanted to avoid carving up Stanley Park, which an alternative — twinning Lions Gate Bridge — would do. He favoured the tunnel proposal, since it would be the least conspicuous. In conversation with a reporter one day, he was asked what was happening with the Burrard Inlet situation and let it slip that the tunnel was favoured.

Announcements of such importance were usually made jointly by Gaglardi and Bennett, and it was a *faux pas*. "I made a stupid mistake."

Bennett reacted by announcing a few days later that the government would build a four-lane bridge parallel to Lions Gate. It would carry four lanes of traffic in one direction, and Lions Gate's three lanes would carry it the other. While Gaglardi's slip was inappropriate, Bennett's announcement was an unprecedented public interference in Gaglardi's territory, and he was flabbergasted. He could only muster an "absolutely no comment." The premier didn't just reject Gaglardi's plan, he scornfully dismissed it as "an engineer's dream," and it amounted to a public humiliation of his highways minister. The next evening Gaglardi was in an elevator at the Hotel Vancouver. It stopped at a floor and there stood Bennett. "You'd better find yourself another man," Gaglardi told him as they rode down together. Bennett told him to take it easy, to think it over. "I didn't like what he said," explains Gaglardi about his threat to quit. "He put me down." Bennett called him the next day and talked him out of it. While it wasn't enough to terminate their friendship, the tiff was a sign all was not right between them and, about this time, Gaglardi began thinking of moving on politically, despite having once rejected a federal nomination in his riding.

Walter Bowden, director of the Manitoba Social Credit League, thought Gaglardi should consider federal politics. The Manitoba party as a whole thought so, too. Robert Thompson resigned as national leader early in 1967, and an heir was needed to lead the federal branch of the party out of obscurity. Gaglardi was seen by many as a natural, and the federal wing of the party believed they had him interested. He'd indicated to Bowden some time ago he would consider switching to the federal arena if Thompson ever stepped down. There was an intriguing rationale to the idea of a Gaglardi–led national party. It had been made obvious in 1963 that Gaglardi was more than a match for Davie Fulton in any election in Kamloops riding. Fulton was back in office as Kamloops' federal MP; how sweet it would be to knock him off a second time. Doubly sweet if Fulton should first succeed in getting the national Conservative leadership. Defeating a national leader would be just the thing the Socreds needed to make the party take off. A Quebec delegation also urged Gaglardi to go after the federal leadership.

There are still buttons around that say 'Phil Gaglardi for Prime Minister.' "I said, 'I don't speak French.' They said, 'That doesn't matter.' I told them, number one, I wanted a jet airplane at my disposal because I'd be travelling the nation like a mad man. Two, I wanted very capable research people, and $3 million so I could keep going for a solid year without being forced to slow down. They said that they could have that in three months, but I couldn't see the evidence of it, so I backed out and that's the last I ever thought of it."

According to Ray Perrault, Gaglardi also thought about switching parties. "Phil said at one point he'd be a federal Liberal candidate if we wanted him. I remember a conversation I had with him. He said, 'By gosh, under certain conditions I'd run for you, but I certainly wouldn't want to be a backbencher.' I said, 'Phil, we must have a talk.' But it was never pursued."

Gaglardi soon rejected any thoughts of a federal candidacy. "I'm not after any national leadership. I'm happy in British Columbia . . . happy in the job I'm able to do here." Bowden was surprised in light of his earlier discussions with Gaglardi. But W.A.C. Bennett privately counselled Gaglardi against getting into federal politics for two reasons. One was that Gaglardi was a strong provincial cabinet minister who still commanded a lot of popularity, vote–getting popularity needed by the B.C. Socreds. Secondly, since Real Caouette had led the Quebec faction out of the national party to form his breakaway Creditistes, Bennett had lost hope of any federal triumph by Social Credit. Bennett was persuasive — Gaglardi was unwilling to enter federal politics without the Old Man's blessing and help.

The Boys

Ye shall eat the fat of the land.
GENESIS 14.18

I'm not a detail man.
PHIL GAGLARDI

My father does not completely, thoroughly, understand business.
BOB GAGLARDI

All the burdens of political office, all the days and weeks spent away from home, all the pressures his career put on marriage and family couldn't keep Phil Gaglardi from his sons. He harboured an almost pathological ambition for them, to see them grow up strong and independent as he did, that they might prosper, make their mark.

"Even to this day I buy most of their shoes for them. I'm an Italian in that respect, but Bob and Bill are my boys and they always will be my boys and I'll do anything I possibly can to help them," says Gaglardi. "If they ask me for anything, or they want me to do anything, I go and do it."

He ensured that politics did not separate him from them, that he maintained not only a presence, but an influence on them. When Phil Gaglardi went into politics, he vowed it wouldn't keep him from his church or from his family, and the weekend airplane shuttle between Victoria or Vancouver and Kamloops allowed him to honour and enjoy that pledge.

Even when he was home, though, most of Gaglardi's time was taken up with church and political business. When he was at the house, there were constant telephone calls and knocks at the door. "People would come to the door, wanting things, always wanting things from Phil," said Jennie Gaglardi. "This has been our life; I never remember being by ourselves. The only time we actually got to see Phil was for Sunday dinner. That was the only time the boys really got to talk to him."

When they did get together, the time was precious. "There never were three people who got along together better than Bob and I and Bill," says Phil Gaglardi, "and still are today, because we're a very close-knit family. There were lots of times when I would take them out when I was able to do it. They understood my situation and I understood theirs."

He usually phoned home several times a week. Rarely, Jennie and the boys visited him in Victoria for a brief glimpse of his other life, his public one. If he was away too long, they wrote to him.

> *Honable Daddy come home and see us we what to see you to have you a snowball fight so come home you will have more fun hear then there. So please come home and have some fun with us and you will feel better.*
>
> *Your Sinserily*
> *Bob & Bill Gaglardi*

But for the most part to Bob and Bill, their father wasn't a politician, whatever that was, but a strong-minded, strong-willed disciplinarian who encouraged them to think for themselves and spanked them when they needed it. Gaglardi tried to imbue his sons with his own belief that the rights and freedom of an individual are all-important, that freedom of choice constituted the right to succeed or fail with the resources and attributes given you by God. So he seldom issued orders to his sons, preferring to guide through logic and explanation, and his own unique interpretation of the Gospel. But when he felt they had strayed too far, he came down on them hard, physically disciplining them even late into their teens.

Gaglardi believes his sons suffered to the point of being mistreated because of his political career. "Both Bob and Bill took a tremendous amount of abuse from the schools. On one occasion Bob was playing basketball and he hurt his back, and one day they were supposed to be doing some practising and Bob said his back was sore, and the physical education teacher took Bob outside and gave him a shovel and demanded that he dig. He still suffers to this day, and we used to get reports all the time about how the teachers were abusing Bob and Bill because of me. But neither Bob nor Bill ever came to me and complained about anything."

The boys were quite capable of looking after themselves in their peer groups. A classmate and neighbour who is now a school administrator remembers well being soundly thrashed by the Gaglardi brothers more than once on his way to school.

Bob was the more aggressive of the two, more serious, more independent and, ultimately, more ambitious. He inherited a mechanical bent from his father and took to tearing down old cars. He also inherited his father's love of fast driving. His own early interpretation of his father's emphasis on individualism was that if you didn't believe in the way something was done, you didn't do it. And Bob Gaglardi couldn't see why he should have to travel in a new car the same speed as a seventy-five-year-old, say, in an old car. That didn't make sense. So he tended to collect speeding tickets.

Bill, three years younger than Bob, was more easygoing, though he had his own driving problems, receiving a hefty fine for driving a truck not covered by insurance when he was involved in an accident. Bill, say friends who grew up with him, felt the absence of his father more deeply than the independent Bob. Bill did not have the same drive for success as his father and older brother. While Bob was in university learning about construction engineering, Bill studied religious music in the U.S. and moved back home to live with his mother and act as music coordinator at Calvary Temple.

Bob had two major reasons for going to Longview, Texas, to study mechanical technology and construction. One was that as he matured through high school, the realization that his father was much more than a minister of the church and a strong authority figure came to him. Being the son of Phil Gaglardi became less easy. Instead of Bob Gaglardi, he was "Phil Gaglardi's son." "I had a bit of an identity crisis. I wanted to escape that."

But his father's career even determined where Bob should go for his education and freedom. Because the second reason for going to Texas was that his father had a good friend down there who, in addition to being acknowledged as the foremost inventor of roadbuilding equipment, was responsible for the operation of a construction and mechanical-engineering college. The man was the very same Robert G. LeTourneau, U.S. Man of the Year, who had acted as official guest speaker at the opening of Calvary Temple in 1958. So Bob Gaglardi enrolled in LeTourneau Technical Institute (where his father visited him often, buying him clothes and other essentials), met his wife-to-be Karen Gieser, a pharmaceutical student, and graduated in 1963 with a Bachelor of Science in Mechanical Technology.

Armed with his parchment, the senior Gaglardi son returned to British Columbia ready to make his career. His first choice was highway construction, because he was well trained in roadbuilding equipment.

That was when the spectre of his heritage returned to daunt, if not haunt, him. He did not find a lot of construction outfits excited about hiring on the son of the B.C. highways minister, lest they be accused of getting jobs because of him, or be unfavourably treated by government bureaucrats wary of the patronage charges flying around Victoria. Being the son of the highways minister entailed certain restrictions. Bob could not go into any business that would have the appearance of conflict of interest. So any industry that even remotely did business with the government was out.

But, just as his father's public life had both forced Bob to flee B.C. and given him the opportunity for the kind of education he wanted, it again came to the rescue just when it appeared to be pushing him under for the third time. An oilman named Mike Latta had been transferred from Castlegar to Vancouver as district manager for Pacific Petroleums in 1962. Latta was to play his own unique role in the Phil Gaglardi story over the years, and would eventually obtain his own measure of political success as four-term mayor of Kamloops.

The vice-president in charge of sales at Pacific Pete was Don Morgan, an acquaintance of Phil Gaglardi's. Morgan advised Latta that Phil Gaglardi would be a good person to get to know, that, in fact, Gaglardi had asked Morgan if he had anything in the oil business that might be suitable for his son Bob. Pacific Pete had come under the control of Phillips Petroleums, and there were plans for expansion. Those plans, which included more service stations, had led to Morgan's conversation with Phil Gaglardi. A survey was needed on a site at Spences Bridge, so Latta sent Bob Gaglardi to do it.

Next, Latta asked him to act as intermediary in the purchase of some other service-station sites, a manoeuvre made necessary and more convenient by the complexities of the real-estate code. Bob Gaglardi was a fast learner. He was soon in business for himself, with a real-estate licence, buying up and selling properties to oil companies.

Bob concentrated on turning over land, borrowing money to buy it and depending on selling it quickly. It was a risky but profitable business. And, at least initially, it seemed like one that was safe from conflict-of-interest charges. "We made a lot of money," said Bob Gaglardi. "I did well; I work hard." His company, Northland Properties Ltd., set up with the help of a $5,000 bank note signed by his father, made $100,000 profit in its first year in 1963-1964.

Bill joined him, and they established more and more companies. Bob continued with Northland, and added Abilene Holdings. Bill set up B and W Developments (for Bob and

William), Karobil Enterprises, and bought out a dry-cleaning firm called White Swan, which he turned into a development company. Savemore Investment Associates Ltd. was set up under Bob's wife, Karen. As they bought and sold land throughout the Interior of B.C., they became known simply as The Gaglardi Boys.

They flipped property after property, sometimes within days of purchase. At Blue River in the North Thompson Valley, Northland bought 118.92 acres on the new highway for $42,000, subdivided it and sold off the lots to various oil companies for almost $100,000 total.

In his dealings with Bob Gaglardi and, inevitably, his father, Mike Latta developed a strong admiration for Phil Gaglardi. "He exemplified what a person in politics should be — flamboyant, colourful. I felt knowing him was a privilege, a thrill." In three and a half years, Latta negotiated three dozen property purchases through Bob and Bill Gaglardi. That first contact with Phil Gaglardi's son had "opened up the door." But Latta grew tired of working for somebody else and decided he, too, would like to get into a business of his own. He decided to get into the wholesale oil business, and Bob Gaglardi offered to go into it with him. They chose Kamloops and established Active Petroleums in equal partnership, setting up five agencies in the vast marketing area served by the Interior hub city. Bob Gaglardi stayed away from it, leaving it to Latta to operate.

The business did well, with the help of Phil Gaglardi. "Phil never had to say he was the minister of highways," recalled Latta. "But he did call a lot of people and asked for business for Active Petroleums. He didn't have to put pressure on anyone. I was never aware of anything unforeseen." The only business Active Petroleums did directly with the government was to sell some oil and fuel to the Highways Department.

Meanwhile, Bob was getting into the building career he'd originally intended. As a sideline to their wheeling and dealing with the oil companies, Bob and Bill had gone into the ranching industry, with Abilene acquiring eight hundred acres of hay-producing land in the Deadman Valley near Savona. It was about this time that the two-hundred-acre Silver Sage Ranch to the east was bought from Les Turcott, a close friend. It was put into the name of Karobil Enterprises and leased back to Phil Gaglardi. The ranch was a fine place for Gaglardi to raise his horses, and he began spending much of his time there during visits home.

But the real change came when Bob Gaglardi met moteliers Ralph Beck and Jim Yates. The latter, the originator of the

Slumber Lodge motel chain, had incorporated a new name, Sandman Inns Ltd., and built a hotel in Smithers. When Yates and Beck scouted Kamloops for a second site, they found one optioned by Bob Gaglardi. Instead of selling them the property, Bob Gaglardi went into partnership with them on the new project, buying a share of the Smithers hotel as well. Yates retired, so Beck and Gaglardi picked up his shares and started expanding the Sandman Inns hotel–motel chain into the biggest in B.C. They built in Blue River, Princeton, Prince George, Vernon, McBride, Terrace, Revelstoke and, eventually, Vancouver, Kelowna and then into Alberta. When you're hot, you're hot.

Opportunities seemed to open up everywhere for The Boys. Along with various partners, Phil Gaglardi's elderly friend Turcott owned 2,500 acres of property along the Merritt Highway stretching from its intersection with the Trans–Canada in Kamloops. Tired and dying of lung cancer, he wanted to put his affairs in order and get out of real estate. Turcott offered Gaglardi two thousand acres. The land was of prime development potential, but Gaglardi resisted. He told Turcott to hang onto his property and to keep busy, that he might be cured. But Turcott died a few months later, and Gaglardi was named an executor of the estate. After the funeral, says Gaglardi, Turcott's widow told him Les Turcott had left instructions that the property be offered first to Gaglardi, for a down payment of $40,000 and a total price of $200,000. He would have a year to come up with the down payment. Gaglardi fully realized the enormous potential of the property for development, but he didn't have $40,000 and saw no way of getting it. However, he had another friend who could raise the money, a crusty local developer named Charlie Bennett. Gaglardi struck a fifty–fifty deal with Bennett, whereby Bennett would come up with the necessary money in return for getting his hands on the prime piece of land, and Gaglardi would pay back his share as it was sold off or developed. There was another twist to the bargain: because of his position in government, Gaglardi didn't want his name connected to it, so he turned over his share to his sons, Bob and Bill, who would be responsible for developing the property. After the smoke had cleared from the proceedings, Turcott's two–thousand–acre property had been purchased by a company incorporated as Del Cielo, owned by an American named Gerald Main, and Bennett, with The Boys as agents and would–be beneficiaries. But, says Gaglardi, his lack of business sense was to lose him and his sons this golden opportunity. "At that particular time I wasn't as aware of technicalities as I am now, and the mistake I made was the fifty–fifty basis which made them as strong a partner as Bob and Bill were. I should have made it 51–49. What went wrong was that they had a sale for it for $2 million or somesuch figure and they forced the sale because they were fifty percent partners and they had as much control as Bob and Bill had. I didn't make a dime. Potentially I lost in the neighbourhood of $25 million to $50 million. All of it was mine."

In the meantime, though, The Boys carried on as salesmen for the project. On January 29, 1968, a piece just under an acre at the intersection of the two highways was sold to Shell Oil for $80,000. With Gulf and Union Oil also interested in the prime intersection area, the Gaglardi Boys stood to make substantial gains there. Instead of granting direct accesses, however, the Highways Department decided to put in a frontage road system.

After years of land–dealing by the Gaglardi Boys' companies, the opposition finally woke up to it and started asking questions. The NDP's Alex Macdonald got wind of the Del Cielo setup. On February 2, 1968, he questioned the propriety of the involvement of Phil Gaglardi's sons in a highway land development in which Gaglardi himself had acted as estate executor. Macdonald was cautious, declining to directly charge Gaglardi with wrongdoing, but he did the next best thing. "I am not talking about highway contracts," he said, "I am talking about the land speculators, who seem to know where the action is — the roadrunners who are so fast they get to the highway interchanges before the highway itself; the speculators who know where to buy cow pasturage and turn it into a goldmine; the speculators who seem to be gifted with second sight." He implied, although he didn't say it, that Bob and Bill Gaglardi had an inside track with the Highways Department in getting the essential accesses for those to whom they sold land.

Actually, getting an access wasn't as simple as picking up the phone and calling the highways minister. Since accesses weren't transferable, the companies that bought the land from the Gaglardis had to apply for it themselves. And accesses within municipal boundaries had first to be approved by the municipality, which, in turn, applied to the Highways Department for approval. That didn't rule out the possibility of influence being exerted from the highways minister's office, but the intervening bureaucratic structure definitely made it more remote.

Nobody ever directly accused Phil Gaglardi of getting highways accesses for his sons or clients of his sons, or of leaking information about where highways would be built. Macdonald, other opposition members and reporters skilfully avoided that charge.

Once again, Gaglardi took to the airwaves on Kamloops television to defend himself and, this time, his sons. That only brought him more problems. A caller, Gordon Guild, claimed his seventeen–year–old son, Don, who worked part time and during the summer at the Highways Department's sign shop in Kamloops, had seen two signs being painted for Del Cielo Heights. A highways employee came forward to say he'd done the work on his own time and had been paid by Del Cielo. Don Guild made out an affidavit, with a lawyer present, saying he'd seen the work being done on Highways Department time and that he'd been asked to erect one of the signs on Del Cielo property during his own working hours.

Gaglardi flew back to Victoria to deliver a speech he promised would "blow the lid of the legislature off." That was one promise Gaglardi usually kept, so the public and press galleries were once again filled when the highways minister delivered his defence. He referred once again to alleged bribery, to a $25,000 offer made to persons he would not name, by persons he would not name, to smear his reputation, to tell dreadful lies in order to bring him down and, therefore, to bring the government down.

"Mr. Speaker, it seems that terrible gangsterism has entered here and some have stooped so low as to use the most despicable methods known to human beings in order to try and bring the dishonour of individuals, the tearing down of integrity and the defeat of the government! I'll hold my head high in spite of what any man says. I have always loved this province with its wild and precipitous mountains, its rolling hills and wooded territories and its open plains!"

As he was wont to do on such occasions, Premier Bennett wept.

Undoubtedly influenced by the Lymburner and Thornton affidavits, his ongoing distrust of the NDP and Liberals in general, and Gordon Gibson in particular, and the constant threats made against him, Gaglardi was convinced and still is that there was a conspiracy to bring him down.

The conspiracy theory is one hundred percent correct. I was walking down the street one time in Victoria and the guy that was the head of the Registrar of Companies said to me, "Phil, for God's sake, watch yourself, these guys are coming into my office at least three times a week and checking on everything that you're doing and finding out everything that they can about you." He never gave me specific names, but the Liberals were in there, too. A man told me, "The Liberal party has gone into your

*background from the day that you were born and has
investigated every part of your life to try to find something
against you but they couldn't find it." I haven't got the foggiest
notion what they were looking for. Gibson was the pawnbroker
that they used to do all these things because Gibson was the kind of
guy who would do anything, he was absolutely unscrupulous. I was
the whipping boy.*

Gaglardi dared the opposition and the media to try to find
anything wrong in his department, and they obliged by trying
their hardest. *Vancouver Sun* reporter Jes Odam went to Kamloops
and pored over land registry records, tracking land back to
companies with short options. The result was a three–part series
of articles outlining the land dealings of Bob and Bill Gaglardi.
Fearful of lawsuits, he, too, carefully avoided any direct suggestion
of wrongdoing, but said The Boys were "making a highly
successful business out of following father's footsteps along B.C.'s
highways" and "seem to have a knack of getting between local
residents and the oil companies."

Phil Gaglardi was madder than ever when he read Odam's
stories. He called them "the most vicious type of propaganda I
have ever seen."

Alex Macdonald didn't back off.

"This is the question: is it right that the family of a minister
of the crown should be involved in companies which deal with the
minister for such things as highway access and subdivision rights?
. . . I believe the public have the right to know the facts, and make
up their own minds about it."

Helping the public make up its mind were innumerable
editorial writers and hotliners waxing indignant at the latest
Gaglardi scandal. But not all of them came to the conclusion,
inferred rather than charged or proven, that Gaglardi once again
had been shown to be a crook.

Emmet Cafferky, a businessman, former provincial and federal
Liberal candidate, and CJOR radio hotliner, was challenged by
Gaglardi after a program to go into Bob's files and try to find
anything wrong. Cafferky immediately accepted and was at Bob
Gaglardi's Vancouver office within an hour. He received complete
access to Bob Gaglardi's files on highway land deals, looked at
correspondence and tax notices and took photostats. Then he put
the radio station's lawyers to work looking for something wrong.
Neither he nor the lawyers could find it.

In an impassioned address to his listeners, Cafferky stated
his conclusions.

"If I could pin Mr. Gaglardi and, more specifically, Premier Bennett, with anything that could be identified as wrongdoing, you better believe I'd do it," the hotliner told them. "I beg you to refrain from judgment on Phil Gaglardi because what was presented in the legislative assembly in Victoria to me appeared to be a flimsy thing." Much of the current case against the highways minister and his sons, he pointed out, was based on an affidavit from a Blue River man who claimed he didn't know he was dealing with Bob Gaglardi in selling his land. "If you sit back idly today and allow this type of dirty, miserable, filthy, evil politics and don't step on a high horse and demand a higher standard from those we elect than character assassination by innuendo and insinuation without facts, then you and I have taken a step backwards in politics today and in government," said Cafferky.

He said the Blue River highway had been surveyed in late 1958 and early 1959 and the farmer who owned the property in question sold some of it to the Highways Department, to Trans Mountain Pipelines, the Forestry Department and British American Oil. After construction had started on the highway, one of the Gaglardi Boys' companies bought the rest of the property at "top price." There was no advance knowledge of highway location, as had been insinuated. The *Vancouver Sun*, he said, had "left out one thing, that's the dates." The Gaglardi Boys bought their property six years after the highway was surveyed.

Cafferky concluded: "To the best of my ability, I have covered every angle I could think of . . . and Mr. Gaglardi, as far as I'm concerned, is cleaner now than he ever was before."

But the blows kept coming. There was the question about the fountain. The Highways Department decided to build an ornamental wall and fountain in front of its Columbia Street works yard in Kamloops. The yard happened to be across the street from Bob Gaglardi's new Sandman, and the cynics among the public found the coincidence too irresistible not to suggest more than a passing connection.

Bob Gaglardi insisted he hadn't asked for the project. "It would have been better if they had not built it. There was some open space there."

The open space being a storage yard for heavy equipment.

"That had nothing to do with Sandman Inn," says Phil Gaglardi. "It was done because the public complained about the eyesore of all those trucks and cars being parked there. It was a horrendous view."

Then Kamloops Highways employee Fred Renk, whom

Gaglardi had helped get work but who, for some reason, didn't like him, swore an affidavit that on May 1, 1967, he was told to transport an I–beam and four shorter pieces of steel to the Silver Sage Ranch leased by Phil Gaglardi from his sons' Karobil Enterprises. Renk claimed he was ordered to charge the work to another job that day. The I–beams, salvaged from a dismantled bridge, ended up as part of a concrete dam on Cherry Creek at the ranch. No invoice or request for payment for the steel had been made.

The NDP took it to the legislature, but Attorney General Robert Bonner, with government backing, referred it to the public accounts committee. Gordon Dowding told the committee a Highways Department engineer in Victoria had designed Gaglardi's dam, which was then constructed contrary to his specifications.

Government members relied on a report from controller general C.J. Ferber to parry the opposition's claims. Ferber had just returned from Kamloops, where he had spoken with highways people involved in the mystery of the dam and concluded that a valid record of the transaction had been kept, even though the ranch was never billed.

His report explained that Karobil held conditional water licences for two dams on Cherry Creek for irrigation and stock watering. "The lower and original dam is just above the CPR tracks on Cherry Creek and of an earth variety. The second dam is higher up and of concrete. Early in the spring of 1967 the large runoff of water caused considerable concern in that if the concrete dam were to break, the lower earth dam would go and wash out the CPR tracks. The Department of Highways district engineer had already been advised of the danger and when approached by Karobil Enterprises Ltd. for assistance made available certain steel to enable reinforcement of the concrete dam. All work to be done by Karobil Enterprises Ltd." Ferber said the department kept no record for stocks of salvaged material because it wouldn't be practical, but a daily diary was kept of usage, and the steel sent to Silver Sage Ranch was on record. Renk's claim that he was told to charge his day to another project couldn't be substantiated.

The opposition pointed out that the steel had been in place for almost a year and could hardly be considered "on loan," as the government record showed.

Gaglardi said he had "absolutely nothing" to do with the decision to reinforce the dam — the district highways engineer had done it on his own.

Having returned from its weekend in Kamloops, the Lear

was now winging its way southward to Wichita, Kansas, to have its wings pulled off for a maintenance job.

Bob Gaglardi had often flown on the Lear, between Vancouver and Kamloops, and to Calgary, Victoria and even Whitehorse. Sometimes he went along with his father for the ride, sometimes it was a convenient and cheap way to travel. The plane didn't go anywhere just because Bob Gaglardi wanted it to go there. If the Lear was going somewhere he wanted to go, he just went, too.

Many people still did that. Other Gaglardi family members, cabinet ministers, friends or anybody who needed a lift. If a constituent needed to go down to Vancouver or Victoria from Kamloops, and the Lear was going there, and there was room, then he had a ride.

So when Bob Gaglardi heard the jet was going down to Wichita for an inspection, it was almost tailor-made. Since his wife Karen was from Longview, Texas, it would be a simple thing to catch a commercial flight from Seattle or Wichita to Dallas and then travel home to Longview to show her parents their new grandson. It was an opportunity to make a trip that otherwise would be expensive.

Karen was reluctant about hitching a free ride, but when Bob's dad said there was room on the plane, Bob went ahead and called Bert Toye, booked the connecting commercial flight to Dallas, and she was set to go.

The Plane, The Plane

They that wait upon the Lord shall renew their strength; they shall mount up with wings as eagles.
ISAIAH 40.31

When I bow out, it'll be flying. I'll get into some scrape with a plane, and that'll be it.
PHIL GAGLARDI

On Tuesday morning, March 19, 1968, Dave Barrett received a phone call from a Victoria airport air-traffic controller who thought he might like to know that the B.C. government jet had taken off for Dallas, Texas, the previous night with several people on board.

Barrett knew that Phil Gaglardi had relatives in Texas. And Barrett despised Gaglardi, was disgusted by the highways minister's flamboyant style, and was convinced that Gaglardi used his government portfolio for his own benefit. In an interview years later with the author, Barrett's anger with Gaglardi still showed. Gaglardi, said Barrett, "has no redeeming value. He isn't immoral, he's amoral."

The NDP member stopped by a table at the parliamentary restaurant where several Liberal MLAs were eating lunch, and told Ray Perrault about the phone call. During a post-lunch stroll around the capital's Inner Harbour, Pat McGeer, Perrault and fellow Liberal MLA Barrie Clark decided they'd better check out Barrett's story.

Clark happened to know a radio reporter in Dallas. Back in their offices, Clark gave him a call. The reporter friend said he'd look into it at the airport. That evening he teletyped back a reply. The provincial government Lear had landed at the Dallas airport at midnight Monday for refuelling. At a private terminal, the people on board were met by two couples — one elderly — and two children. The Lear then took off, without the passengers, on a flight plan to Wichita, Kansas.

Was Phil Gaglardi now using his jet to fly relatives to far-flung corners of the continent to vacation?

Wednesday morning, Perrault took the information to a closed meeting of the public accounts committee. He was the only opposition member in attendance, since the NDP members were boycotting the committee after staging a walkout over calling witnesses on the Silver Sage issue. Perrault asked the Socreds to call Gaglardi and Toye before the committee to explain the flight. The Socred members, who had just completed a committee report exonerating Gaglardi in the Silver Sage affair, refused.

"Gentlemen," said Perrault, "you have left me no choice."

He and Barrett called a quick meeting with reporters in the press gallery and told them the story of the mystery flight of the Lear.

"We want a complete accounting of this last trip," said Perrault. "If the minister is not going to give the information, he should resign forthwith. If he doesn't, his colleagues should ask him to resign."

The reporters found Gaglardi in the Hotel Vancouver, where he'd just had an operation to fix an impacted tooth and cyst in his jaw, and was feeling none too well. Gaglardi readily confirmed that the jet had made the trip to the Lear factory in Wichita.

Had it dropped off his son or daughter in Dallas on the way?

Dallas? This was news to him. No, his son or daughter wasn't on the plane, as far as he knew. In fact, he wasn't sure who was on the plane. It probably just stopped in Dallas "to get gassed up." Better ask Bert Toye, the pilot.

Toye was contacted in Wichita. He refused comment. Ask Gaglardi.

By now, Gaglardi had checked the jet's exact itinerary. It had flown from Kamloops to Vancouver to Victoria to Seattle, then Denver, Dallas and Wichita. It wasn't supposed to go to Dallas, but weather forced a diversion.

When Toye landed in Denver, he said, the aviation weather office told him the cloud base was less than one thousand feet over Wichita, with winds gusting up to forty-five miles per hour and visibility three miles in rain. Toye, being unfamiliar with the area or its airports, decided to divert to Dallas, an extra twenty minutes' flying time, rather than leave his passengers stranded in Denver until the Wichita front blew over.

And, asked reporters, was Gaglardi's daughter-in-law a passenger?

Yes, she was, said Gaglardi. Karen Gaglardi had hitched a ride on the Lear with the idea of catching a commercial flight at

Seattle if one was available, but apparently there hadn't been. "She was to get off at Seattle."

But when reporters checked on commercial schedules, they found flights from Seattle to Dallas almost duplicating the Lear's flight plan, and arriving ahead of the Lear.

Yes, said Gaglardi, but Karen didn't have time to catch a Seattle flight because the Lear didn't arrive there on time for her to make the switch.

It was pointed out to him that U.S. weather officers at Denver reported that at no time after 5 p.m. Sunday had there been a ceiling below four thousand feet or was visibility less than ten miles. There had been no reports of a weather front between Denver and Wichita. Winds were sixteen miles per hour, gusting to twenty–seven.

"The ceilings were real good," a U.S. Federal Aviation Administration spokesman was quoted as saying. "There was no weather to interfere with a Lear jet."

That didn't mean anything, said Gaglardi. "I've checked with the weather office many times and got a different report to the one my pilots have been given. Bert Toye is the best pilot I have got. He would not lie for all the tea in China."

What the press didn't know was that Gaglardi genuinely hadn't expected Toye to take the side trip to Dallas to deliver the passengers. Hadn't expected it, because he'd given specific orders against it. He was wary of Karen riding at all. In a conversation at the Kamloops airport, he warned Toye against it. "Bert said, 'What difference does it make? I have to go there anyway.' I said, 'The difference it will make is what some people might make of it.' He said, 'It has nothing to do with you.' " Gaglardi was worried about the publicity he'd been getting over The Boys' land deals, and couldn't afford any more controversy. He says he was left with the impression that Toye and co–pilot Ron Page understood they were to take no extra passengers with them. Lou Iverson's recollection backs up Gaglardi on the caution to Toye, although he says he knew Toye intended to take Karen with him on the trip. Toye was to let his passengers off in Seattle, where they would catch a Continental Airlines flight to Dallas. McNeill confirms Gaglardi's concern. "I was standing right there," he said. "Phil did not want those ladies carried to Dallas. Now if the pilot got down there, and if the pilot decided something different, I don't think Phil should carry the can for it." The Lear headed out of Kamloops, dropped Gaglardi in Vancouver and continued to Victoria and then south. Karen Gaglardi and her son were on the plane. By the time she got through customs, it was too late to catch the Continental flight. They went on with Toye, and from that point, all the flight decisions were up to him. The weather, said McNeill, was not a problem for Toye. The collaborated version of events now provided by Gaglardi, Iverson and McNeill indicates very strongly that Gaglardi took a bum rap, a rap that caused him grievous political harm, in order to protect Bert Toye. "I can tell you categorically that I did not make that decision," he says of the extra leg. While Toye could not be interviewed for this book, he was a favourite of Gaglardi despite not being well–liked by other pilots, one of whom described Toye as "always trying to score points for himself." Yet Gaglardi's sense of loyalty made it impossible for him to absolve himself by blaming Toye. The contradiction between his statement that he didn't think Karen was going to be on the plane, and comments attributed to him at the time that he thought she was going as far as Seattle, might be attributable to his protection of Bert Toye. "In the final analysis, I was responsible for everything that happened with that plane. I couldn't very well stand up and say I wasn't to blame, because who would believe it?" He would have had to fire Toye to back it up. Even if Toye had come forward and taken responsibility, people would have thought he was covering up for his boss. So Gaglardi didn't try to cast doubt on Toye's story; he never, in fact, even talked to Toye about it after the scandal broke. There was speculation of deeper motives. Iverson believed Gaglardi was set up from within the Social Credit party, a theory that gained some limited support at the time.

Any hope Gaglardi had that this controversy would die a natural death the way so many others had was doomed. It was an instant scandal. Partly, it was timing. It fed on the other controversies of recent days: the land deals, the ranch work and fighting in public accounts over keeping logs on the Highways Department's air fleet.

To Dave Barrett, flying your daughter–in–law on a government plane, even if it was purposely diverted somewhere especially for her, was a minor indiscretion. But in politics, you used what you had for ammunition. In politics, you were guilty unless proven innocent.

Ray Perrault was demanding a judicial inquiry, comparing the plane scandal to the Bob Sommers case. "The public must be reassured that every effort will be made to ascertain the complete facts and, if necessary, that appropriate action will be taken in the interests of the citizens of B.C."

In retrospect, even Ray Perrault would find that position a trifle pompous. The Lear's price tag was a quarter that of Prime Minister Lester Pearson's Lockheed Jetstar, which had been used only recently to take Pearson and his wife for a vacation in Jamaica. The federal jet was fully equipped with special electronics, a bar, a galley — all the comforts of home. All federal cabinet ministers used the Jetstar, and all MPs flew free on Air Canada or Canadian Pacific Airlines, as well as on Department of Transport aircraft. And, other provinces had large fleets of aircraft. Perrault was also aware of the growing use of aircraft by private companies. It was becoming a necessity. "Gaglardi's contention that he needed an airplane was justified," Perrault said in an interview with the author. "In retrospect I would revise some of my judgments."

But in 1968, without benefit of hindsight, all the Liberal leader saw was the minister of highways giving himself and his relatives rides on an expensive jet paid for by the taxpayers. Perrault's view was shared by more than a few members of the Socreds' own caucus. Several who had been uncomfortable with Gaglardi's way of doing things for a long time, who had become increasingly alarmed at the trouble caused by his sons' land deals and everything else that had blown up to the delight of the opposition recently, were horrified at this latest *faux pas*. Cyril Shelford of Omineca, always outspoken, told anybody who wanted to know that he felt Gaglardi had to go. John Tisdalle of Saanich and Dudley Little of Skeena felt the same way, and were confident others would take the same stand when it came to voting on Gaglardi's estimates.

Within cabinet itself, whatever reluctant support Gaglardi had enjoyed in the past evaporated. His competence had never been questioned — though he often cut red tape when he should have unravelled it — and no cabinet minister ever said Gaglardi wasn't doing the job. But it was Gaglardi's spending that had resulted in the premier's clamp-down on budgeting in the early 1960s and that had often resulted in money taken from the coffers of another ministry to go into Gaglardi's projects. ("I didn't spend a dime without the premier saying it was OK.") It was Gaglardi who missed many a cabinet meeting ("W.A.C. did stop me on the stairs one day in the legislature and say, 'Phil, we need you to be at cabinet meetings,' "), yet managed to get most of the press and somehow remained second in popularity with the public only to Bennett. And it was Gaglardi who got the perks, who drove government cars with radio telephones, who maintained a room at the Hotel Vancouver, who flew around in a jet. Some cabinet ministers still hadn't figured out where the money came from for that jet, or even how he'd been able to swing all the past spending on other planes. Other cabinet ministers used the jet on occasion, and some used other government planes as well, but never to the extent or in the manner that Gaglardi did it.

Most of all, Gaglardi's refusal to hold back on the bombast and the flaunting of the amenities of his office had become an acute embarrassment to the government.

Ken Kiernan: "A good many of the cabinet were tired of taking flack over the aircraft. It had reached the point where the Dallas trip was just the last straw. It was one of those little things that in terms of dollars and cents didn't amount to anything, but in terms of public criticism did. There was no support for Phil on that."

And Wesley Black, who was to "come as close to hating" Gaglardi as he had any man, came to believe the highways minister changed over the years leading up to the Lear scandal. "Phil, by his methods, by the fact he knew what the media were all about, exploited that, but something happened, Phil became power hungry, Phil became an ego–maniac and, in fairness to Phil, some of the public helped him out."

Bennett didn't go to cabinet for advice, but he was getting the message. Though it was highly unlikely, there was speculation that enough Socred members might vote with the opposition against Gaglardi's estimates the following day to defeat the government and force an election.

Gaglardi returned to Victoria with his aching jaw and assured the premier he could bring everything under control once again. Gaglardi would go into the House to speak on his estimates and deliver a rip–roaring speech in defence of the Lear and in explanation of the Dallas fiasco. Then he went away to work on the speech. He almost always delivered his speeches from the cuff, but this time he worded it carefully, and had it typed out for him to read.

"I would like to make a statement to the House concerning some of the utterly ridiculous, small–minded and inaccurate non-sense which has been levelled at me over use of my department's jet aircraft," the draft speech began. Then it lambasted Pearson, Art Laing and John Nicholson of the federal Liberals for using publicly owned aircraft for private trips. "Now, Prime Minister Pearson, I'm told, frequently takes newspapermen with him on Department of Transport aircraft, and I'm told that other cabinet ministers do likewise. The bar opens the moment the plane takes off and one newsman has described the twelve–hour flight to London as twelve hours in which to get stoned."

The eight–page draft said that, "I have absolutely nothing to hide, although I freely admit that because of the outrageous character assassination and the campaign of innuendo that has been directed against me in the last few weeks I have not always been as candid with the press in the last few hours as I would normally like to be."

On page six he got around to the question of the Dallas flight. "The answers are childishly simple. . . . I am the guilty monster here. I am the errant cabinet minister who suggested to my daughter-in-law that seeing as the jet had to go anyhow, she might as well go along as far as Seattle, where the plane had to stop for customs, or to Wichita, and take a regular airline from there. . . . In one place I am reported as saying I didn't know who was on the plane. And I didn't. I didn't volunteer that it could be my daughter-in-law and not my daughter."

Gaglardi's speech concluded: "If it's a flight log the people of the province want, I would be happy to do this. I have nothing to hide. The planes save the taxpayers millions of dollars.

"The opposition has not found one single, solitary instance of dishonesty or improper use of my office, so they want to investigate and unearth twenty minutes of extra flying time."

The speech was remarkable in several respects. One was Gaglardi's insistence on taking full blame for supposedly suggesting that his daughter-in-law make the trip in the Lear — a scenario readily accepted by the public and press — even though his son Bob had made the request, and Toye had promoted it. Another was that his assertions about use and abuse of public aircraft by other politicians were absolutely correct but, of course, other politicians weren't Phil Gaglardi and they didn't receive the attention Gaglardi received. Then there was the admission that he hadn't been entirely candid about who was on the plane. Later, he retrenched to the position that he had tried to be honest. (Bennett got very upset with Gaglardi for telling him his daughter wasn't on the plane, but not explaining that it was his daughter-in-law. Today, Gaglardi admits to "sidestepping" the question of who flew on the plane when Bennett asked him, and that Bennett felt misled. "But I told the truth as I saw it." In his own defence, he says he may not have had a chance to tell the whole story. He has trouble recalling the exact circumstances of that particular conversation with the premier, but believes it may have been in a situation in which he was interrupted before he could fully explain. "I didn't have any daughters and everybody knew I didn't have a daughter. There could be a possibility I would say, 'No, that's not the case' or some such thing.")

And there was his ready agreement to maintain detailed logs on use of government aircraft, a practice he had brushed off many times in the past, and soon would again.

Finally, there was that concluding statement, his refusal to resign and the rationale that he must stand before the opposition and refute their charges.

Gaglardi never got to make his speech. Only twenty-four hours later, he was to be condemned by the opposition for failing to face the legislature to answer to the airplane scandal.

In the highways minister's Victoria office, Edith Valen (the longtime Gaglardi secretary had married the previous year) received a phone call from Katherine Mylrea, Bennett's secretary. It was essential that Gaglardi see the premier before going into the legislative assembly that day. Gaglardi had not yet shown up at the office.

Lieutenant-Governor George Pearkes took the eleven o'clock ferry from Swartz Bay to Tsawwassen, planning to attend a luncheon in Vancouver. Part way across, he received a message to return to Victoria immediately. Upon docking at the Mainland at 12:40 he would be driven to Vancouver International Airport where a plane would be waiting to return him to Victoria. Bennett's secretary had arranged for the highways plane to be there, instructing the booking clerk to tell no one, not even Valen, who normally had approving authority for anything other than routine flights.

Gaglardi, now in his office, continued receiving phone calls and visits from reporters. "There is nobody, but nobody, to blame but me," he told *The Province* in explaining the jet scandal. "I am responsible for the plane. It has nothing to do with the premier or the cabinet. I am the culprit, nobody else."

As the noon hour approached, Katherine Mylrea called Edith Valen again. Gaglardi was tied up.

Shortly after 12:30, she was on the phone again "in a very disturbed state and wanted me to make sure that Mr. Gaglardi had to talk to the premier before attending the session," Valen recalled. "I passed this message to Mr. Gaglardi and he then left the office to see the premier."

Only two people knew for sure what was said at that meeting: Gaglardi and Bennett. Both of them, at the time, maintained that Gaglardi submitted his resignation voluntarily. Gaglardi still maintains it; Bennett later said otherwise.

Said Valen in thinking back to that day: "It is obvious to me that everything had been arranged for Mr. Gaglardi's resignation except for the fact that Mr. Gaglardi was not aware of it."

Ray Williston: "W.A.C. forced him out. It had nothing to do with the aircraft; it had to do with Phil not levelling with him. That was one thing you didn't do with W.A.C." Williston was referring to the question of whether or not Gaglardi's daughter

Gaglardi with "The Chief," Premier W.A.C. Bennett, who stuck by his controversial highways minister through controversy after controversy, but who was forced to accept his resignation during the Lear jet scandal of 1968.

flew on the plane — the highways minister taking the same tack with Bennett as he did with the press, refusing at first to acknowledge that his daughter-in-law had taken the trip. "Phil's weakness was that unless something was right in front of his nose, he didn't admit it existed," said Williston. "He swept it under the rug."

Years later, Bennett told an interviewer he had, indeed, fired Gaglardi for that very reason, though Gaglardi says the premier would never have said such a thing. "I resigned and that's it."

Bennett certainly never gave any outward hint that Gaglardi faced the axe during the first tense days of the crisis in 1968, and neither did Gaglardi. But the dramatic defense Gaglardi had been planning to deliver to the House the afternoon of their meeting was cancelled. The feared revolt in party ranks would be rendered irrelevant.

The issue of whether Gaglardi quit or was fired may be academic, since it's clear Bennett wanted the resignation. Even Gaglardi doesn't pretend Bennett didn't want him out of the Highways portfolio, but says he beat the premier to the punch, and that Bennett was adamant about Gaglardi remaining in the government. "A lot of people say Cec Bennett asked me to resign. That's a packa hogwash. Not that he couldn't have. He didn't get the chance. I said, 'I've been looking for an opportunity to get out of politics anyway, and this is it.' " In their meeting in the premier's office, Gaglardi and Bennett came to the conclusion one way or another that Gaglardi must go. The government could no longer afford him as highways minister. But he wouldn't be simply tossed to the slavering wolves of the opposition.

> *When the premier asked me to come into his office, he told me that I had embarrassed the government, so I said to him, "Mr. Premier, I'm not in the business of embarrassing anybody," and I said, "Give me a piece of paper," which he did, and I scribbled out my resignation and he very forcibly said, "I'll accept your resignation as minister of highways but you're still going to be in the cabinet." I said, "What in the name of common sense are you talking about?" He said, "You have to remain as a minister in the cabinet." I said, "What kind of a minister?" He said, "A minister without portfolio," and I said, "Cec, I've worked hard, I've worked fourteen– to eighteen–hour days for sixteen years, I've never let you down." I said, "Cec, in all the years that we've been working together have I ever given you one bum steer?" and he said, "Phil, you're right, you haven't." That's how much confidence he had in me. Now why would he fire me if he wanted me to stay in the cabinet?*

Gaglardi reluctantly agreed to stay on as a minister without portfolio, with a cut in salary and allowances from $25,000 to half that. It would be temporary, Bennett assured him; the time would come when there would be a new job for Phil Gaglardi. In the meantime, he would sit on the Harbours Board, and take it easy.

Now, they had to deal with the caucus, the opposition and the press. Half an hour after their painful meeting had begun, they left Bennett's office on the ground floor for the Socred caucus room one flight up. Each day before the 2 p.m. sitting of the legislature, the government members gathered there for a brief strategy session. It wasn't familiar territory for Gaglardi, who attended few such meetings. This day, the members had been promised an explanation of the jet scandal.

Bennett entered first, with Gaglardi behind him. But Gaglardi didn't stay. He looked around at the MLAs, and strode out, leaving the legislative building for his office in the Douglas Building across Government Street.

Bennett was left to stave off the caucus unrest, telling them to give him a little more time. They would soon have their answer.

It was going to be a tough day for Bennett. Although he was acknowledged as a hard–nosed politician, he had a streak of loyalty that was difficult to break. When his troops strayed, he tended to give them a lot of line. The colourful Gaglardi more than most. It wasn't easy cutting him loose. Bennett returned to the House for only half an hour more, then left with reporters trailing him. His limousine was waiting along with his executive assistant and deputy provincial secretary L. J. Wallace. "It's a nice day for a drive," he said.

The limousine drove over and picked up Gaglardi, then headed toward Government House, where Pearkes, summoned back from his Vancouver appointment, awaited them.

"We had a lovely cup of coffee," Bennett told reporters when they emerged thirty–five minutes later. That's the most any of them would say. Bennett said he would make a statement in the House. A few minutes later, he was back at the Legislative Building, where the House was debating Ray Williston's resources estimates.

"I ask permission of the House to make a statement of public interest," said Bennett.

"I wish to announce to this House that with great regret, at 3:15 p.m. this afternoon, his honour the lieutenant–governor accepted the resignation of the minister of highways and appointed him as minister without portfolio. He will continue to be an adviser. And two minutes later the premier was sworn in as minister of highways."

Despite the unrest among members of all parties over the plane scandal, Bennett's announcement was a shock. Socreds were as surprised as the opposition. "Oh, no," someone moaned.

But it was Herb Capozzi, Gaglardi's friend, who expressed his shock and disappointment most vehemently. "Shame!" he exclaimed. It forced its way through his lips from his heart before he had a chance to think about it. While Phil Gaglardi liked to call many people "friend o' mine," Capozzi was one who returned the feeling, sincerely. He had been all in favour of Gaglardi's airplane fleet as an entry into twentieth–century politics. He admired Gaglardi for his accomplishments. And while the latest airplane screwup should never have happened — "It was more stupid than wrong" — it was, he said in retrospect, "an act that didn't cost anybody any money."

Capozzi felt Gaglardi trusted too much in his own judgment. "Phil had difficulty realizing that just because he was a church minister and never thought things could be wrong, it didn't mean they couldn't be wrong. If he thought it was right, then, according to him, it was right. He didn't realize that it must also seem right." So on that Thursday afternoon in 1968, in the House, hearing that a personal friend was paying the price of an illustrious career for a small indiscretion, Herb Capozzi couldn't stop himself from gasping out, "Shame!"

And as Bennett left the House to be surrounded by clamouring reporters, Capozzi left, too, to console his fallen friend.

Bennett struggled to keep his composure in the face of the onslaught in the hallway. "I feel very sad," he said when asked about his personal feelings on the resignation.

Was it really a resignation?

"I talked to him for quite awhile but he insisted. I suggested that if he did resign I certainly wanted him to stay in the cabinet."

Why had Gaglardi quit?

"I'm sure it was ill health. As you know, he had an operation on his jaw and the trouble he's had since. . . . He's lost fifteen pounds and his health is not good."

On the way back into his office, Gaglardi told Edith Valen he was no longer the minister of highways. Surrounded by the paraphernalia of sixteen years in office, he had calls to make to his family, to tell them what had happened. At one corner of his huge desk was a small model of the Lear. In a glass cabinet, a helmet with "Flying Phil" in large black letters. On the wall, portraits of Bob and Bill and other family members. Beside the Lear model, a large, leather–bound Bible.

His first visitor was Capozzi, but the phone was soon ringing, and reporters were crowding over from the press gallery wanting to talk to him. Capozzi stayed as he let them all in. Girding himself, Gaglardi determined to maintain his composure and his humour, though he could not hide some of his bitterness, reminding them of who they had brought down. "I have no regrets. I have worked with a dedication and determination that have brought to a conclusion some of the most fantastic projects the province of British Columbia has ever seen and, I venture to say, will ever see. What I have accomplished has been for the people of B.C."

They wanted to know if he might quit politics completely and go into business.

"I am a young man, a working man. My business in life is never to be cynical and always to be helpful to those people I can help, even when they are kicking me in the teeth. The fellow that cuts my throat can ask me ten minutes later, 'Phil, can you lend me ten bucks?' and I'll lend him ten bucks. That's always been my attitude in life."

They asked if he thought he'd done anything wrong.

"I have a positive, straightforward answer to anything that can be said about me. The only thing I know that could be wrong was that decision to allow my daughter–in–law to fly south in the jet. That was an error and an indiscretion, and I shouldn't have done it."

They asked why he'd lied about his daughter–in–law's flight in the Lear, and this very day about his resignation.

"I didn't lie. I never lie. Are you so stupid as to think I don't know what I'm doing!"

Later that day, he left Victoria for his hotel suite in Vancouver, leaving the NDP and Liberals calling for his head. They wanted Gaglardi on the carpet to answer questions on the jet, on highways access and on the ranch work. And they wanted him out of government.

Several Socred caucus members agreed with the view that Gaglardi should have been kicked out of cabinet altogether. Cabinet members themselves had difficulty holding a middle line. Asked if Gaglardi had done wrong, Robert Bonner said, "I think that is apparent in the minister's decision to resign."

Bennett instructed highways deputy minister Tom Miard to have the Lear returned from Wichita as soon as possible and "grounded until further notice." And only government people would be allowed on government planes. "No passengers, no members of families or other passengers."

As he went about mopping up the remains of Gaglardi's ministry, Bennett was almost as lavish in his praise of Gaglardi as Gaglardi himself. "B.C. highways will always be Gaglardi highways even if we have twenty–two highways ministers. They talk about Roman roads in Europe, but they don't compare to Gaglardi's highways in B.C. He had sixteen years without a holiday but there was that darn jaw and all. . . . The poor guy."

Jake Krushnisky, Gaglardi's former Kamloops engineer now working in Vancouver, heard of his old boss's resignation on a radio newscast while driving down Burrard Street in Vancouver.

Krushnisky contacted him by phone at the Hotel Vancouver, but Gaglardi wasn't very talkative. His jaw was bothering him again, he said.

Alone, Gaglardi sat at a window in the Hotel Vancouver, looking down seventeen floors onto the street below. In the darkness, automobile lights streamed by, their occupants off to their clubs and theatres and rendezvous.

For sixteen of his fifty–five years, he had served the people of this province.

Gaglardi thought about it. He thought about the window, and the street below, and about how someone who had lost so much might consider jumping out of a window. He understood.

Then he pulled away.

A Stranger in the House

A prophet is not without honour, save in his own country, and in his own house.
MATTHEW 13.57

What does it matter what happens to you today or tomorrow as long as your faith in God is intact?
PHIL GAGLARDI

Gaglardi flew home, as usual, on the weekend. But he flew on a commercial airliner. "I'm warning you, no pictures," he told the local press at Kamloops airport. "You've had your day."

On home ground, at least, he was still Phil, the little Zephyr who got things done. But even here, there was discontent. Saturday morning, he met with the executive of the Kamloops Social Credit party. Afterward, the party, through president Rick Wanless, issued a statement reaffirming its "confidence in Mr. Gaglardi" as "the most capable man the province has had in its history." There were dissenters to that. The party's vice–president, Jack Ernst, resigned in protest over Gaglardi's refusal to step down as MLA. "They haven't got the guts to say what they really think," Ernst said of the Kamloops executive. "You should hear them when Gaglardi isn't there." Wanless, a teacher by profession, a breeder of fine horses by avocation, a Socred since his teenage years, and a full–time admirer of Phil Gaglardi, was having some doubts of his own. Behind the public statements of confidence and support were misgivings. "There was at least a glimmer of suspicion that some things weren't being done right, and we would have been wearing rose–coloured glasses not to wonder about it." Wanless worried about the Gaglardi boys' highway deals and about plane rides. "I don't want to be holier–than–thou, but I thought it was wrong (the plane rides). I wasn't about to make a big fuss about it; I just thought that I wasn't about to do it."

Gordon Britton, like Wanless, a teacher, and a constituency director and provincial Socred director, got a phone call from

Gaglardi about that time for a lengthy chat about what was going on, and what could be done. "My feelings were quite clear at the time, which he couldn't accept — there was no way that what he was accused of doing could be made palatable." Gaglardi argued that he was a victim of circumstance. "As I look back I have a certain amount of embarrassment," said Britton, who soon left the party because of Gaglardi and because he felt W.A.C. Bennett was losing touch with the people.

But in the immediate aftermath of the resignation, the show of support came through from the *omnium gatherum* of the local party because Jack Ernst was viewed as having political ambitions of his own, and because nobody was about to try to dump a man of Gaglardi's stature over unproven allegations or relatively minor indiscretions.

That evening, Gaglardi and Jennie were boisterously cheered at a Lions Club district spring conference banquet. Sunday morning, he told the congregation at Calvary Temple: "Believe me, with your help and my strength and with my spirit and my faith in God, I'll lick the world. Amen!"

Mike Latta, Bob Gaglardi's partner in the bulk-oil business in Kamloops, was appalled at Gaglardi's forced resignation. When Charlie Bennett, Gaglardi's acquaintance and temporary partner in the Del Cielo deal, received a phone call from Victoria asking for help in organizing a pro-Gaglardi demonstration, Latta gladly agreed to go along with it. The plan was to get a group of supporters together from Kamloops, link up with another group in the Lower Mainland, and bus over to the legislature. A Vancouver contractor named Bill Gallaher rented a bus, backers were assembled, and signs painted. A group of pilots was lined up to fly over the legislative buildings at the same time the demonstrators would arrive. But the best-laid plans. . . .

Not everybody in the Kamloops party, first of all, thought it was a tremendous idea. Wanless and others thought it better to let things run their natural course. To make waves now would just perpetuate the scandal stories. So Latta and his wife Emily didn't achieve the groundswell of support they were hoping for, but that wasn't their biggest problem.

"It was an astronomical screwup," Latta recalled. "It was mostly government people who organized it, but the day before, they were called in and told not to participate in any demonstrations." Latta and Bennett went ahead anyway. Two dozen people drove down from Kamloops to meet with about fifty more ready with the bus at the Broadway Pentecostal Tabernacle in Vancouver.

A warehouse had been rented for the day in Victoria as the marshalling area. When they arrived, it was pouring rain. "There were stacks of placards, enough for an army," said Latta. "A guy in a trenchcoat came in and said participation was cancelled." Not only that, but the miserable weather had all but grounded the air show, with only three planes able to get off the ground. Charlie Bennett was ready to give up and go home, but Latta, aware that the media had already been tipped off, knew cancelling out would look even worse for Gaglardi.

Instead of marching to the legislative buildings as planned, they decided to go in their bus. When Charlie Bennett saw the reporters waiting for them at the legislative building front steps, he got even more gun-shy. Latta saw that seventy people standing around in the rain with placards, aided by three airplanes, wasn't going to be a very effective show of strength. They would have to go inside the House.

Up they trooped. But the sergeants-at-arms divested them of their "We want Phil Gaglardi for Highways Minister" placards, which were stacked against the hallway walls, as they quietly entered the public gallery that overlooks the House, and sat in the area above the speaker's chair. (Edith Valen came over from her office to watch, but didn't join the protesters.) This wasn't going to get them anywhere, either. Latta passed the word around to be ready with "We want Phil!" when the signal was given. Then he sat there in nervous agony, knowing he was about to do the unmentionable, to disrupt the proceedings of the legislature. Besides being incredibly rude, it was an offense that could get them all thrown in jail. Latta wanted to wait for an NDP member to speak, but Liberal leader Ray Perrault was debating on and on a piece of welfare legislation, so Latta decided it would have to be now or never. The crew-cut oil dealer stood up and shouted, "We want to protest the character assassination of Phil Gaglardi!"

The chant began: "We want Phil . . . We want Phil . . . We want Phil!"

"You can have him," said Alex Macdonald from down in the House, never at a loss for a quick repartee.

"There's a stranger in the House!" proclaimed Perrault, using the traditional parliamentary warning to the speaker of an unusual occurrence. As the chanting continued, he gave up on his speech, tossing his papers into the air. They rained down on the desks and floor like giant confetti.

Bennett smiled and waved at the chanters.

Speaker W.H. Murray called a quick recess.

"Lousy communists!" hissed one middle–aged Kamloops woman. "Phil is the best man of all of them. Phil has done more than all of them put together!"

As they walked en masse through the corridors on their way out, the demonstrators continued their "We want Phil" chant. Charlie Bennett dodged questions from reporters, but Latta was more forthright, identifying himself and his business and explaining the reasons for the protest. "The people of the province will realize a great man has been unduly handled," he said.

As the demonstrators headed home, the reporters began the chore of trying to track down the origins of the protest. Latta's association with the Gaglardis was quickly identified. Gaglardi himself, who had been in Victoria earlier in the day but returned to Vancouver before the demonstrators arrived, acted surprised when questioned about Latta's business relationship with Bob Gaglardi. He denied he had any knowledge of the show of support for him, also denying knowing of any business link. "I am positive they are not business associates. I am as positive as I can be."

Bob Gaglardi, who had known in advance about the rally, said, "What he (Latta) meant to say . . . was that we just knew each other. We are not associated."

Latta, Charlie Bennett and the protesters, meanwhile, made their long trip home. Latta climbed into bed back in Kamloops at 3 a.m. the next day. He was baffled about the claims of Phil and Bob Gaglardi that he had no business connection with Bob. "I remember thinking, 'Why would they say that?' Phil was just furious with me, I guess maybe for what I'd said."

Bennett shuffled his cabinet a month later. He intended to carry out further changes some time in the summer, probably after a series of needed by–elections. He brought one new member into the cabinet. That was Waldo McTavish Skillings, sixty–one, a Victoria insurance man who had been a close bridge–playing friend of Bennett's for years. He had extensive experience in municipal politics. An MLA since 1960, he had been kept well informed of cabinet activities by Bennett, and was happy to be brought in as minister of industrial development, trade and commerce. Ralph Loffmark would move from that portfolio to minister of health services and hospital insurance. Wesley Black would move from there to highways, retaining the provincial secretary's job he had held since 1952.

The shuffle of portfolios also meant a shuffle of offices. Black moved out of his office in the main legislative building and into Gaglardi's office across the street in the Douglas Building. An angry Edith Valen packed up Gaglardi's files on the brusque orders of Black and sent them to Gaglardi's home in Kamloops. There was no way she could work for Black, whom she found to be abrasive and rude. She wasn't going to have a choice, anyway, since Black moved his own secretarial staff in with him. So Valen transferred over to Skillings' Douglas Building office, taken over from Loffmark, who was moving to Black's former office.

Gaglardi, once deemed the man most likely to succeed Bennett, once the darling of the province's common folk, the greatest Roman roadbuilder, had no office at all. That, claimed Bennett, was because Gaglardi had wanted it that way. Seeing that her former boss was going to be humiliated by being given neither office nor staff — even the three ministers without portfolio shared one among them — Valen asked Skillings if she could handle Gaglardi's phone calls and correspondence. Skillings readily agreed. Gaglardi decided to keep his Hotel Vancouver accommodation.

Despite the trauma of losing the Highways portfolio, Gaglardi managed to make light of his fall. "I was a prominent politician up until a couple of weeks ago," he told a convention of doctors in Vancouver. "Of late, I mostly used an airplane to get around the province and became quite famous for it until they took it away from me. Now I am grounded, but I still get there because I am sure I am going to make the grade somehow."

Black, meanwhile, was making some changes in the Highways Department. "My first task in the Highways Department was to reorganize, which, I must admit, was easy. In simple terms, I put Tom Miard back in his rightful job as deputy highways minister. I took the round pegs and I put them in round holes, and I took the square pegs and I put them in square holes. It's as simple as that. I put people back in their own slots." He also told the engineers he would not be making engineering decisions. "I told them at our first meeting, 'What I know about operating a slide rule you could put on a postage stamp, so I won't interfere.' But as far as politics are concerned, I said, 'I make the decisions as to what the priorities are,' and even though they submitted a priorities list I changed them. I got along with them very, very well. I'm not a small boy, I know that Phil Gaglardi's act was pretty tough to follow. However, the whole organization needed a change. Phil had a direct line. You'd go into Phil's office about a road or something and the doggone phone would ring and Phil would talk for twenty minutes and you never did get your answer."

The new and the former highways ministers clashed when,

Gaglardi says, he was told by several contractors that Black was asking questions about alleged improprieties.

> *Three different contractors came to me and said he was saying things that sounded like I had done something wrong, so I phoned Edith (Valen), my secretary, dictated a letter to Wes himself, and I said, "It appears you have been saying some things that put me in a bad light," and I stated right now categorically that, "If there is any further continuance of this on any kind of a basis, I demand an absolute judicial inquiry into the entire affairs of the department from the day that I went in there until the day that I left," and I sent a copy to the premier, and I never heard anything more from my friend Mr. Black.*

Black did have questions in his own mind about what Gaglardi had done as highways minister. "All kinds of things were alleged vis-a-vis God, Ginter and Gaglardi, and so on. I did have suspicions, but I think that part of it has to be water under the bridge." As for contractors, some of them came to him with allegations about Gaglardi. "But that's a two-way street. Contractors are going to get as much money the easy way as they possibly can. Phil, as far as they were concerned, was pretty tight-fisted and he didn't let them get away with too much. I didn't either. I cut out all the overages." He put a stop to paying contractors extra when they claimed to run into trouble, he said. "If you were the low bidder and everything was right about your specs, you got the contract, but you blinking well did it for whatever the sum was; no sense in bellyaching about it. Never listen to that because that's how you milk the cow."

But Gaglardi wasn't impressed with his successor. "The people in the department felt that Wesley Black was like a bump on a log; all he was there for was merely to sit in the chair." And, according to Gaglardi, road-construction costs started going up.

Phase two of the cabinet shuffle came earlier than expected. On Monday, May 27, 1968, word got around the legislative press bunch that a plane had been sent to Penticton to return Lieutenant-Governor George Pearkes from a Canadian Legion convention to Victoria. That meant something big was brewing, and the betting was that Gaglardi was going to be returned to a full cabinet post.

But Gaglardi wasn't at Government House that afternoon when the shuffle was made official. Backbencher Cyril Shelford, forty-seven, logger and farmer from the Burns Lake area, was sworn in as agriculture minister. That was a surprise, since Shelford, elected in 1952, had constantly criticized the government. Mines

Minister Don Brothers was moved to education, and Frank Richter to mines and commercial transport. Les Peterson was announced as the new attorney general.

Bennett surprised everyone by announcing that Bob Bonner had resigned the cabinet to accept a position in free enterprise. Bonner, who had served Bennett for sixteen years, was regarded after Gaglardi's fall as the clear choice to succeed Bennett. But the private sector, specifically a plum of a job as McMillan Bloedel's new senior vice-president, lured him away.

His departure touched off new speculation about the party leadership. Now that he was gone, could a comeback by Gaglardi be far behind?

Gaglardi had come to believe it wasn't. When he said it was only a matter of time before he made his comeback, he wasn't relying entirely on his eternal faith in his own tensor strength. Bennett had led him to believe there would be a resurrection, that Gaglardi would be politically reborn. If he couldn't get Highways Department back (in fact, he wasn't even sure he would take it), Gaglardi wanted something new, something where he could put his old talents to best use. He knew what he wanted. . . . The northern half of the province was still largely untapped. It was in even more of a pioneer state than southern B.C. had been when Gaglardi started building roads in 1952. Tackling the job of opening up the resources of northern B.C. would be a lot like it was in the old days. One of the major jobs that needed doing in the north was the paving of the Alaska Highway, a project Gaglardi had supported for years. Clearing the hurdles in Ottawa and Washington to accomplish it would be a big job in itself. It involved not just paving, but upgrading and realigning. A paved Alaska Highway would channel traffic up an International Highway 97 that started in California, ran through Kamloops and eventually became the Alaska Highway in northern B.C. The north half of the province, rich in coal, hydro and a plethora of other natural resources, was on the verge of a giant economic boom. The vast region north from Vancouver right up the coast to Prince Rupert, and through the Chilcotin Plateau east to the existing highway to Prince George was also ripe for development.

> *I had all that planned. I was the fellow that built the road into Whistler and then into Pemberton. I was going to go straight into Prince George, and then a route would go into an area that's uninhabited today, where there are hundreds and hundreds of opportunities in the tourism business. The fishing is out of this world; there's mining up there; that area is completely*

undeveloped. Jumpin' Jupiter, I put highways places where people still don't know they're even there, because that meant development. So when the premier said to me he wanted me to go out and get entrepreneurs interested in the province and developing the north country, that was part of the program I'd been working on for years. We could stand to have another ten million people in the province within a number of years that would be happy and proud to be living in those areas. That was the plan, that's what I was working on.

Bennett's dream of a new northern empire had always gone hand in hand with his plan for total development of the province. In 1956, a Swedish multimillionaire named Axel Wenner-Gren had devised a grandiose scheme for constructing a $1-billion monorail through the Rocky Mountain Trench to the Yukon border. His representatives signed a memorandum with Bennett undertaking the plan, which would lead to timber and mineral developments, pulp mills, a huge hydroelectric dam on the Peace River. All of Wenner-Gren's schemes evaporated by 1960, but the idea of a Peace River dam had stayed firmly in Bennett's head, and his vision of extending the Socred economic commonwealth into every corner of the province was more focused than ever. Gaglardi understood clearly Bennett's dream, and saw clearly that he, Phil Gaglardi, was the man to once again take the impossible, reduce it to the feasible, and make it reality. Bennett had promised him he would have an important role in the province's future development, and Gaglardi wanted it to tie in with the north. Be patient, Bennett said. Gaglardi was not naturally a patient man, but he was trying. "I'm not built for sitting around. It drove me crazy."

Politics weren't the only part of Gaglardi's life causing him trouble. There were problems with his ministry at Calvary Temple as well. On the evening of July 26, 1968, several families met in the Valleyview Hall just outside Kamloops to discuss a most urgent and trying proposal. By the end of the meeting, they had resolved to break from Calvary Temple and establish their own church. The Bethel Pentecostal Tabernacle stands today as a monument to what is described by those who abandoned Gaglardi as a "family" dispute that ruptured the Pentecostal community in Kamloops. Trouble had been broiling for a long time, partly because of Gaglardi's continued absence from day-to-day operation of the church, and partly because of dissatisfaction with his methods when he was there. One church member approached Gaglardi and complained he didn't give members enough say in how the church was run. "They kicked up a fuss," says Gaglardi. "I said, 'It looks to me like there are some people here that are dissatisfied and I agree with all of that. Let's call a congregational meeting and let's have a vote,' and every time that I would ask for a vote they would say, 'No, we don't want a vote' because the majority of the people wanted me there." Gaglardi recommended to the Pentecostal Assemblies that the discontented be given a piece of property the church owned on the city's North Shore. The group sold the land and used the money to buy a lot east of town. "It was a tough situation for me because I was never in that situation in my life except when they were trying to get me out of government. I broke my heart to do everything in my power to make sure everybody was treated on a fair basis. Sad to say, neither church ever recuperated after that. So the only one who ever got any benefit from it was the Devil himself."

The beginning of 1969 brought good news for the NDP. The party had taken a Vancouver South by-election the previous May. It was looking to new leadership, with a tired Bob Strachan announcing he would step down as leader in April, and Tom Berger expected to take over. A January 13 by-election in Burnaby-Willingdon saw forty-five-year-old lawyer James Lorimer handily elected. The result left standings in the legislature at Social Credit thirty-two, NDP seventeen, Liberals six.

The NDP wasn't the only party showing renewed life as the new session opened. Dr. Pat McGeer, a medical researcher, had been elected Liberal leader to succeed Perrault.

Gaglardi wasn't expected to show much interest in the new session, especially since he'd attended only thirteen of ninety-five cabinet meetings between the previous February 16 and the end of the year. But he was there faithfully, though he was given to taking frequent sojourns down the hallways when things got too boring. He was relegated to the back cabinet row, at the very end in a place of even lower status than the other three ministers without portfolio.

But he would soon be given something to do. In the United States, Henry Ford II had been asked by President Lyndon Johnson to organize a movement that would help get the hardcore unemployed into the workforce. Ford set up the National Alliance of Businessmen, which encouraged employers to hire those they normally would not have. Government subsidized the wages of untrained workers until they learned their skills; then the employer decided whether or not to hire them. Gaglardi's friend, Herb Capozzi, studied the idea and liked it.

"There was certainly interest in it," Capozzi recalled. "The government was a lot less inclined to social programs — there was enough trouble trying to get enough money for welfare — but it was beginning to see the moral responsibility." Pressure from government backbenchers for more emphasis on people programs coincided nicely with Bennett's dilemma of what to do with Gaglardi. Capozzi's project had a ring to it. "Bennett didn't want to put Gaglardi out of the cabinet," said Capozzi. "He wanted to shuffle him, not necessarily into oblivion, but certainly shuffle him somewhere between less publicity and obscurity."

"Phil, do your own organizing," Bennett told Gaglardi in bestowing upon him his first real job since he'd left the Highways Department. Budget considerations and responsibilities were vague, but Gaglardi was glad to have something to do.

On February 13, almost a year after he left highways, Gaglardi made a long and windy one–hour speech in the legislature, exchanging the usual insults with the NDP. At the end of it, he announced the formation of the Provincial Alliance of Businessmen for Human Resources. "It's just a temporary job as far as I'm concerned," he said, explaining it would probably be taken over by the Labour Department after he got it operating smoothly.

By spring, after a session featuring more controversy over his continued use of government planes, and a public accounts committee grilling over the cost of his room in the Hotel Vancouver, Gaglardi was growing tired of waiting for Bennett to come through with the real job he had promised. That promise had kept him going, but Bennett hadn't come through. Gaglardi had thought about quitting politics several times before, including in 1963, but the challenge of E. Davie Fulton had changed his mind, made him want to stick it out. Now, though, he was tired, dispirited, bored. He went to Bennett in the premier's office and told him he didn't want to wait any longer. He would not be a candidate in the next election. Bennett pointed to the date of August 27 on a big wall calendar, and told him that would be the day. And Phil Gaglardi had to be a candidate. "He said, 'Phil, we can't win without you.' He said he would give me the most important portfolio in the cabinet if I stayed on. He said, 'Phil, you've done an outstanding job, and you're going to be well–looked–after. You have to run.' This was strange to me," says Gaglardi, considering the sorry state of Gaglardi's political stock. Years later, he says, he discovered Bennett had received petitions of support for Gaglardi with thousands of signatures. But Bennett never told him. "He was that kind of a guy in a lot of ways."

Gaglardi didn't even know by now whether he had any kind of political base intact in Kamloops. Constituency president Wanless, whatever misgivings he might now have about his MLA, saw to it the base was there. The executive declared itself still solidly behind Gaglardi, and by the time a nomination meeting was set for the end of May, he had all the support he needed. And the 150 people at the meeting gave him a standing ovation and a banner reading, "We want our 'Phil' of The Good Life," a reference to a recent Socred propaganda film. The show of support at the nomination meeting touched Gaglardi. "The delegates here tonight have given me a strong indication of their continued support. It's because of this show of confidence in me that I've decided to stay and fight."

If ever the oppositionists smelled blood, this was the time. Jack Ernst, the former first vice–president of the Kamloops Socreds who resigned after unsuccessfully demanding Gaglardi quit during the Lear scandal, went after the Liberal nomination. But he was defeated by former rancher Mack Bryson. McGeer intended to pour everything he could into the Kamloops race. "The most significant win in the province is going to occur right here," he told 236 party members at Bryson's nomination meeting.

Bennett called the election for August 27, 1969, as he'd told Gaglardi he would, catching the NDP without a candidate. Tom Berger, now the party's leader, flew up to Kamloops for his party's hurried nomination meeting. The Tories, under new leader John de Wolfe (the first the party had since Fulton), didn't have a candidate, either. But that was no surprise. De Wolfe planned to muster only three or four candidates, and Kamloops wouldn't be among the chosen ridings.

The NDP nominated accountant Jim Jacobs. Berger spent much of his day in Kamloops denying Bennett's accusations that the NDP was a party of Marxist socialists. He urged voters to tell Gaglardi, "Sorry for the inconvenience, but you've got to go."

Responded Gaglardi: "They all think they're giant killers. They want what they call the honour of beating the giant."

The issue of a new cabinet post for Gaglardi presented Bennett with a delicate situation. Aside from the public controversy brought on by the prospect, Bennett had to decide how to bring Gaglardi back on stage without giving him back the spotlight. Many political analysts think Bennett was afraid that if Gaglardi were given another responsible, senior post he would again pose a potential challenge to the leadership. Gaglardi had believed for years that Bennett was jealous of his accomplishments and of his popularity. "I think there were some other things that the premier had in his mind but who am I to say? The premier did not want me to be premier of the province because if I did what I did as minister of highways you can imagine what I'd do as premier of the province." Bennett was faced with the problem of pacifying Gaglardi's supporters by keeping him in cabinet, and putting him somewhere he wouldn't cause much trouble or rebuild his political base. Gaglardi had decided long ago, however, that he would never openly challenge Bennett's leadership. Gaglardi believed Bennett knew that, and that Bennett hung onto the party's reins past his prime because of it. "I thought that when Bennett retired I would have the opportunity. If he had resigned in the middle of a term, mister, I would have taken it, and I'd be still there today." About three weeks before the election, Bennett hinted that Gaglardi's new cabinet job would relate to Gaglardi's record of helping people, his church background, his "Sunday school work and so forth," that it would be some sort of ombudsman's position. That didn't sound like the northern development portfolio Gaglardi wanted.

The campaign was up and down for Gaglardi. At an all-candidates' forum, he was roundly booed and was unable to complete a statement. A few nights later, he was given a standing ovation and renewed confidence at a rally in North Kamloops. His biggest campaign boost came with the visit of Bennett on August 18. Bennett and Gaglardi, wearing cowboy hats, rode together in an open convertible at the head of a parade of 150 cars, dune buggies, buses and logging trucks.

At the Paramount Theatre, where the Bennett-Gaglardi rally preempted Peter Pan, all eight hundred seats were filled in a replay of the 1963 election visit by Bennett that had seen Davie Fulton headed off at the pass. The difference this time was that there were about forty hecklers concentrated in the back row and sprinkled throughout the crowd. A scuffle broke out when one of them refused to stand for "O Canada."

"The people of Kamloops are going to give the answer to the critics of Gaglardi," said Bennett. "Gaglardi's greatest victory is going to echo and re-echo across this province, across this great nation, and across the great continent of North America." Bennett never was one to underestimate the effect of anything the Socreds did.

"Go, Phil, go!" chanted Gaglardi workers.

"Lies, lies, lies!" chanted the hecklers.

The premier spoke for just under half an hour, a short speech by his campaign standards, but as enthusiastically supportive of his wayward minister from Kamloops as it could be.

Enthusiasm alone wouldn't do it, and the punch line was this: "And he is going to be a full-fledged member of the cabinet after the election is through." He concluded: "The premier wants Phil, Kamloops wants Phil, and the government needs Phil! Vote for Phil!"

Bennett refused to give details about what he had in mind for Gaglardi as a cabinet post. He simply said it would be a major department, and that Gaglardi would be in the people business. "The new portfolio I have in mind for Mr. Gaglardi is not Highways. Of course, we had to build highways to get the country moving. But Mr. Gaglardi's main interest is in people.... Our interest is mainly in people."

There were many who thought Bennett doomed the Socreds with his promise of reinstating Gaglardi. Canvassers were finding, in some ridings, that Gaglardi was losing them votes.

In the final days of the campaign, all eyes turned to Kamloops. The Liberals and New Democrats were atwitter with confidence. McGeer and Bryson led a parade of fifteen hundred people through downtown Kamloops. "It's got to be unreal," said the awe-struck Liberal leader. "It makes the PNE parade look bush league. It's fairly obvious Gaglardi is going to be defeated by a fairly wide margin."

Tom Berger was even more confident of destroying the Socreds and forming the next government. Bennett had launched a desperate sounding attack on the NDP "barbarians" and their "Marxist socialism." Berger felt certain he had beaten off the "pathetic old man," and sensed Bennett was going to fall hard. The thirty-six-year-old Berger started talking about himself as the youngest premier in Canada.

The press was just as sure Gaglardi was going down with Bennett. "Philip Arthur Gaglardi is fighting for his political life," wrote a *Victoria Colonist* reporter. "Former highways minister Gaglardi is on the defensive in what could be his last campaign," said the *Vancouver Province*. "A little man with large shoulders, greying hair and darting eyes, he looks almost as subdued as one of the few old bulls that roam the hills in this cattle country."

Nobody, apparently — neither the press, the Liberals nor the NDP — had spoken to the voters. At least, not those who mattered. On August 27, they gave Gaglardi a record 7,305 votes, trouncing Bryson with 4,641 and Jacobs with 4,051. The trend became clear as soon as the first polling stations began reporting in.

"This is a win for the people of this area," declared a happy Gaglardi. "I'll do my best for you." He was besieged with congratulatory phone calls, including one from Bennett, who had cause to be pleased himself. Social Credit became a clear winner less than an hour after the polls closed. B.C.'s voters boosted the Socred seat total to thirty–eight, leaving the NDP only twelve, and the Liberals holding on to five. Tom Berger, as Bennett had predicted during the campaign, met personal defeat in Vancouver–Burrard along with incumbent running mate Dr. Ray Parkinson. Beating them were Harold Merilees and, making a comeback after defeat in a previous election, Bert Price.

Bennett's hysterical anti–socialist bombast had worked with a B.C. public suspicious of the left. The aging premier had been written off by the pundits, but welcomed heartily by the public.

In September, a news report from Ottawa announced that the wives of Members of Parliament would now be allowed to travel on government aircraft with their husbands free of charge, as long as extra seats were available. The new policy included holidays as well as government business. The policy was implemented after it had been revealed that some MPs were taking their wives along for European junkets on Defence Department aircraft. Such had actually been the quiet practice for years.

His Brother's Keeper

Am I my brother's keeper?
GENESIS 4.9

Nobody seems satisfied with what God gave them.
PHIL GAGLARDI

"We're talking about human resources, not handouts. Handouts remove incentive. You've got to restore the dignity of the individual, give a man back his pride and put him back in society as an entity and a contributing force. Everybody who has need will be looked after. But believe me, the deadbeats have got to be weeded out."

Phil Gaglardi was announcing how he would be the roughest, toughest, but most effective welfare minister in history. It was October 27, 1969. Bennett had waited until after the election to offer Gaglardi a specific portfolio. How would Phil like to be minister of welfare? Gaglardi was horrified. He hadn't the slightest interest in the welfare department. The Provincial Alliance of Businessmen was one thing, but it was almost humiliating to think of himself as playing nursemaid to a bunch of hippies and types who didn't want work or couldn't find it. Bennett insisted Gaglardi's background made him the perfect man to minister to the ill, the underprivileged, the unemployed, the halt, the lame. In some ways, it would be an expansion of the Alliance. He would be a sort of ombudsman for the poor and the handicapped. Another incentive was that Bennett made it plain it was a take-it-or-leave-it situation. "I said, 'Jumpin' Jupiter, I'm not a welfare man.' He said it spends the most money and I fought with him and eventually he said, 'Phil, you've got to take it.' "

Though Gaglardi regarded it as a broken promise, having believed he would get a new northern development department, the welfare portfolio was, at least, a real job. He accepted it on the condition that he be allowed to revamp the department, change its name, give it a new look, with emphasis on getting people off welfare and into work, instead of handing out free money. Gaglardi wanted to do things his own way. Bennett agreed.

So Gaglardi, Bennett announced, would take over the welfare portfolio from Dan Campbell, who would be left with his other cabinet job, municipal affairs. The name of the department would be changed at the next legislative session to the Department of Rehabilitation and Human Resources. It would include in its functions administration of the Provincial Alliance of Businessmen.

At fifty-six years of age, Gaglardi had made his comeback. Taking on the welfare challenge was no small job. B.C. had almost 100,000 people on welfare. During the past four months, 24,000 people had got themselves off welfare. Thirty thousand new ones had gone on it.

Reaction to the appointment and to Gaglardi's comments about weeding out deadbeats varied. "I don't really think he knows anything about welfare, and has a typical churchman's punitive attitude towards the poor," said Reg Clarkson, executive secretary of the Victoria Low Income Group. That wasn't altogether fair, since Gaglardi, whatever his faults might be, was generous almost to a fault. His willingness to help people in distress, whether they needed food or help changing a flat tire, had become legend from his first days in the church ministry. He often lent people money, sometimes a few dollars, sometimes much more, never expecting to get it back. On one occasion, one of the parishioners who had helped lead the rebellion against him that resulted in the breakaway church in Kamloops in 1968 came to him begging for help. The man had been caught by his employer juggling books, and unless he paid back $10,000 he faced the prospect of jail. Gaglardi signed a bank note for the money, the man never paid it back or thanked him, and Gaglardi had to pay it off. (Not long after becoming mayor of Kamloops many years later, Gaglardi borrowed $20,000 from a bank and lent it to a man so the constituent could save his business and stay in Kamloops.) Gaglardi also spearheaded construction of Silver Threads, a twin-tower senior citizens' low-rent apartment building on property formerly occupied by the Gaglardi home in Kamloops. When he asked his congregation to sponsor building the first tower, some of the same people who eventually deserted Calvary Temple opposed him, saying it was too risky. Gaglardi worked out a land swap whereby the property on which his house sat was used for the Silver Threads project, and another piece given to the church in return. He personally arranged financing and grants through CMHC, and oversaw construction. In the meantime, he took out a mortgage and built a new home on a bluff overlooking the city. Several years later, he donated a prime lot next door to the apartment block to build a second tower. "I donated that piece of property as the sponsor of the second unit on a personal basis. I would think that the two units together have cost me somewhere in the neighbourhood of $250,000." Yet such acts of philanthropy didn't impress people like Reg Clarkson, who knew only his hardrock attitude toward society's non-productive sector.

Letters to newspapers ranged from "I felt shocked and terrified at hearing Phil Gaglardi's first remarks" to "More power to Phil Gaglardi, we need more men like him to clean house once and for all."

Social workers were tentatively approving, with the exception of the deadbeat comment, which they felt harsh. Feeling swamped by an increasing welfare roll and a lack of resources with which to handle it, they welcomed an approach that would cut red tape. But to give people jobs, as Gaglardi proposed, you also had to give them training. That would require cooperation from big business and labour. The social workers generally viewed the picture with pessimism. While the general birthrate was about equal to the death rate, the birthrate among the poor was doubling every twenty years. The number of "deadbeats" was going to increase. "That must be the most frustrating job of all — the worst job in the whole cabinet, because it is impossible to do anything about the problem," sympathized one social worker. "As a social worker I can help one or two individual families on the small scene, but over the large spectrum, there is no hope."

The province waited with anticipation to see what the man who had bulldozed his way through mountains and over rivers would do with the complex welfare system that dealt not with concrete and asphalt but with human pain and suffering. Despite the fact Gaglardi didn't want the welfare portfolio, his return from political purgatory buoyed his spirits, and he felt more his cheerful self again. He had a sounding board from which to proclaim his homespun brand of political gospel, a lectern from which to sermonize on the ills of society as not even his highways job had provided him.

He had an office again, too. He'd been able to hang his hat at the Victoria P.A.B. offices after getting that off the ground, but now he had a proper office in the legislative buildings. And it was a nice one, a large room over the main entrance to the buildings. With an office of his own, Gaglardi needed an office staff. Edith Valen gladly returned to his employ, though she liked Waldo Skillings.

" . . . Workshop? . . . Remember those 'sorry for the inconvenience' signs you used to make for me . . . well, start making them again . . . "

The P.A.B. seemed to be functioning pretty smoothly. It had offices in Victoria, Vancouver, Kelowna, Prince George, Nanaimo and Kamloops. For 1970, it would be working with a budget of a half–million dollars. Early advertising of the P.A.B. service didn't include addresses of the P.A.B. offices, a fact some people found perplexing, but Gaglardi explained it. "All kinds of kooks that you can't do anything for would flock to them and I'm not geared to that. I don't want a whole bunch of people at the office. I select the people I want brought in."

Ron Price, in charge of the Victoria P.A.B. office, didn't look at it as a matter of keeping out kooks, but it was a practical consideration. The office staff included only him and a secretary, and they were getting fifty calls a day. Those who called were sent application forms, and suitable applicants were assisted in finding jobs.

The 1970 legislative session was something of a celebration for the Social Credit government. Not a single cabinet minister had been defeated in the election of the previous August. It was a bright new decade, and Bennett looked at it as an opportunity to officially change gears. One of the biggest criticisms levelled against Bennett through the years had been his failure, or refusal, to recognize people needs. He had always said you couldn't do that if you didn't have the economic base to work from. Now, he said, B.C. had it. The speech from the throne read by Lieutenant-Governor John Nicholson outlined the de-emphasis on blacktop and development and the attention to human problems: increase social allowances, boarding home and nursing rates, and the provincial old-age pension supplement; legislate protection of the rights of housing tenants; boost assistance for housing for the elderly; build a Workmen's Compensation Board rehabilitation centre.

Gaglardi, moved closer to the premier in the legislature in recognition of his return to a full cabinet post (Les Peterson was ensconced beside Bennett with Wes Black beside him), was set to roll up his sleeves and get down to work. He had, he said, received information on "lots and lots" of welfare fraud cases.

"By the time I get through there will be no problems at all," Gaglardi said on the way to cabinet one day. "Soon there will be no such thing as being on welfare as such, on that kind of basis."

As Gaglardi would learn, bombast worked better with hard-hatted rednecks than it did with the down and out. Tough talk had to be tempered with understanding, and even within his own party, offence was taken at his tone. In his first speech of the session, Herb Capozzi teed off against his friend Gaglardi for using the word "deadbeats." It was an obsolete and outdated word, he said, and he hoped "a properly worded retraction" would be forthcoming.

Capozzi probably would never make it into the cabinet, for just such statements. He had a habit of criticizing the government, and no amount of chastising would make the millionaire ex-football player toe the line. The baby he had spawned or, at least, adopted — the Provincial Alliance of Businessmen — was not being handled properly, in his mind. Gaglardi said the P.A.B. had found work for 1,150 people by the end of January, 350 of whom had been taken off welfare. But Capozzi told the House the P.A.B. was duplicating the services of Canada Manpower, backing up concerns from within the federal job-finding agency. By then, though, Gaglardi couldn't hear what Capozzi was saying. He'd walked out of the House.

If Capozzi wasn't impressed with the P.A.B., one of the men closest to its operation was. Ron Price, almost two decades later, would remain convinced that it had worked, and worked well. "It did work. It produced tremendous results." The program, he said, built self-esteem in those it helped. Working for Gaglardi wasn't easy, but it was effective. "He was not an easy guy to work for. He's a maverick. He's a motivator, not a particularly good administrator, in my opinion. But he's gutsy. One of the things I appreciated about Phil Gaglardi was that he would make a decision."

Neither the challenge of his new portfolio nor the scepticism of his fellow politicians daunted the new welfare minister. In mid–February he announced his plans for a new welfare deal. Welfare recipients would be handed questionnaires, and placed in categories as fully employable, partially employable or unemployable. They would then be given the appropriate job–finding advice and/or retraining. "I'm a builder, and I'm going to build human beings."

Twenty–five percent of those placed by the P.A.B. came off the welfare rolls, said Gaglardi. By saving $200 a month in welfare payments to those with jobs, the government was saving hundreds of thousands of dollars. In one month, April, it saved as much money as it had cost to operate the entire program up to that time. Which, a few sceptics supposed, must be where all the money came from for the plush P.A.B. offices in Vancouver on the eighteenth floor of a new tower, next door to the Hotel Vancouver where Gaglardi still kept his room. Gaglardi's car was parked beside the fountain in front of the courthouse across the street. ("It was the Department of Public Works that got me that office. It was the only one available. It was a nice office but there was nothing posh about it.")

Then there was the staff. Vancouver regional director was Norm Delmonico, a former right–of–way agent with the Highways Department when Gaglardi had that portfolio. And, of course, Ron Price, Bert's son, in Victoria, defeated as a Socred himself in the Burnaby–Seymour riding in the 1968 federal election. Price, a former radio–TV sales rep, now doubled as Gaglardi's executive assistant and Victoria P.A.B. director. And there was Doug Stewart, a friend and former garage operator, now the P.A.B. director in Kamloops.

The other three P.A.B. directors appeared to have no particular political connection to Gaglardi, who admitted to hiring them outside the civil service commission but with commission assistance. They had no special social–science abilities, but that didn't matter, said Gaglardi. "What I wanted in these men was merchandising ability. They have to be top–notch boys, these fellows, you know, they have to be able to manage an office, carry on interviews, guide young people, and check them out. I don't care if a man has fifty–five degrees after his name, without practical experience."

While he tried in vain to keep tax money from going to those he felt shouldn't get it, Gaglardi also bent the rules for those who should. He paid part of the wages of an overweight bricklayer so the man could work at his own pace until he got back in shape and earned his paycheque from his employer. He bought tools for mechanics, and a licence for a fisherman who had had a heart attack and lost his boat. "I broke every blasted rule in the book. I made that department tick like a Swiss watch." But despite these efforts, and his bluff and bluster about weeding out deadbeats and giving people back jobs and dignity, the overall situation got worse, not better. In 1970, more than 9,000 more employable men and women went on welfare in B.C. than in the previous year; more than 48,000 employables were on the dole. In total, there were still well over 100,000 people collecting welfare in a given month. For all his promises of saving the taxpayers money by cracking down on fraud, only fifty-six people were convicted of welfare fraud during 1969-70, and nineteen of those won appeals. It was almost impossible to figure out how many people the Provincial Alliance of Businessmen was actually helping. One week, Gaglardi would talk of the P.A.B. finding jobs at a 1,500-per-month clip. Then, he'd give a more realistic figure of just over 2,800 for a twelve-month period. Then, suddenly, it was up to 5,000 per year. In fact, a joint federal-provincial program to give in-industry training to ten thousand unemployed British Columbians per year had to be dropped, due, said Gaglardi, to the inflexibility of Canada Manpower regulations. The bad economic times weren't Gaglardi's fault, and he hadn't created the welfare problem, but it was obvious there would be no quick fix. Little wonder that calls for his resignation and demonstrations on the steps of the legislature were in vogue.

Gaglardi redoubled his efforts to weed out the undeserving. A new assessment form asked applicants questions on financial and marital matters and whether or not they had drinking or drug problems. ("How can you help people if you can't find out their problems?")

He also decided to deny welfare to anyone on strike or locked out, which didn't endear him to the province's labour force.

As the province headed into winter, Gaglardi stepped up efforts at tightening payments to foil the abusers who collected more than once. He decided also that welfare recipients would get no extra food money this winter except in emergencies.

Gaglardi's feelings about welfare had roots in his own upbringing to the work ethic. He had been raised to appreciate the value of individual initiative, the pride of providing for yourself and others. Hippies, for example, were totally foreign to his way of thinking, though he tried to understand them. It was a time of long hair, beads, marijuana and protesting the Vietnam war, a time of rebellion by young people against the traditional values held by Gaglardi and his generation. Man had walked on the moon, and colour television was the latest home appliance, but young people were rejecting materialism and the system that had created them. As Richard Nixon struggled to extricate the U.S. from Vietnam, Pierre Trudeau battled the FLQ and the October Crisis. Young people blamed the world's problems on anyone over thirty, and withdrew from society, comforted by their own simplistic solutions and slogans. It was the age of Woodstock, Flower Power and "Make love, not war."

Gaglardi couldn't sympathize with anybody who wanted to lay around instead of work. He saw the hippies infesting the cities and he could feel them mocking the system. "I don't hate a hippie, but I don't like him to walk down the street shaking his long hair while living on my money." He spoke against them at every opportunity, telling one Kiwanis Club meeting, "You are shirking your responsibility by not speaking against hippies. I think a community does a disservice to itself when it sits back and lets hippies do as they want."

He got one young man a job in a store, but the store manager told his new employee he'd have to cut his long hair. When the young rebel refused and was fired, Gaglardi cut him off welfare. "I said as far as I'm concerned, if you want to grow your hair long, you can grow it down to your ankles, you can swallow it and have it for breakfast, but I don't think the taxpayers should have to pay for it if it stops you from getting a job."

Gaglardi saw all kinds of abuses in the welfare system by those who didn't want to work. Some people started out taking welfare because they had no choice but, after an initial loss of pride, it became a new way of life. "You have taken away his pride, his guts and his integrity, but he has also found an easy way to live."

Despite his fight against the kooks and the deadbeats, and his claim that there were ten thousand jobs available in B.C. if only people were willing to go after them, welfare costs hit $9 million a month by the end of 1970, quadrupling in only five years. Gaglardi blamed it all on emigration to B.C. from other parts of Canada, loose screening of applicants, the federal government's anti-inflation measures, and exceedingly high unemployment. But whichever way he cut it, it was the worst welfare year in B.C. history. P.A.B. was making a minimal dent, and the "rehabilitation" in the Rehabilitation Department was nowhere near reality. His department exceeded its budget by more than $30 million in 1970; $20 million more was spent than during the previous year.

The 1971 legislative session opened with a nasty demonstration by unemployed that got out of hand. NDP leader Dave Barrett went outside to try to stop it, but the Socreds tried to blame it on him anyway.

On August 30, 1971, the thirty-six-year-old Social Credit government of Alberta was destroyed in a provincial election. Conservative leader Peter Lougheed took his party from six seats to forty-eight, while the Socreds under Harry Strom dropped from fifty-five to twenty-six. The next day, Mike Latta, the man who had helped organize the pro-Gaglardi legislature demonstration three years earlier, telephoned Dennis O'Rourke, a brash young reporter working for the Kamloops News Advertiser. Latta had a startling story for O'Rourke.

"The Alberta election has shown the writing on the wall," Latta told him. "We need new blood in the provincial government, young men. And I don't mean in the backbenches. Bennett is getting old, and with age comes his arrogance. He's lost his touch with the people and lives in a world of his own importance."

Latta admitted to O'Rourke he was planning another pro-Gaglardi move, but this time he was going after Bennett's job. The plan was to challenge Bennett in the backrooms between now and the annual Socred meeting in November. He knew Bennett would be solidly backed by the old guard, and that if it came to an open fight on the convention floor, the Old Man would win. The Gaglardi camp would have to convince Bennett to quit for the good of the party.

There was one catch to the story. Latta insisted on anonymity. O'Rourke agreed. His story led page one, headlined "Kamloops to lead Bennett ouster."

Latta, in fact, hadn't consulted Gaglardi about running him for the leadership, but he figured Phil would go for it if enough support could be demonstrated. Latta firmly believed Gaglardi wanted more than anything else to be premier; it was his ultimate, absolute goal.

O'Rourke's story quickly hit the major newspapers in Vancouver and Victoria, and suddenly the entire province was talking about a Bennett-Gaglardi confrontation. Gaglardi rejected the rumour. "As long as W.A.C. Bennett remains premier, Kamloops will be loyal to him . . . one hundred percent." But he added, "I'm not seeking the leadership of anything, but if the people of B.C. want me, that is the Social Credit party, I'll consider." Gaglardi phoned Bennett to assure him he had nothing to do with the story. "He just said, 'Thanks for letting me know, Phil.' "

Curious about the *News Advertiser*'s source, other media began nosing around Kamloops to try to find out, but the oil dealer's identity remained a secret except to a few Kamloops newsmen. The plan for the leadership revolution continued, with Charlie Bennett, the man who had co-organized the legislature protest with Latta, helping out. They bought dozens of hats and noisemakers intended for a brassy demonstration in favour of Gaglardi at the convention, and tried to line up support within the party. Though Bennett showed no sign of even thinking about quitting, they were determined to force a leadership review one way or another. Whether or not their work would translate into action at the convention was yet to be seen.

The leadership bid, which seemed to be gathering so much steam or, at least, controversy, fizzled suddenly at the convention itself. Socred president George Driedeger collared Latta and Charlie Bennett and angrily informed them that if they tried anything, he would cancel the convention. He meant it.

Latta and Charlie Bennett returned home to Kamloops that weekend with their hats and noisemakers, once again having failed to give Gaglardi what they believed was his rightful place in government.

Trying to dump provincial premiers wasn't Charlie Bennett's only political pastime. He became a politician, of sorts, himself. He wasn't a politician at heart; he was a developer. His involvement in the controversial Del Cielo acreage in Kamloops had brought him to the public's attention a few years before. Del Cielo, embroiled in the debate over highway accesses and involvement of Gaglardi's sons in highway development, was still there. In fact, it was there more than ever. (So were Bob and Bill Gaglardi, who continued to buy and sell land, prompting opposition charges that the premier had not followed through on a promise to put rules in force to prevent such speculation along new highways.) Greater Kamloops, in the early 1970s, was a case lesson in how not to plan a municipality. It was a collection of suburbs, some incorporated, some not. One of them was Dufferin, a tiny municipality that contained the always controversial Del Cielo residential development, a piece of a rail line and part of an existing residential area on the border of Kamloops — fifteen hundred people in all.

The mayor of the new District Municipality of Dufferin was none other than Charlie Bennett. He and his six fellow interim councillors were appointed by the government; Bennett was elected mayor by the other appointees. The new municipality, operating out of the Del Cielo offices in an old house at the

Merritt and Trans–Canada Highway intersections, enjoyed a mill rate a third that of Kamloops.

Bob Williams, the acerbic Vancouver East MLA, saw the whole thing as a plot to make Charlie Bennett money by setting him up with the zoning he wanted and a nice little tax break. Williams called Dufferin the "gerrymander of the century," pointing out that the boundary had been drawn so carefully that it split a hotel in two, leaving the beer parlour in Dufferin. Municipal Affairs Minister Dan Campbell, he said, had taken directions from Gaglardi in setting up Dufferin. "Oh, he may have little squabbles with him in public, but what the member from Kamloops wants, the member from Kamloops gets."

Throughout the new session Campbell tried to shrug off opposition harangues on Dufferin, saying it had been set up by democratic vote. Dave Barrett claimed there was a major cabinet rift over Dufferin, but Campbell wouldn't commit himself on any changes to its status.

That issue was barely out of the way when whisperings were heard around the legislative buildings that Pat McGeer had something good on Gaglardi. The something good happened to be some pertinent questions about Gaglardi's expenses and who paid for them on some of his many trips. Even during his banishment to the company of the three women ministers without portfolio (Grace McCarthy, Pat Jordan, and Isabel Dawson), Gaglardi had soon got back into the flying mood. Now, a full–fledged minister again, he was once more the flyingest of them all. He flew between Vancouver or Victoria and Kamloops sixty–three times in 1970, including one trip when he was accompanied by his grandson. That had forced Wes Black to reinforce an order that only government personnel fly in government aircraft. But it was the flights to more exotic locations that most interested McGeer.

In 1970, McGeer explained, Gaglardi had submitted $382 in expense vouchers for a trip to South Bend, Indiana, and others for trips to San Francisco, Portland and Edmonton. He said Gaglardi had received expenses from the organizers of a "non–denominational Christian group in the trucking industry" in Indiana. "Was that part of the trip done on government business?"

Repeatedly questioned by McGeer, Gaglardi replied that "as far as I know any money that I'm reimbursed usually goes to my office and not to me." He said he couldn't remember details of who paid what because he received two hundred requests every month to speak at various functions.

"When I make a statement, I usually think the statement is true."

As opposition MLAs laughed, he shouted, "In fact, I know it is true."

"You're almost positive it's true, aren't you?" laughed a scornful Dave Barrett.

As the day droned on, phone calls were made to the U.S. When the coordinator of the South Bend conference was asked if Gaglardi received any direct payment, he said a collection had been taken up for the minister, and his airfare was paid. Gaglardi denied it. He admitted, however, that his hotel room, and some of his meals, were prepaid by his hosts.

The San Francisco trip was just as baffling. Gaglardi said it was to check on welfare procedures of the Bay Area Council on Alcohol, but the executive director of the council, when asked, didn't remember Gaglardi's name, according to Barrett.

Gaglardi looked through his desk and then his pockets. "I thought I had the name on a slip in my pocket from the last time I was there. If I remember correctly, it was the name of a lady as well as a gentleman."

Williston, Kiernan and Skillings got up and walked out of the House. Bennett had already left.

Every aspect of Gaglardi's expenses was probed for new information. Gaglardi himself acknowledged that he'd been paid for appearing on *Front Page Challenge*. "Of course they paid me. They paid my way down and back, and my hotel." (He'd appeared on the television program three times in all, "more times than anybody, I guess.")

Gaglardi's personal wealth came up for discussion, too. People talked about his posh Kamloops home, the ranch, his summer house, his horses. He protested that he was worth very little, that he took not a dime from Calvary Temple, that he could be making much more money if he wasn't in government. In truth, while he wasn't poor, he wasn't rich, either. Most of his personal property was heavily mortgaged.

"It makes me angry, these people telling me I am a millionaire. That's a lot of crap. Some day I am going to declare my worth to show these stupid jerks. I am not a man of wealth at all."

It was among the strongest, angriest language Gaglardi had ever used in a public statement. Those who still had faith in him believed him once again, and put all the criticism down to a sensationalist press and a deceiving opposition.

This Little Government

He that diggest a pit shall fall into it.
ECCLESIASTES 10.8

No pressure group is going to push this government around.
PHIL GAGLARDI

If anniversaries mean anything, 1972 should have shaped up as a triumphal year for the government. It had been twenty incredible years since W.A.C. Bennett and his scrappy band of Socreds bloodied the noses of the establishment parties; for twenty years they had proudly clasped office like an icon, seemingly ordained by God — to whom, after all, they had a direct line through Phil Gaglardi — to rule. There was no serious reason to believe or hope they wouldn't reign for twenty more.

What wisdom we are afforded by hindsight. It seems so obvious now to latter-day pundits, armed with their newspaper clippings and tape recorders, that the dynasty was about to tumble.

In 1972, though there were signs of weakening in the Socred armour, the thought of the unthinkable happening was, well, unthinkable. There was a growing realization within the party that renewal was necessary; Bennett felt it himself to a certain extent, but he feared the consequences of his departure more than he feared the consequences of staying. So any regeneration would have to come either at his hand or in spite of him.

There was some change within the government, but it came more in the form of chance transition than orchestrated movement, a seasonal shedding of skins rather than a rebirth. At the opening of the 1972 legislative session, five cabinet ministers including the premier had served as MLAs since 1952 — Ken Kiernan, Wes Black, Phil Gaglardi and Cyril Shelford, though the independent-minded Shelford hadn't made it to cabinet until 1968. Several others were almost as politically long in the tooth: Ray Williston, Leslie Peterson, William Chant, Dan Campbell, Donald Brothers, Waldo Skillings, Frank Richter — all traced their legislative roots back to 1960 or before. The likes of Pat Jordan and Ralph Loffmark, though having several years in office under their belts, were comparative newcomers. There would be room for a couple of more, because Chant, the seventy-six-year-old public works minister and one of the original B.C. Socred organizers, decided in April 1972 that he would not run again. The following month, Ken Kiernan made the same decision. Though there was some youth and talent left in the backbenches, there was no guarantee, by any means, that the most talented or deserving would be rewarded with elevation to cabinet. Herb Capozzi, for example, had sat in the legislature since 1966, but was no closer to a cabinet job than when he started. Shelford's long sentence in the backbenches had illustrated that, if you tried to do it your way, you'd better be prepared to do time purging yourself. Likewise, Grace McCarthy, though handed a ministry without portfolio in Bennett's grand sop to womanhood, seemed to be going nowhere. Such intolerance and lack of upward mobility did not make for totally contented foot soldiers. Occasionally throughout Bennett's regime, an unhappy MLA pocketed his marbles and went away to sit as an independent or to join one of the opposition parties. Though Bennett had once done just that himself before seeing the light as a Socred, he invariably wrote off such people as turncoats who were never good Socreds to start with. There were two recent defectors, both of some consequence. Scott Wallace, the physician who held the Oak Bay seat for Social Credit, finally succumbed to his anger over Bennett's medicare policies and to the courting of the new provincial Tory leader, Derril Warren, and crossed the floor in August 1971. In March of 1972, he was joined by Don Marshall of South Peace River, who was disenchanted with Bennett's failure to help the financially stricken farmers of his region.

Clearly, the boardroom power within Social Credit was still being wielded by the right-wing, fundamentalist, old-line party warhorses, while the innovators and interns were kept waiting in the lobby. Though not in particular favour with the premier, nobody represented that Old Guard better than Phil Gaglardi. Bennett had kept his party in power for two decades through a divide-and-conquer strategy by which, with political sleight of hand, he constantly aligned the government with the common man against what he called "pressure groups." A pressure group could be organized labour, in which case he would side with the lunchbucket schmuck against the high-paid union hierarchy. Or it could be the new boys on the block, the environmentalists; it then became a case of rabble–rousers with beards and dirty feet trying to take jobs away from good British Columbians. When, in a burst of Puritan morality he sought to ban liquor and tobacco advertising, not to mention topless and bottomless dancing, Bennett was forced to battle Big Business on behalf of clean–living people everywhere. Always, it was "this little government" against the "pressure groups." Nothing more epitomized this confrontation than the dastardly New Democrats, who represented to Bennett everything evil in politics. He succeeded in election after election in convincing voters to help him fend off The Horde. Keep them from the gates, he would urge, and fearful electors would oblige, heeding his cautions not to waste support on the Liberals or Tories and risk letting the sneaky Godless Socialists in the back door. Vote for the party that stood for "fair treatment for all and special privileges to none." In all of British Columbia, it was said, you couldn't find a man or a woman who would confess to voting Social Credit but, come election day, somehow the little government racked up victory after impressive victory.

Bennett himself, though given to tearful excess in public, was not a charismatic purveyor of the message. Time after time, when a particularly important subject needed to be addressed in the House, or the board–of–trade circuit was in need of being inculcated with the government line, Bennett called upon Phil Gaglardi to do the job for him. Who better to defend "this little government" than "this little fellow"? David, ever ready with his slingshot. The non–smoking, teetotalling Christian versus the foul–mouthed atheists.

"Never before has there been more social trouble," Gaglardi would say in explaining Social Credit's crusade. "All over the world there is human upheaval; we have ruled God out of society." To the women's liberation pressure groups, he said, "If God didn't want you to be women, why didn't he make you men? . . . It seems to me it's the men who should be liberated." To the anti–American pressure groups, he said, "I'm not one of these buy–Canada–back artists. I love the American dollar as long as it is spent in B.C. If there is any takeover it will be Canada or British Columbia taking over the United States." To the pressure groups that protested pollution: "I know that some people can't stand the smell of pollen in a flower. You may be allergic. I'm amazed about people who make a great emotional demonstration about the death of one seagull from oil." And, "I think there is a sensible and sane basis for pollution, but the moment some people find a smell in the air, they think everything is pollution.

God put the tree on the mountainside, not to be worshipped but to be cut down. And God put fish into the stream because they are beneficial, dead or alive." He called the stench of pulp mills "the smell of money."

When Bennett was fighting for his Two Rivers Policy in which he wanted to build a hydro dam on the Peace as well as the Columbia River, Gaglardi advised the procrastinators and the doubters, "We are not interested in the politics of power. We want to turn on a switch and see the lights come on. If Washington takes half as long as Ottawa did to do something about the Columbia, you people will be walking around in the twentieth century with candles in your hands." To those who would speak against profiteering: "Greed has been given to us by God." But when the union pork-choppers got too demanding, he warned against the "tremendous greed" of labour. "The working man knows that this government, as well as myself, have been their greatest champions, and they are never swayed by the haranguing of certain labour leaders who are really out of touch with the common needs of the ordinary people." To the anti-censorship lobbyists: "There are certain sets of rules in any society which sustain and strengthen that society, and any type of licensed basic lewdness is what has caused destruction of many nations. The disintegration of an empire begins with the degeneration of womanhood." The intellectuals and academics who complained about the education budget were told, "The educational system needs a real overhaul. Students receive a fine academic education but can't fill jobs in society. I'd like to tell those cotton-picking professors to run their universities and leave me alone." Of the NDP, the worst pressure group of all, he said, "Socialism in a democratic nation is dangerous. Nothing can put the brakes on our economy and progress faster." Rounding it all out was his modest conclusion that, "I'm fantastic because I'm with a fantastic government, and that's fantastic."

While Gaglardi didn't like to think of himself as a populist politician, Bennett candidly described his own style and that of the government as very much populist. They governed, he said, for "all the people," not for those pressure groups. Socred programs were designed to be populist, to market a feeling of prosperity and growth. For most of the government's twenty years, the sound of heavy machinery working on highways, buildings, bridges and dams had been an ever-present reminder that B.C. was moving ahead, moving in spite of the detractors and crepehangers. The choice was always clear come election time:

"Social Credit or Chaos," "Economy with Efficiency," "Progress, not Politics," or "Forward with Social Credit." Free enterprise or socialism. In the spring of 1969, to be sure everybody appreciated the bounty given to them by the government, Bennett had toured the province with a film he had commissioned entitled *The Good Life*. In 1972, though, the consequences of growth were catching up with the government. Any government ignores changing times and attitudes at its peril, and the new generation was redefining flower power into a sophisticated critique of establishment values. Phil Gaglardi's analysis of the pollution issue would have made perfect sense to the immigrant farmers and labourers of Silverdale at the beginning of the century, to the corporate elite of the day and to his still considerable and faithful personal following throughout the province. But to a whole new constituency, it sounded like the facile chattering of Bonzo the chimp. To Gaglardi and his ilk, on the other hand, the suggestion that trees and animals were somehow more important than growth and jobs was insanity. The entire premise of Social Credit was set on growth. The government did pay lip service to environmental concerns in each throne speech, but the Pollution Control Act brought in during the 1967 session was a toothless document that did nothing to hinder the mines, mills and pulp companies or to suggest that the province's natural resources wouldn't last forever. Short-term material gain, growth, was all-important.

The short-term gain for long-term pain mentality, of course, would inevitably have a rebound effect. It was an economic narcotic, building expectations like a drug tolerance. Everybody wanted in on the lolly. While Bennett preached restraint, warning against the dangers of inflation, pressure groups such as the teachers grew more militant each year in their demands for more and more. That old greed was taking over. Labour unrest that marked 1970 and 1971 continued into 1972, with building trades, steelworkers, civic employees and forest workers either on the bricks by the thousands or on the verge. The new generation hadn't been around for the creation of B.C. Hydro, the building of universities, the launching of ferries, the salvation of medicare. They saw waiting lists in hospitals and fights between the government and doctors over income and licensing, believed the teachers' federation propaganda about crowded classrooms, were offended by a chaotic public welfare system. They interpreted all of this as the by-product of a government that no longer cared for the average Joe. They saw internal squabbling between cabinet ministers like Gaglardi and Dan Campbell (who said a personality clash was "the fairest way" of describing their differences), and they interpreted that as a government that was losing control. And they saw the aging Bennett and his geriatric cabinet and concluded that this was a tired government.

In large measure, they were right. Bennett had tried to redirect some of the emphasis of his government toward people programs, but the shift in values came too quickly for his old brand of packaging. A government of bumpkins once so attuned to the people with their simple, unpolished style now seemed out of touch. The political skills of this government of toothpick–chewing, anti–intellectual rednecks, once so invaluable in reading the masses were suddenly out of step with the new high–tech liberalism. Bennett tried, in the 1972 session, to acknowledge the new reality, adding a few dollars to the homeowner grant, hiking payments to pensioners and even earmarking several million dollars for reforestation and development of parks. Bennett promised "clean" industries and greenbelts, better urban planning, more time for leisure, more of the good life.

Though it seemed to some that Bennett's heart wasn't in these new initiatives, he had genuine and legitimate concerns about inflation. He wasn't blithely cutting his government adrift from public opinion or, at least, not purposely doing so. Far from it. His balance–the–budget, pay–as–you–go monetary policies that kept a parsimonious string on spending during boom times were designed to avoid calamity as the economy levelled out and downturned, as it inevitably would. The premier firmly believed most British Columbians would not only appreciate the absolute necessity of restraint in government spending in 1972, but that they would rise up in a taxpayer rebellion if it wasn't done. So he put a 6.5 percent ceiling on teacher pay increases and told school boards they could hold referendums if they wanted more. And he was stingy on health care, slowing down the release of funds for hospital extensions. He aimed several bills at labour, including Bill 33 to restrict bargaining rights of public employees, and Bill 88 to remove the rights of unions to include job protection clauses in union contracts. Even then, the Socred government's budget for the year set aside its greatest portion of $448.6 million for education, up almost $45 million from 1971. Health services was allotted $388.8 million, a jump of $48 million. Though that would never be enough for some, Bennett expected the emphasis of the budget along with the commitment to limit tax spending to once again align the government with the vast majority of British Columbians against the gluttony of the pressure groups. A full decade later Bennett's son Bill would turn restraint into a virtue, selling it with the most successful Madison Avenue sales campaign since North Americans were tricked into liking yogurt. But W.A.C. ran a little government to which the multimedia science of numbers crunching, issue polling and opinion moulding was unknown. The Old Man relied mainly on his own experience and intuition, and he was giving a scrambled message and getting garbled reception. The pressure groups were coalescing.

Though Bennett didn't realize the depth of his political problem, it had at least become apparent to him that some repair work on the parapets was required. But when Gaglardi went to him and told him the government was more unpopular than at any time in its twenty years, Bennett brushed it off, saying the government remained in high esteem with the people.

Indeed, though that judgment was a delusion, there was not yet any serious thought within or without the government that the Bennett regime was in terminal danger. In times of trouble, when everything seemed as though it would fall apart, the government, at worst, would lose a few seats. It had, after all, lived under siege for two decades. And in 1969, when an electoral disaster for his party was widely predicted, Bennett had pulled off instead a glorious victory. With the third year of the government's term almost up — Bennett's traditional time for another election — a testing of the waters was needed. One of his patented Odysseys to the provincial hinterlands seemed in order.

In the spring of 1972, Bennett and his cabinet went on the road. They headed north into Prince Rupert, Kitimat, then to Ray Williston's Prince George riding, stumping the white-spruce capital, receiving briefs from the locals on the need for rail construction, environmental control, energy. Then they aimed south through the Cariboo and on toward Kamloops. It would be, they hoped, a headline-grabbing adventure of communing with the masses, of cheering crowds, of handing out goodies and receiving parchments and pins and other trinkets of civic etiquette.

They started down from Prince George to Kamloops on May 31, travelling in a long convoy of cars led and trailed by RCMP black and whites. Gaglardi took the wheel of a Chevy himself, and nearly got into a scrape when a couple of motorists panicked as the caravan approached and accidently put the squeeze on him. He wheeled expertly between them and never skipped a click.

"He drove like a bloody maniac," was how an RCMP constable driving behind Gaglardi described the incident, but an investigation cleared the minister of blame.

The cabinet excursion continued on to Kamloops, with less than gratifying results. Kamloops unionists, not missing a chance like this one to hassle their least favourite politicians, arranged a welcoming party. Pickets in baggy blue jeans, plaid shirts and baseball caps hounded the cabinet at a local hotel and then at the official opening of Cariboo College. They carried placards demanding greater bargaining rights, protesting Bill 33 and calling Gaglardi "a Phink." Their bovine shuffling and squalling was loud enough to disrupt the ceremony.

It was not an auspicious beginning to the cabinet's muster, but the Okanagan was more hospitable. Gaglardi temporarily deserted at that point, and so did Shelford, Loffmark and Kiernan, who had other commitments. In his home riding at Kelowna, Bennett unveiled a new "Kelowna Charter," a five-point package of financial-assistance proposals that included cancellation of provincial succession duties and gift taxes. It also promised a supplementary allowance to senior citizens, though Bennett gave no figures; an increase in social assistance benefits to those handicapped through age, mental or physical disability; a minimum-wage hike, again not specified; and social assistance to high school and university-aged youth for training on the job via a government subsidy for wages and salaries.

Its unveiling spurred talk of a summer election, and invited obligatory condemnation from the opposition parties, but they needn't have worried. Bennett's tablet fell with a thud upon the populace, which was supposed to be swept up in the bravado of its fearless leader. But there was no excitement, scarce interest, and little understanding of its substance.

Bennett and his entourage plodded onward down Highway 97 as it wound among the cherry blossoms and idyllic lakes of the Okanagan to Osoyoos, and the respite from picket signs continued until they hit the Kootenays. They were greeted in Nelson and Cranbrook by sign-carrying, booing demonstrators. "Stop the Socreds now — twenty years of arrogance is enough," read one placard. "Get the bloody maniacs off the road, rehabilitate the speed freaks," read another imaginative entreaty, obviously referring to Gaglardi's latest driving incident.

After Fernie, they turned west again, to Salmon Arm, Merritt and through Kamloops, where Gaglardi rejoined them. Provincial-government employees picketed them in Lillooet, demanding collective bargaining rights.

Wednesday, June 7 was going to be a long day for the cabinet. They pulled out of Lillooet in the morning. Although they had collectively decided not to complain about it, the ministers were very unhappy with the press coverage the tour had been getting. It was not, to say the least, the hurdy-gurdy *tour de force* that had been envisioned. Instead of chronicling a reaffirmation of the government's grass roots, news media were heralding the cabinet's travels with stories about Gaglardi's driving and the protesters who greeted them at almost every stop. The cabinet's annoyance was somewhat understandable. Most of the demonstrators were instant-protest roughnecks enlisted solely to make headlines for labour's lengthy bitch list. The tour gave them a rolling, ten-day photo opportunity to be seen pressing their righteous grievances. It wasn't hard to do. The building trades alone had eighteen unions locked out by their bargaining employer, the Construction Labour Relations Association; there was plenty of available manpower. Les Peterson facetiously deduced that the only way the embattled roadshow troupe was going to get its own message across was to put it on a placard.

Hope was hospitable, but as if it was too good to be true, the pattern reemerged at Chilliwack and Mission. "Make us an offer you can't refuse!" demanded one demonstrator, stealing a line from the movie *The Godfather*. "What's the speed limit today?" asked another.

Meanwhile, at New Westminster's Royal Towers Hotel, a mob of labourites was building. There weren't a half-dozen pickets or twenty or fifty, as there had been in other centres in which labour had rallied the faithful. The Provincial Council of Carpenters, with help from the International Brotherhood of Electrical Workers and the International Woodworkers of America, had organized five hundred protesters, who were downing liquid courage and psyching each other for the confrontation. They were a mix of the sincerely indignant and the kind of four-by-four-driving, side-burned, unquestioning unionist hyenas who guffaw at each other's coarse jokes. They carted their printshop pickets — directed mainly at the construction dispute — reading "Collective bargaining yes, compulsory arbitration no," and hung an effigy of Labour Minister Jim Chabot from a lamppost with a sign, "Chabot must go." Impatiently they milled outside the hotel, waiting for the subjects of their fury, built up during weeks of frustration over the dispute with the CLR. Twenty-five New Westminster police and ten RCMP members were there with them, ready to prevent anything inappropriate, but under orders not to arrest anyone, only to keep them under control.

At 5:30 p.m., the premier's limousine arrived. It stopped directly in front of the hotel door, and Bennett and Ken Kiernan were inside almost before the mob realized what was happening. A few of them, angry at missing a chance to hassle their adversary, kicked at the limousine and banged it with their placards as it pulled away. By now, other ministers' cars were arriving.

"Sieg Heil!" they shouted.

Pat Jordan leaned out her car window to say something to a demonstrator, who swore at her and gave her the finger.

As each car arrived, the union gibbons slashed at it with their signs and pounded it with their fists. When Gaglardi drove in, a man in an undershirt jumped in front of his car in an effort to stop it. Instead of hitting the brake, Gaglardi inched forward, pushing the man in front of him. Police yanked the would-be human speed bump away.

Peterson, meanwhile, was out of his car and had stopped on his way into the hotel to speak into a microphone thrust in front of him by a shaggy young man. "The government pays attention to the public interest and not any special group . . . " he was saying when a clutch of demonstrators, attracted by the microphone, suddenly recognized him. Attention was temporarily diverted from pounding Gaglardi's car to Peterson, as the attorney general now attempted to head for the hotel door a hundred feet away. Two policemen found him and escorted him in that direction, but the demonstrators caught up, shoving him and throwing signs at him. A placard slammed down on top of his head and Peterson bent over under its force before being hustled along by the policemen.

Gaglardi parked his car and walked toward the hotel with his bags as two cops got to him. Near the hotel, the pickets again turned their attention to him.

"Get that little Mussolini, Gaglardi!" someone shouted. They pushed at him from behind, pounding him on the back with their arms and swinging their placards. One demonstrator consistently poked at the back of Gaglardi's head and at his back as he moved toward the hotel. Gaglardi didn't retaliate, keeping his Latin temper in check. "I laughed right in their faces." More policemen came to help out, forming a ring around Gaglardi to protect him. One cop had the wind knocked out of him by the surging mob. The police were nervous but they remembered their orders to do nothing more than push back when pushed. The union goons were determined not to let Gaglardi get into the hotel. He could hardly be seen under the sea of taller, bobbing heads. They were angrier now, past a nasty bit of fun; they were dangerous, losing control of themselves. "Kill 'em, kill 'em, kill 'em!" some were chanting. At the door, one of them lunged at Gaglardi, but he was discouraged with a well–aimed boot from one of the minister's police guards. The demonstrator shoved the cop, who shoved back. Finally, Gaglardi was inside.

But the attention paid Gaglardi had left Cyril Shelford, Isabel Dawson and Frank Richter stranded in the crowd without protection. The sign–swinging started. Shelford shot out an arm to shield Dawson as a heavy sign descended, and felt a two–by–four smash against his left arm. Outdoorsman and ex–serviceman Shelford had been swung at with two–by–fours before, but this was the hardest he'd ever been hit and he grimaced in pain.

Chabot arrived a full fifteen minutes after Bennett and, luckily for him, was not readily recognized by the crowd. Somehow, they all got inside, shaken, bruised and angry. Peterson had a bump on his head, Jordan had a wrenched shoulder, Black had a sore stomach from a jab with a placard, Richter had a lacerated and bruised back from similar treatment. Shelford uncovered a bruise the size of a softball on his upper arm. The bone itself was bruised, perhaps a hairline fracture.

Mercifully, the tour came to an end the next day with stops at White Rock, Richmond and Delta. In the aftermath of the Royal Towers fiasco, the recriminations began. B.C. and Yukon Building and Construction Trades Council president Jim Kinnaird, in an interesting twist of logic, blamed the disgraceful actions of the unionists on the cabinet and the police. "If the cabinet ministers had walked calmly from their cars to the hotel, there might have been some shouting but no violence," he claimed.

Bennett declared at a news conference that mob rule would never force the Social Credit government to yield to pressure groups. "I think democracy is in danger when we've got economic pressure groups, no matter what group they are, trying to force their will by force. But have no fear, this Social Credit government will stand firm."

The government went ahead with its order to the construction unions to get back to work and back to the bargaining table. "You can have labour unions run the country or the government can run it," Gaglardi told a dinner meeting of the South Vancouver Kiwanis Club. "This is a democracy. And if you want the unions, then you can vote them in. But no pressure group is going to push this government around."

Bennett and his cabinet, in the days following that shameful afternoon in New Westminster, pressed home their advantage.

The tour had been an obvious strategical misfire by the premier. It had provided the government's enemies — organized labour in particular — a golden opportunity to sully the government's image. But then, as if the labourites couldn't live with the success of their incursion, they handed Bennett a near-perfect election issue. British Columbians were disgusted, outraged by the sight of vulgar unionist rabble mishandling their politicians. The Gaglardi scandals, the economic woes, the petty complaints were momentarily forgotten. No matter the disparity in opinion or basic ideals, whatever personal animosity there might be, the premier and his executive council deserved a certain level of respect by dint of their positions. It was all tailor-made for a pressure-group alarm. Never had the elected representatives of the people been so shabbily treated. Never had the Big Labour pressure group acted so irresponsibly. The choice at the polls, if Bennett should call B.C. to the hustings, would be clear: order or mob rule. Responsible free enterprise or the chaos of socialism. Would the people give this little government another mandate?

Bennett had a decision to make.

Square Pegs

I was born dangerous, I live dangerous, and I'm gonna die dangerous.
PHIL GAGLARDI

How are the mighty fallen in the midst of battle!
II SAMUEL 1.23

Some people say, "Why do you make so much noise?" It's because I'm P.A. Gaglardi and that's the way I am.
PHIL GAGLARDI

On Sunday evening, July 23, Kamloops Socred constituency association president Bill Vincenzi gathered his directors together to talk election. He had been told by Socred headquarters to get the nomination set up. Although even Phil Gaglardi didn't know the date, the Victoria grapevine had Bennett calling an election for late summer or early fall. And the announcement would come within a day or two. The Kamloops executive decided to act immediately, and set Friday, August 4 for the rubber stamping of Gaglardi's nomination. At 7 a.m. the next day, Vincenzi began telephoning the local media to announce the nomination meeting. "All signs indicate an election," he declared, adding, "within the next twelve months."

Two hours later, Premier W.A.C. Bennett walked into a press conference, called at a half–hour's notice, in the Hotel Vancouver. The great province of British Columbia, said the premier, was experiencing unprecedented prosperity. In every way, B.C. was "the best in Canada." Its economy was sound, new energy sources had come on stream, it was out of debt, its highways and communications systems were second to none, and its leadership was as strong as ever. "People can see now the great results of Social Credit in government. Before they took us on faith. Now they can see the benefits everywhere."

The government would ask for a new term of office in a provincial election on August 30, 1972. Bennett excitedly showed off a thirty–seven–page Socred campaign pamphlet (entitled *A Personal Report from the Premier – Twenty Years of Achievement*) and announced that the basis of his party's platform would be the Kelowna Charter. Social Credit didn't need to run against anybody, said the seventy-two-year-old Bennett, it only had to run on its record and on its new ideas. But he added, "We're presenting here the alternative to state socialism, genuine, competitive private enterprise."

As the press conference was wrapping up, a boyishly good-looking stringbean of a man walked up to Bennett, extended his hand and said, "Hello, Mr. Premier, I am Derril Warren. Good luck in the election."

Bennett, who had mistaken the Tory leader for a reporter, woodenly shook his hand, forced a smile and said, "How do you do, nice to see you." A photographer's camera flashed, and Bennett walked away, scowling. In the old days, the Old Man would have beamed back at his young rival, pumped his hand and dismissed him with an assurance that Warren would probably make a good opposition MLA . . . someday.

Bennett's curious lack of humour that day was part of the change his advisors and political colleagues had seen come over him in the past year. "He sort of lost his touch," Gaglardi said later. "The premier made mistake after mistake after mistake because the man was completely fatigued. He did want to quit and he had promised he would quit after seventy years of age, but his friends implored him to run." There was widespread opinion in and out of the Socred caucus that Bennett should have resigned the year before, giving a new leader a chance to establish himself before the next election. But the premier decided to hang on, and the issue was no longer a leadership campaign but an election campaign. Gaglardi, who felt the election should not have been called that year, remembers Bennett's odd lack of consultation with cabinet ministers. "It was the strangest election call that we had ever been marshalled into. He came in, the cabinet met, he never even spent any more than just a few minutes, and simply stated that we were going to have an election on such and such a date, and as I remember it that was the end of it. He never asked a question of anybody."

While there was nervousness about Bennett's timing, there was little opposition expressed by his cabinet. Ken Kiernan: "As I recall, most of them didn't say too much. You have to remember that we had been through seven elections, and W.A.C.'s strategy had worked in every one of them. When W.A.C.'s opinion was that it was time to go, and you've got that kind of track record, you've got to be pretty hard-nosed to oppose it." Black's assessment agreed: "There were a few (ministers worried about the timing), but there were always a few. Amongst cabinet ministers and MLAs there are always those people who are afraid to put themselves on the line. Why? Because some of them hadn't got their homework done, hadn't got their fences mended. They were afraid of their own nomination."

Bennett understood the concern about having an election that summer. He had hesitated for several weeks after the rhubarb in New Westminster, losing what temporary advantage, and issue, the government had. But the premier was certain the dark cloud of inflation was about to rain on B.C.'s parade, and that waiting another year before going to the polls would enfeeble the government's chances of reelection even more. Kiernan explained: "There were two or three major issues shaping up. For one thing, in his (Bennett's) best economic judgment, we were heading into a slump, and this was partly why he had been building up reserves, and he felt that by mid–summer of 1973 we would be in a serious slump." Kiernan, though he wasn't running again, worried about the unpopularity of Bennett's restraint program. "You have a chance to stop inflation in its early stages, but if you fail to stop it in its early stages, it's almost impossible to stop in its late stages. W.A.C. was convinced that if he couldn't slow it down at this stage, it was about to take off. The storm didn't develop until a little later on. Of course, we've all got 20–20 hindsight."

Wesley Black: "We felt we were going to be, certainly as far as the premier and I were concerned, and the attorney general and others, you know, that we ran the risk of losing a few seats, but there was certainly no idea that we were going to lose the election."

Which explains why Bennett called the election in the summer of 1972, but not why he was hanging onto the leadership of the Social Credit party and to the premiership of the province. Why didn't he grandly pass the torch after twenty fine years and retire to his beloved Okanagan to smell the blossoms and sip Ovaltine? After being told by voters seven straight times that he was doing the job they wanted him to do, it's not difficult to understand his reluctance to fade away. It's likely, though, that he somewhat arrogantly believed there just wasn't anybody suitable to whom he could hand the torch. He had given thought to his retirement, and personally favoured Les Peterson as his successor, but when asked if he would retire after the election, he responded that he fully intended to serve a full term. Herb Capozzi, and others, attribute Bennett's reluctance to quit to fear of a Gaglardi premiership. "We went into the election with the idea it was going to be Bennett's last election, that he would call a leadership campaign in the middle of it," said Capozzi. "Well, Phil forced the premier into a statement that he was going to run and that he was not going to resign. It made a helluva difference. He never saw Phil as his successor, that's for sure." Bill Vincenzi also saw that the fifty-nine-year-old Gaglardi's grass-roots popularity in the party was very real, and that Bennett was "absolutely" worried about it. "His (Gaglardi's) biggest single problem was that W.A.C. saw him as a threat. Phil was a man of the people, W.A.C. wasn't. Phil could stand a crowd on its head; W.A.C. could do handstands and they wouldn't notice him." The supposedly nonexistent leadership campaign would, as it turned out, become very tangible quite soon.

So it was that the little government, in the summer of 1972, uncertainly but bravely set out once again across the moraine of B.C.'s body politic to smite the Marxists who, for their part, dodged behind rocks, as their leader Dave Barrett put it, "trying to keep our heads down and survive." It had dawned on Barrett and his New Democrats, after several generations on the opposition benches flailing impotently at the establishment parties, the Coalition and, more lately, Social Credit, that if a socialist in British Columbia poked his head out from behind cover, he was likely to get it blown off. Pinstriped suits and assurances of moderation slipped off the electorate like water from a duck's back; they simply didn't buy it. Barrett's strategy, in his first election since taking over from Tom Berger following the rout of 1969, was to quietly court the same "pressure groups" Bennett disdained. Those pressure groups had grown both in influence and in their disaffection, and Barrett said to them, point blank, that if Social Credit was to be the government of B.C., then B.C. must give Social Credit a more effective opposition. "People must understand that this government needs more pressure on it."

The other two parties had a youth movement going on. Both Tory leader Derril Warren and Liberal leader David Anderson were only thirty-five. Warren was easygoing and likable, Anderson — a former MP — intense and articulate. The Liberal leader, who had defeated Surrey mayor Bill Vander Zalm for the position, made a strange charge: that there was a conspiracy between Social Credit and the Conservative party, with the Tories acting as spoilers for the Liberal vote. "Encouraging the Tories to run is the greatest thing Premier Bennett has got going for him."

In Kamloops, Gaglardi and his campaign hardly considered the Tory candidacy an advantage. Though official party spokesmen always denied it, there had long been assumed a gentlemen's

In Victoria, Gaglardi posed for this 1972 election-campaign picture in front of the legislative buildings.

agreement in Kamloops between the Socreds and Tories, with the Socreds staying out of federal campaigns and the Tories ignoring provincial elections. That was the opposite of the kind of conspiracy Anderson saw, but it had always been there. This time, a thirty-six-year-old allergist and paediatrician named John Willoughby was running for the Conservatives and it had everybody a little nervous. Whether he would take votes away from the Liberals, as Anderson suggested, or from the Socreds or even the NDP, would be the subject of debate for many months after this election. Willoughby had no personal dislike for Gaglardi. He remembered, as a child, walking by Calvary Temple one day shortly after Gaglardi had taken over the ministry of the church. He watched as Gaglardi hopped in his old car and began backing toward the street. Suddenly, the car jerked to a stop, Gaglardi leaped out, picked up a tumbleweed and put it in the garbage. "Because he cared enough," Willoughby explained.

There was no such feeling of esteem for the sitting member

on the part of thirty-four-year-old Bill Mercer, a social worker and former newspaper reporter carrying the banner for Anderson's Grits. Mercer had gained prominence as chairman of the Kamloops School Board, and had a reputation for hyperactivity and a sound grasp of finances. His social conscience smarting under Gaglardi's handling of the welfare portfolio, Mercer very badly wanted the incumbent MLA beaten. It was, Mercer admitted, a "personal thing with me."

Unlike Mercer and Willoughby, oil-refinery worker Gerry Anderson had no profile in the community. He had something that might be better: the well-organized political machine of the Kamloops New Democratic Party. Anderson was an easygoing party loyalist who fell into the candidacy because nobody else wanted it. He had no illusions about beating Gaglardi, but he worked hard to get his name known, especially in the northern reaches of the riding where Gaglardi had been indestructible for twenty years. The NDP was expected to poll the usual solid number of hard-core party votes.

There was a fifth candidate, an unemployed independent named Terry Shaw. His sandy shock of hair falling over his eyes, Shaw loved to spout rightist pseudo-political dogma to anyone who would listen, but he wasn't a factor.

Gaglardi didn't expect to lose the election but, despite Vincenzi's assurances that he would walk away with it, he knew he couldn't take it for granted, that it could not be a battle of personalities, that it must be a battle of issues. He had more than ever riding on this election. Earlier in the year, he had formally relinquished his pastorate at Calvary Temple. The conflict within the church over his absences from the pulpit had become too much; as well, Jennie was unwell, and had resigned as Sunday school superintendent the year before. Though he intended to continue his association with the church, and to carry on his radio and TV work, he would turn over authority to his associate pastors. "The church started to fall apart because of dissension. I felt that it was about time to go. Jennie felt that she had had enough, so when she took that stand there was no use in my trying, so I resigned." In light of what was soon to follow, Gaglardi admits, "It was very bad timing, but I don't think that anything happens in your life really by chance. Of course, I could have continued, and I'm sure I could have whipped it all back into shape, but if I didn't have Jennie working with me it would have been difficult to maintain a big Sunday school like that." The church work Gaglardi had once sworn never to give up would now take second place to politics.

Point Grey Liberal candidate Garde Gardom shattered the delusion that this could be an election fought on issues or even on basic differences of principle. "A vote for Bennett is a vote for Gaglardi," he declared. Gardom (who, not quite three years later, would discover his entire political life had so far been sham, and switch to the Socreds) claimed the Kamloops MLA was the obvious successor to W.A.C. Bennett.

It was the first attempt of the campaign to put the scare of a Gaglardi premiership into the voters, one that would often be repeated, even within Gaglardi's own party. A province–wide controversy rapidly formed over Gaglardi's alleged designs on numero uno. While Saanich and the Islands Socred candidate Foster Isherwood was telling a rally Gaglardi had no chance of becoming premier, Oak Bay Socred candidate Howard McDiarmid, battling popular Socred defector and Tory incumbent Scott Wallace, was making exactly the same prediction the same day. "I bear Gaglardi no ill will," he said, "but I have to say this because people have been asking me point blank, 'Do you think Gaglardi will succeed Premier Bennett?' and I tell them there's not a chance."

Bennett's flaccid style of campaigning fed the leadership debate. But did Gaglardi really want the leadership? Gaglardi himself maintained throughout that he never sought any office, let alone premier, and that he was one thousand percent loyal to Bennett. He often said that as long as Bennett was premier, Gaglardi was his biggest supporter. "When he steps down I'm always there if the people want me."

Legislative colleagues and political and non–political friends say Gaglardi deeply coveted being The Boss. Mike Latta, his Kamloops friend and political supporter of many years, concluded, "Phil wanted more than anything to be premier. It was his ultimate, absolute goal." Today, there is no doubt about that. To the question of whether or not he really wanted to succeed Bennett in 1972, Gaglardi himself replies simply, "Yes, one hundred percent."

On August 22, Gaglardi sat down with Chris Dennett, senior national reporter for the *Toronto Star* based in Calgary and assigned to cover the B.C. election. Dennett's recollection was that he was told to assign himself his own stories on the campaign; Gaglardi's claim was that Dennett was a Liberal puppet sent specifically to do "a hatchet job." At twenty–nine, Dennett already had almost thirteen years of experience, starting in his native England and continuing with the *Star*, where he had worked in several bureaus and covered election campaigns in several provinces. He arranged to meet Gaglardi, whom he had never previously talked to, in the Provincial Alliance of Businessmen offices across the street from his room in the Hotel Vancouver. The interview wasn't taped, so we have only the conflicting accounts provided by Gaglardi and Dennett upon which to judge. Dennett: "It was basically a very informal interview. I am surprised to this day that it went the way it did. It wasn't a matter of putting one calculated question after the other hoping for some lively response about Bennett. My memory of the interview is that it suddenly took off in that direction. Gaglardi seemed keen to talk about the issue, he seemed genuinely sore about the way he was being treated by the 'Old Man,' as he called him, and seemed to want to talk about it in a very straightforward, informal way."

The story that was to result from this interview quoted Gaglardi as expressing his disenchantment with his cabinet job, with fellow cabinet members and with the premier himself. But Gaglardi's version is quite different. "He misrepresented everything that I said. He would say, 'The premier of the province is out of touch with all of the young people and a major portion of the people of the province,' and I would say, 'That's your statement, that you think that the premier is out of touch with the young people of the province, and I want to tell you that's one hundred percent incorrect.' So he used the statements that I would repeat back to him, but he wouldn't put my whole statement in the record." To accept Gaglardi's account, you would have to believe, first, that Dennett misrepresented everything Gaglardi said to him. You would also have to believe that Gaglardi repeated every question that Dennett later quoted him on. It's also true that nothing Dennett quoted Gaglardi as having said in that interview is much at variance with what Gaglardi has said in part at various times before or since. Gaglardi is an easy man to interview in that he always has plenty to say. But he usually takes a question and runs away with it, rambling from place to place for many minutes at a time before eventually returning to the beginning to tie it all together with a logical–sounding conclusion. Gaglardi acknowledges his opinions on the subject, but his main defence is that he would never have said anything so politically suicidal during an election campaign.

There was another person present at the P.A.B. offices: Betty McLeod, director of the P.A.B.'s women's division. The six–foot–tall McLeod, a member of Gaglardi's Kamloops church, was acting as his secretary that day and arranged the interview at Dennett's request. "I felt it was a setup. It was a gut feeling. I didn't feel he should do the interview." She heard a small part of the discussion between the two, and got the impression Dennett was well prepared, but nothing specific stuck in her mind.

The reporter walked out of the office thinking to himself that he'd just got a remarkable interview. "I know what a good story is. I can remember being absolutely surprised that he would do something like that. A lot of people have said since, 'Gaglardi's been doing that for years. Everybody's heard him say that before but that was the first time anybody printed it.' " Dennett returned to his hotel room, wrote the story, and phoned it in.

The following day, one week before voting day, a Dennett–bylined story that proved to be the biggest bombshell of the campaign appeared in the *Star*. Up to that point, Gaglardi had publicly continued to profess full support for Bennett. But now, according to Dennett, the gloves were off. It was a bitter Gaglardi reflected by the interview.

"He (Bennett) would have retired after the 1969 election, but he didn't want me to be premier," Gaglardi was quoted as saying. "That is the only reason he stayed on — to stop me."

When Dennett asked Gaglardi if he would be a candidate to replace the aging premier, he replied, "Yes, I think I'm the only real choice for the job." According to the story, Gaglardi called Bennett "a great politician," and said, "There's no enmity between us. But the Old Man doesn't understand what is happening with the young people of this province. The Social Credit cabinet is filled with square pegs in round holes. If I got in (as leader) there would be some fast changes. The government would have to become more responsive to the people."

Gaglardi, wrote Dennett, admitted he wasn't well–liked by his fellow cabinet ministers. "We go to a public meeting together and I get nine standing ovations in an evening, they don't get any. No wonder they dislike me."

B.C. newspapers and radio and television stations leaped on the story, and Gaglardi denied almost everything about the interview except that there was an interview. He told reporters Dennett's story was "hogwash." Two days after the Dennett story appeared in the *Star*, the *Vancouver Sun* reprinted it verbatim, and a rewritten version bylined Peter McNelly was published in the *Vancouver Province*.

Betty McLeod offered to make a public statement about the interview, but Gaglardi told her not to worry about it. "He said, 'Why bother?' "

The premier was as surprised as anyone else by the story,

and at first simply said he was certain Gaglardi didn't make the comments. He added that he was not about to retire. Gaglardi called Bennett and assured him he hadn't said any of it, and was pondering a libel suit.

CBC *Hourglass* interviewer Jack Wasserman asked Bennett later in the day what would happen if Gaglardi failed in his lawsuit. "It's clear enough," Bennett replied. "He must clear himself of these accusations. M,U,S,T. Must." He made similar comments to other reporters.

Gaglardi was back in Kamloops when he read the morning papers. Bennett's reaction bothered him. In the old days, Bennett would simply have accepted Gaglardi's public denial and left it at that. Now, by talking about the libel action, he was keeping the controversy alive. So Gaglardi called a press conference on ten minutes notice to confirm his intention to begin legal action, though he didn't elaborate. He claimed there was a move afoot to create dissension within the Social Credit party, and the opposition parties had something to do with it. Unlikely, but they would have had to be deaf or stupid to ignore what was going on.

Dave Barrett, who only in the past few days had begun to realize he might actually win this election: "I have no comment on the vicious internal struggle within the Social Credit party." After which, in the remaining days of the campaign, he proceeded to comment substantially. So did Derril Warren and David Anderson.

On Monday morning, lawyer Tom Braithwood filed a writ in B.C. Supreme Court on Gaglardi's behalf against Dennett, Pacific Press Ltd., *Province* publisher Paddy Sherman and *Province* reporter McNelly alleging libel.

At 11 a.m., radio CKNW's Ed Murphy waited for the introduction to his Vancouver hotline show to end before starting an hour of nonstop talk. With him was Premier W.A.C. Bennett. Murphy started off with the libel case. There was, he suggested, nothing very libellous about calling cabinet ministers square pegs in round holes.

"Because that's not true," replied the premier. "But the whole . . . let 'em deal with the whole thing, let it all come out in court, because Mr. Gaglardi has got to make it clear in court that he didn't say these things."

And if he didn't win?

"There'll be a replacement in the cabinet."

Murphy, Bennett and Gaglardi all knew it was going to be almost impossible to prove the libel, but Bennett insisted, "It's a question of Mr. Gaglardi's got to show in the evidence before the court that he did not say these things and he was misquoted and it was completely false. Got to show that."

Thirty–five days after it started, the campaign was over. The major issue of the campaign wasn't the Socialist Horde versus good old Free Enterprise. The issue was, to some extent, economic restraint, but more so the ability of the government and the man at the head of the government to lead the province through it. The issue was the ability of W.A.C. Bennett to continue to govern, and the ability of possible successors, Gaglardi included, to fill W.A.C.'s shoes. The issue was what the departure of Bennett in mid–term might do to the Social Credit party in B.C. and, therefore, what it might do to British Columbia. Ultimately, of course, the issue was whether or not the aging Social Credit government was relevant to the times, and whether or not any of the other parties or leaders was any more relevant. It was almost as if that spring cabinet tour was a foreboding, an election campaign in miniature. The game plan was twenty years of progress, and fear of The Horde. It had worked so often before, but in 1972 its authenticity was in doubt. In retrospect, of course, the issue of Bennett's longevity should have been obvious, yet he had no strategy for countering it. He had left the government and the party vulnerable where it hurt the most. Its entrails were strewn along the campaign trail in open view, and it wasn't a pretty sight.

Yet B.C. awaited the opening of the polls expecting Bennett to once again pull it off. He would have fewer MLAs than he was used to having, he might even have a minority, but there was little doubt he would sit at the head of a Socred government until retirement. Voters would give him a well–deserved slap on the wrist, just to remind him it was time to reassess, then retire him to glory. But lose the election? Never.

In Kamloops, Phil Gaglardi would surely be reelected. Lesser lights like Waldo Skillings, Don Brothers and Ralph Loffmark had cause for concern, but Gaglardi was close but safe. The effect of the leadership foul–up, particularly the Dennett interview, was difficult to gauge. While it hurt him and the government provincially, it might well help him in his home riding. "I felt very negative about the election. I still had a feeling that we wouldn't get in by very many but down deep inside I felt we were gonna make it. I never, never expected I'd be defeated."

Provincially, the party leaders were attending windup rallies in the Lower Mainland on the last day of campaigning. Bennett had finally abandoned his disappearing act in the last few

On parade, Gaglardi saddles up for his last election campaign in Kamloops, 1972.

days, appearing on open–line radio shows, including Murphy's, in television interviews and at rallies in Greater Vancouver. Province–wide, 1,343,445 people were eligible to vote; in Kamloops riding, 33,527. There were 11,000 new voters in Kamloops for this election. Turnout for the advance poll, 1,230, was termed "heavy" by chief returning officer Frank Arnish. Party standings at the end of the 29th legislative assembly: Social Credit thirty–six, NDP twelve, Liberals five, Progressive Conservatives two.

When the polling station at the Christian Education Centre in Kamloops opened at 8 a.m. Wednesday, August 30, sixty people were waiting in line to vote. Among the first two dozen through the doors was Gaglardi. Throughout the riding officials were saying it looked like an excellent turnout, maybe as high as seventy percent, a riding record. It was a tense day, and when polls closed at 8 p.m., thousands inched toward their television sets to await the first returns. Only minutes later it began with a few small polls sending in tabulations of only a dozen or two votes.

At 8:45, Gaglardi had drawn 116 votes, almost double the totals of the NDP's Anderson and the Liberals' Mercer, with Willoughby the PC just beginning to show on the board. At the Socreds' Stockmen's Cabaret Room election–night headquarters, the three dozen supporters broke into scattered applause.

Kamloops News Advertiser editor Mel Rothenburger (the

author) and *Kamloops Sentinel* reporter John Pifer watched the first results come into Gaglardi's headquarters with interest, but they knew it would be a while yet before a clear trend developed. "How'd you end up spending the night covering Gaglardi?" Pifer asked. "I figure I may as well cover the winner," said the editor.

Ten minutes later, Anderson had drawn to within eight votes of the incumbent and, at 9 p.m., they were tied with 501 each. It might be the start of the trend, or it might mean little, since the three largest polling stations wouldn't be in for at least another hour.

But across the province, Socreds were worried. NDP candidates were leading everywhere. Even cabinet ministers were in trouble. In Kelowna, Bennett appeared briefly on television at his party's headquarters to admit the trend was toward the NDP. Looking tired and disappointed, Bennett wished Dave Barrett luck. The NDP, he said, could be thankful the Socreds had left B.C.'s finances in good shape.

Back in Kamloops, the Socreds sat stunned at the unremitting march of The Horde, while across the river in the old Elks Hall, the NDPers were at least as stunned. Not only was it becoming obvious the NDP would probably form a majority government, but Gerry Anderson had opened up a 200–vote lead over Gaglardi. Anderson was now winning almost every one of the outlying stations.

Gaglardi arrived at the Cabaret Room at 9:30 p.m. With Jennie and their son Bob, he settled in front of a television set to watch the disaster. Anderson's lead was down to 128 votes, 1,542 to 1,414.

In Prince George, the once–invincible Ray Williston was going down to defeat. "It's hard to figure out how Williston would lose," said Gaglardi. "It's got to be some kind of a strange trend."

A larger Kamloops poll reported in. Anderson took 587 votes, Gaglardi 464. Gaglardi shook his head sadly. "What kind of thinking must be going on there?"

Bennett reappeared on the television. This time he officially conceded to the New Democratic Party. He had been reelected in Kelowna, but the slough of despond in which he wallowed was reflected in his face and words. He said he had no regrets about the election. "I've nothing but gratitude for the people of this province with no ill will to anyone."

Gaglardi's own fate was about to be sealed. The decisive Kamloops South polling station was reporting in: Gaglardi 1,298, Mercer 1,300, Anderson 1,241, Willoughby 722, Shaw 11. The last hope was gone.

Asked by a reporter if he intended to continue with his

lawsuit against the *Star* and the *Province*, the fifty-nine-year-old replied, "It's up to my lawyers." He added, "It doesn't seem to matter if I do."

It was 10:40 p.m. and Gaglardi called together his subdued supporters to officially concede. He was bitterly disappointed ("I was flabbergasted, it just staggered me; couldn't happen"), but he hid it well, launching into his characteristically agitated rhetoric. "We've given the province of British Columbia the twenty finest years of government it's ever had in its history. We have everything to be proud of. I'll wager that in three or four years' time the people will be happy to get a free-enterprise party back in office. We'll be back in there fighting again. God bless you."

In addition to Gaglardi and Williston, the cabinet fallen included Les Peterson, Cyril Shelford, Don Brothers, Ralph Loffmark, Dan Campbell, Wes Black, Waldo Skillings, Grace McCarthy, Isabel Dawson. Only Bennett, Frank Richter, Jim Chabot and Pat Jordan of the cabinet ministers survived.

The CFJC television station was abuzz. Some of Anderson's supporters had transferred their celebrations to the lobby of the station, continuing their whooping and back slapping. Mercer and Willoughby supporters were also there in large numbers, joining the NDPers in their party mood. It was a night for gloating. In the studio, which was also crowded, newsmen and politicians spoke in whispered tones. When the late-evening national and local news reports were completed, candidates and their campaign directors were seated in front of cameras to make their statements.

Mercer said he was "happy the incumbent was beaten." Even Kamloops-Cariboo Liberal MP Len Marchand told the television audience that "everyone wanted to defeat the incumbent Phil Gaglardi because his government had forgotten about people."

When Gaglardi arrived, he smilingly congratulated Gerry Anderson and posed for photographs shaking the winner's hand. Rothenburger, a witness to Gaglardi's last hurrah, later noted to Anderson the grace with which Gaglardi accepted defeat that night. Anderson professed no surprise. "Some people said that if Phil Gaglardi was beaten he would fall apart. He's a hardrock. I knew he wouldn't fall apart."

Despite the celebrating, there was an underlying sadness in the air, as there must always be at the end of an era. There was a special significance to it ending at twenty years. Not nineteen years, or twenty-one years, but an even two decades of power. Gaglardi, the embodiment of Socred fundamentalism, suddenly wouldn't be there in the headlines, as he had been for those twenty years, basketweave shoes among sensible black oxfords. He was the lampshade wearer of the party, never reluctant to laugh at himself or the vagaries of politics. He was dynamic, impatient, egotistical, outrageous. He would be remembered as the man who had flown his daughter–in–law to Dallas on our money, built more highways than anybody, collected speeding tickets and brought down the Socred government.

The extent of Gaglardi's responsibility for the defeat on August 30, 1972, remains open to debate. Gaglardi rejects the idea he had anything to do with it. If the voters had been unhappy just with him, then he alone would have lost, he reasons. He blames, instead, Bennett's refusal to step down. If he had, says Gaglardi, the Socreds would have won again, and Gaglardi would have been premier. "(Bennett) was tired. He was plumb played out. He was finished. Do you think Ray Williston would have lost his seat? Do you think I would have lost my seat? We didn't lose our seats. He lost our seats for us." Wes Black was certain that, if Gaglardi didn't defeat the entire government, he was entirely responsible for the defeat of some cabinet ministers in close ridings, including his own and Don Brothers'. Dan Campbell acknowledged Bennett's role in the defeat, but believed Gaglardi was a contributor. "I indicated it to Bennett at the time. (Gaglardi) was lipping off during the election campaign. It left the impression that the only salvation for British Columbia was Gaglardi." Ken Kiernan, in an interview with the author in 1980, long after the government's defeat but several years before Bill Bennett made restraint a respectable word, probably best assessed Gaglardi's part in the fall of the first Socred dynasty, and prophesied what was to come: "I don't think it made two percentage points difference, if that. There was a great feeling, almost a revolt, and perhaps no place was that more visible than at the hotel in New Westminster that spring. I'm almost inclined to think that today, if a government were to take the position that we did in 1972, and the public now being aware of the kind of devastation that inflation is racking up, that we would have won that election hands down, but the public was not aware of the dangers of inflation in '72. We were too far ahead of our time. And you know, people tend to get restless after awhile and you can sell the idea that it's time for a change, and if there are other little contributing factors, like the question of leadership being vastly uncertain. Phil didn't help it a bit. He put the fat in the fire, but it was already sizzling anyway." Cyril Shelford, who also hadn't wanted the election, was of much the same opinion. "So many people had grown up who had never known another government and thought they should have a change." But Gaglardi's controversies added to the problems, he said. "It was a sign of things not running smoothly from within."

Whatever the combination of causes, the NDP was the benefactor of Social Credit's troubles. Gaglardi's fear of a split free-enterprise vote came to pass, though an analysis of voting patterns showed that had Social Credit kept all its free-enterprise votes it would have won only seven additional seats. Gaglardi's would have been one of them. Final seat totals left the NDP with thirty-eight, Social Credit ten, Liberals five and Tories two.

In the Kamloops TV studio on election night 1972, Gaglardi told an interviewer: "The press won't be able to write so much about me anymore. It'll be a big relief to get all that responsibility off my shoulders."

To John Willoughby, he said, "John, you took my votes." But there were no other recriminations, no other excuses. Six hundred eighty-five votes — the number by which he had lost to Gerry Anderson — had separated him from twenty years of work, and that was that.

A few minutes later, "It'll be a different world tomorrow morning."

And Phil Gaglardi went home for some rest. It would, indeed, be a different world tomorrow.

Resurrection

And he was restored.
MARK 8.25

It seems to be one of the quirks of my life that I get into everything I don't want to get into.
PHIL GAGLARDI

Phil Gaglardi, in the little dining room just off the coffee shop in the Kamloops Sandman Inn, finishes off his coffee. He's remembering that night in 1972 when his political career ended, and his feelings about it. "The next morning I woke up, and looked over at that briefcase and said, 'What do I do now?' So I jumped in the airplane and went down to Vancouver and I've been doing it ever since." There was no money in his bank accounts, so Bob gave him a thousand dollars to see him through until his legislative pension cheques started arriving. "That's more or less what I lived on. I phoned the federal government and asked them what about unemployment insurance, but they said, 'No, you are not eligible.' That was about two weeks after. And then I said, 'Well, then give me back my money.' They said, 'There's no legislation on the books that will allow that.' I said, 'Then you're a pack of crooks. You took my money illegally.' But I never did get it."

The years after the voters dismissed him from public office were busy but, by comparison, muted. Family and friends say the shock of being out of politics hurt Gaglardi deeply, though he doesn't admit to it. He worked with his son Bob on development projects, including Sandman hotels, flying home from Calgary and Vancouver on weekends. After W.A.C. Bennett's resignation as MLA and party leader in 1973, Gaglardi briefly flirted with the idea of taking a serious run at the coveted job that was now, finally, vacant, but backed off when the Old Man endorsed son Bill. "There was a definite move to get me to run when Bill Bennett was running but in respect for the premier I didn't." Five years later, a group of anonymous supporters filed papers nominating him for the leadership of the national Social Credit party, but without a guarantee of full-time use of a jet aircraft, he declined. He had aspirations for his weekly *Chapel in the Sky* television program on CFJC to go national, but it faltered through personnel changes and lack of money. In 1974, federal income tax investigators and RCMP raided his home in Kamloops and his office in Vancouver with fourteen search warrants, seizing documents and even personal letters. No charges were ever laid, but Gaglardi doesn't want to talk about it. Frequently, he got his name in headlines and his picture in the newspapers when he spoke to Rotary or chamber of commerce luncheons, or even an occasional political gathering. He sometimes lent his "endorsation" to political hopefuls, and worked actively for Bill Vander Zalm at the Whistler leadership convention in 1986. He believes he could have beaten Vander Zalm himself. "I'm absolutely certain that, if I'd wanted to, I could have got in there. I could have done it." Even as he entered his seventies, the passion was still inside Phil Gaglardi, along with the conviction that he could fix what's wrong with the country if only given the chance. He could, he often said, get back into politics any time. People still wanted him. "People still come up to me and ask for my autograph. This staggers me!"

If W.A.C. Bennett had stepped down instead of running in 1972, he would "absolutely" have become leader and premier. "Cec and I were a lot closer than people think," he says, holding up the first two fingers of his right hand, pressed together. "We always thought exactly alike, we were two peas in a pod."

All of that may have seemed like the fond reminiscences and wishful thinking of a defeated old politician, were it not for some biological facts and recent events. While Gaglardi grows older chronologically, his body and his mind have trouble believing it — he in no way acts like a man in his late seventies. He's as stubborn as ever, his voice as unfailing, and he can still run circles around men forty years younger. All of that didn't answer the question of his political longevity; his talk of a comeback still sounded more wistful than realistic. As the years passed after his defeat, Phil Gaglardi remained a curiosity, but hardly a current political force.

There was never any serious talk about Gaglardi running for MLA again. A series of Kamloops MLAs have since held prominent cabinet posts in Socred governments.

But talking about how he still owned the hearts and minds of British Columbians — and not doing anything about it — was never enough for Gaglardi. Deep down inside, he must have harboured a curiosity about his stature with the public. In 1986, Expo year, when Bill Bennett passed the torch to Vander Zalm, the city of Kamloops had a civic election to go along with the provincial vote. The winner of the mayoralty that year was a public relations man named John Dormer, who defeated the incumbent, Jim Walsh, as well as another past mayor, Mike Latta, the ex-oilman and Gaglardi fan. Almost a candidate was Phil Gaglardi, talked into running by realtor and neighbour Babe Nicholson, with support from a group of Kamloops businessmen who saw the former highways minister as just what the economically depressed city needed to get it in gear. Nomination papers were taken out and filled in, and would have been filed were it not for the fact that Bob Gaglardi's business operations took a turn for the worse. The Boys' father had been the companies' troubleshooter in several financial crises, travelling from Hong Kong to the Middle East and elsewhere to raise capital to keep the vultures off his eldest son. "Bob said, 'Dad, I need you.' I wasn't about to do anything else but help him out."

Two years and several multi-million-dollar refinancing deals later, it was a different situation when Nicholson approached Gaglardi once again about the mayoralty. Dormer was dubbed Captain Fantastic by the local press for his boosterism and bombast, but Kamloops continued to wallow in deep unemployment and in self-doubt. The city needed a take-charge kind of a guy at the helm, someone who could make things happen just by virtue of being there.

> *Babe was the main man behind the pushing. When he was first after me, and Bob and Bill said no, I was relieved and happy when they said no. But in this particular occasion the company was on the basis when the election time came that I wasn't needed as critically as I was previously, and so I had absolutely no concrete excuse to offer, and so on that basis it sort of tipped the scales. I never wanted to run for mayor of Kamloops any more than I wanted to run in the political arena when they dragged me in and I became minister of highways. Although I have an ego, no two ways about that, I've never seen myself as anything other than a servant of the people.*

Gaglardi, though he may have entered the fray reluctantly, didn't enter it blindly. He knew himself well enough to realize that a one-man show wouldn't function well in the grass-roots, consensus democracy of municipal government. He needed to be able to take complete charge of whatever he did, without wasting time lobbying and assuaging feelings. As mayor, he would be only one voice in nine, subject to the whims of the council majority, and the prospect didn't thrill him. If he was to be mayor, he insisted, he must have an on-board council, a group of aldermen who would follow him, not fight with him. The answer was the formation of Action Team '88, a sort of municipal political party with a vaguely pro-development policy but, more importantly, committed to Gaglardi as the final word. In convincing Gaglardi to run, Nicholson enlisted the assistance of Randy Black, manager of the Thompson–Nicola Manufacturers Association. Black, known for his unfailingly optimistic boosterism of the city, was looking at running for an aldermanic seat, and he suddenly found himself heading up the recruiting of candidates for the Action Team slate. Frank Luciani and Wayne McRann, a pair of active community businessmen, came onside to help recruit and run Action Team '88. Their job wasn't easy; bringing together a credible slate on such short notice required fast work. They ended up with a group of mostly unknown aldermanic candidates that included Black, an NDP college instructor, a lawyer and a realtor recruited by phone the evening before nomination day. Gaglardi had no idea who most of them were. As unexciting a roster as it seemed, it was unveiled with appropriate fanfare and Gaglardi bombast at a press conference after the nomination papers were filed. It was immediately clear what the strategy would be. Vote for Phil Gaglardi, and vote for his Team because Phil Gaglardi wants you to.

The media received Gaglardi's nomination with considerable glee. Municipal politics had for years been a pretty boring venue, other than the fact that Kamloops councils were infamous for their bickering. Dormer had been the latest in a succession of mayors who were more grandiloquently optimistic than effective. With Gaglardi, they could at least look forward to a lively campaign, even if he didn't win. And Gaglardi was by no means a betting favourite. The question on the minds of the local armchair pundits was whether or not enough of the population would remember a career that had ended fully sixteen years before, and whether those who did remember it would admire, condemn, or absolve him. Was that career a badge of honour or over–limit baggage? Many Kamloops voters were barely of school age when Gaglardi and the W.A.C. Socreds were beaten that night back in 1972. Was he simply an old has–been injected into the campaign for a little fun?

His opponents in the mayoralty weren't pushovers. There was Dormer, back for his second run at it. Others included Doc

Calder, a retired salesman; Ray Dunsdon, a retired armed forces major and incumbent alderman; Tony Milobar, a popular physician, Socred, businessman and ex-alderman; and Kenna Cartwright, an alderman and NDPer who had almost beaten Bud Smith in the 1986 provincial election. Cartwright was considered at the outset to be the front-runner. She had served for many years on the local school board and city council, displaying a knack for coming down on the right side of issues and staying out of trouble.

The question of whether or not Gaglardi could generate enough excitement in a short, three-week campaign — when most of the other candidates had been working on theirs for the past several months — was answered within the first week. An initial sense of wonder turned to curiosity and then to the start of a groundswell. Gaglardi's presence was the major topic of conversation about the civic election, and everywhere in Kamloops voters began comparing him to what had come and gone before. They told each other there was nothing to lose, why not put the little guy in city hall for a couple of years and see what he can do? This caused alarm bells to ring at the campaign offices of the other candidates who had viewed the election, before Gaglardi's belated entry, as being up for grabs. At all-candidates forums, Gaglardi's often tenuous grasp of civic issues was hammered by his opponents. Particularly vitriolic was Calder, smarting because a Gaglardi lieutenant suggested he withdraw from the mayoral election and run for an aldermanic seat instead. There was some attempt to make Gaglardi's age an issue, but it didn't seem to be of interest to anyone. They went at him, with slightly more success, about his absenteeism from Kamloops. He answered that one with a firm assurance that he would be a "one hundred percent" mayor who would spend as much time on the job as was necessary. When one resident demanded to know what he'd ever accomplished for Kamloops, he waded in happily with stories about the Rogers Pass and other highways, and how they had opened up unprecedented opportunities for the city. When someone tried to suggest that if he was such a smart businessman the companies he was involved with wouldn't be in such financial trouble, he responded that it was all fixed up, that the bank had been paid, that Bob was back in the chair, and that everything was fine. Though his height jokes didn't tickle the same fancies as they had in his heyday, he was unquestionably the star of the podium anywhere he went. Gaglardi concentrated on slamming the incumbent council and city hall administration for scaring away investors, guaranteeing voters that if he were elected "you better believe I'll turn this city around within six months."

Part of the little man's attraction was his national profile. The national media truly enjoy writing about Gaglardi because he's easy to write about and he makes entertaining reading. No other politician on the face of the earth gives a reporter quotes like Gaglardi gives them. So the television networks and metropolitan newspapers flew in to do their reprise pieces on the comeback bid, and Gaglardi loved it. "Juda's Priest, there's an article about me in Australia," he said proudly. "That's the kind of attention I bring this city."

A public-opinion poll jointly commissioned by the *Kamloops Daily News* and radio station CHNL a little more than a week before election day found Gaglardi and Cartwright in a dead heat, with Dormer a poor third and the others trailing far behind. In a follow-up poll a few days later, Gaglardi pulled away. The numbers were a bitter disappointment for everyone but Gaglardi, but especially for Cartwright, who had firmly believed, and had every right to believe before Gaglardi decided to run, that she would be the next mayor. The decision to run was something she had agonized over for months, and now Gaglardi had walked in out of nowhere and taken it away from her.

Election day, November 19, the public-opinion poll was confirmed. Phil Gaglardi, sixteen years after being rejected by Kamloops voters, was redeemed. He took forty-four percent of the votes, beating Cartwright by more than three thousand. Two years later, when Gaglardi bowed out, Cartwright became the first woman mayor of Kamloops with a landslide victory, only to die from leukemia in July 1991. Dormer was another five thousand votes behind and the rest may as well not have bothered. After all those years, at the age of seventy-five, Gaglardi still had the magic. Donning a cowboy hat and standing before jubilant campaign workers, he said, "I guess the fat lady has done her singing." Proving he'd lost none of his self-confidence, Gaglardi repeated his campaign promise: "Within six months' time, I'll guarantee you there'll be a change in the atmosphere of the city. If I don't put it on the map like it has never been done before, then the next time it comes to voting, I'll ask you not to vote for me."

Gaglardi got his second wish, too. Four of his Action Team '88 members — Randy Black, Shirley Culver, Ron Watson and Bill Walton — were elected along with him, giving him a majority on the nine-member council. The man who didn't want to be mayor would be the boss of the chair in city hall for the next two years.

I said to myself (before the election) I've always been guided by the highest principles that it's possible to be guided by and I said to the Lord, alright, if I run and if I should be the mayor of the city I will be and if I shouldn't be I won't be, and I'll be the happiest fellow on this earth if I lose. And that's the way it came about and I won and the amazing thing is I won with such a resounding vote that was the highest in the history of the city and it was rather flabbergasting.

If the good people of Kamloops thought they were getting a rococo little master of malapropisms who would, when it came down to the real thing, play by the rules, they were mistaken. Gaglardi wasted no time in assaulting the status quo. He immediately discovered there was no way to get along with Colin Day, the headstrong chairman of a civic committee that had engineered approval of a borrowing bylaw that would be the basis of a $13-million (estimates later rose to more than $18 million) multi-purpose arena. So, using his Action Team '88 majority, he dismissed Day and his committee, putting in its place one of his own. (When it was suggested he didn't do it very diplomatically, he explained, "When I kill a chicken, I don't pet it for three hours first. I chop its head off.") Then, convinced that potential investors were being given the cold shoulder by city hall administration, he decided the place to fix that was at the top. He made the chief administrator, Pat Anderson, feel so unwelcome that Anderson quit, taking with him a fat settlement that included $100,000, a pension deal, use of an office, secretary and car, and a free trip to Africa as a "consultant." The rookie mayor lost another employee when his secretary, Heather Duthie, quit after only a few months on the job. Officially, she would say only that her reasons were personal, but privately admitted she could no longer take the stress of being compared to the perfection — at least in Gaglardi's mind — that was Edith Valen. Gaglardi, she said, offered no sense of direction, expecting his secretary to know what he was thinking. The mayor admitted he was a difficult man to work for.

There were other signs that Gaglardi was the same guy he used to be. Though he didn't gather any speeding tickets as mayor, he was nailed for not wearing his seat belt ("God bless me, I'm so short they choke me.") And he issued orders to his administrators that only he was qualified to make public statements, but insisted publicly they could say anything they wanted to, and that he wasn't trying to muzzle anybody.

He proved he still loved to travel, too, when he asked his council for a credit card with a $5,000 spending limit so that he could hop a

Back in politics after all those years, Gaglardi in his mayoralty robes, 1988.

plane any time he needed to go somewhere for an important meeting. Council members almost gave it to him, but when the legality of it was questioned, and they asked him to provide regular reports on his expenditures, an insulted Gaglardi dropped his request.

He did succeed in doing away with the city's economic development office and turning it over to a free–enterprise agency. Although views differ on how much the city "turned around," the love–hate relationship between Gaglardi and the public indeed created a more vibrant attitude. "I'm not saying it's all because of me," Gaglardi would tell visitors as he wheeled his big station wagon around town. "Maybe it's just coincidence. But I'd say I would have to have had something to do with it. Look over there, there's another building going up. That's what I mean, everywhere you go the city is moving again."

A day usually didn't go by without Gaglardi — nicknamed Mayor Yoda by the locals — making headlines in his home town and often across the country for his extravagant opinions and ideas. Half the town was outraged when he reacted to a riot of partying teenagers by attacking permissive parents and unionized teachers. The other half thought it was about time somebody said it.

His opinions on all of the major social issues of the day

haven't been shaken by time. He still expresses profound disbelief at the stupidity of society. Whether it's abortion ("Murder is murder, no matter what; you can't dress up murder") or the work ethic ("I don't think it's a good thing to make people retire too early in life") he states his opinions unequivocally, without hedging and without caution. One of the things few people still realize about Gaglardi is that when he says he wasn't a populist politician, he's being absolutely truthful. One of his great flaws, but also one of his great charms, is that he doesn't care what anybody thinks about him. He says what's on his mind and moves on to something else, never thinking or much caring about whether people agree or disagree with what he's said. In that sense, he was always a poor politician, because he doesn't shade his words according to what the public is likely to want to hear, and he doesn't straddle fences on tough issues. Had he learned that fine art, there's no telling how far he might have gone in politics, but he also would have given up the thing for which he's most famous — his candour.

> *What I miss in the world today are forthright, capable individuals who aren't afraid of what the public thinks. It seems that in public life there are so few people who are not intimidated by what the public says and what newspapers say, and that was one of the things that I excelled in. I didn't care two hoots what they said about me because your enemies always believe everything bad that's said about you and your friends never do, and I seemed to have more friends than I had enemies, so because of that I didn't care what people said. When I was positive that I was doing the right thing I did it. The thing that's lacking in the political arena today is guts enough to make decisions that are proper, and stick by them. We've got so many mealy-mouthed politicians running around the country today in provincial government and in municipal government and in federal government that it's disgraceful.*

Gaglardi, as mayor, found himself wrestling not only with municipal problems, but with the concept of municipal democracy itself. It was frustrating work for a man who had been used to doing things his own way all of his life. He found the red tape of bureaucracy and the process of politics standing in his way much the same as when he first became a cabinet minister in W.A.C. Bennett's government way back in 1952.

Gaglardi wasn't impressed with most of his aldermen, including those elected on his Action slate, but he remained determined to tackle the job, as usual. His lack of regard for his aldermen, however, was returned by his council throughout the term. One of his arch non-Team critics, Alderman John Cowell, called Gaglardi "a fish out of water" in civic politics. "I don't think he had much of an understanding about the role of a mayor." Even Randy Black soon became disillusioned. "He's the most difficult man I've ever dealt with in my life. When he decides something he makes it up in his mind as if it's true and then he really believes it."

The Action Team slate never did provide the cohesive council Gaglardi wanted, falling quickly into confusion as each of its members went his or her own way on voting. Black, however, felt Gaglardi served a purpose as mayor, bringing the city much-needed publicity with "his name, his infamy and his belligerence."

Others who backed him feel his mayoralty was a success. "I thought he was the right fellow to shake things up and he did that," said Nicholson. "I'm not disappointed." Neither was Luciani. "We wanted to get the town turned around and Phil did that. He has done what we wanted him to do — we wanted him to get Kamloops back on the map. He's not one hundred percent but who is?"

Did it ever cross his mind to be more than a one-term mayor?

"In a pig's eye."

In a bizarre footnote to his political career, the seventy-eight-year-old Gaglardi briefly flirted with going after the Social leadership at the convention that ended up confirming Rita Johnston in July 1991. Due to a misunderstanding of the nomination deadline, his papers weren't filed. "I'll bet you a dollar to a pinch of snuff, my friend, that I'd win the premiership without batting an eye," he said.

As we prepare to settle up the tab and head for the parking lot, a man at one of the tables recognizes Gaglardi and introduces himself. They exchange small talk for a moment, the man explaining he was once in Gaglardi's Sunday school. Gaglardi accepts being recognized matter-of-factly — he's used to it — but he looks pleased. The old days are still the best, and being remembered from back then is still the most gratifying.

The former pupil leaves, happy to have exchanged a few words with the man who has made such a mark in British Columbian and Canadian politics. Then Flyin' Phil Gaglardi is on his way to work, as always, to straighten things out.

Sources

Primary:

Legislative Library of B.C. Proceedings in Committee, in the matter of the hearings of the Select Standing Committee on Public Accounts and in the matter of the hearings relating to certain material tabled in the House on February 26, 1963, Victoria, B.C. Irvine S. Corbett, Esq., Chairman.

Report of the British Columbia Royal Commission, The Honourable Sherwood Lett, Chief Justice of the Supreme Court of British Columbia, Commissioner. Second Narrows Bridge Enquiry. Queen's Printer, 1958.

Books:

Bannermann, Gary & Patricia. *The Ships of British Columbia, An Illustrated History of the British Columbia Ferry Corporation*. Surrey: Hancock House Publishers Inc., 1985.

Barr, John J. *The Dynasty: The Rise and Fall of Social Credit in Alberta*. Toronto: McClelland & Stewart, 1974.

Gibson, Gordon and Renison, Carol. *Bull of the Woods – The Gordon Gibson Story*. Vancouver: Douglas & McIntyre, 1980.

Hill, Annie L. *People, Places, Things*. New York: Carlton Press, 1980.

Holten, E.S. *The ABC of Social Credit*. New York: Coward, McCann, Inc., 1934.

Hutchinson, Bruce. *The Fraser*. Toronto, Vancouver: Clarke, Irwin & Company Ltd., 1950.

Keene, Roger and Hymphreys, David D. *Conversations with W.A.C. Bennett*. Toronto: Methuen Publications, 1980.

Nichol, John Thomas. *Pentecostalism*. New York: Harper and Row, 1966.

McGeer, Patrick L. *Politics in Paradise*. Toronto: Peter Martin Associates, 1972.

Mitchell, David J. *W.A.C. Bennett and the Rise of British Columbia*. Vancouver: Douglas & McIntyre, 1983.

Moore, Vincent. *Angelo Branca, Gladiator of the Courts.*
     Vancouver: Douglas & McIntyre, 1981.

Robin, Martin. *Pillars of Profit: The Company Province,*
     1934–1972. Toronto: McClelland & Stewart, 1973.

Simpson, Jeffrey. *Spoils of Power, The Politics of Patronage.* Don
     Mills: Collins Publishers, 1988.

Sherman, Paddy. *Bennett.* Toronto: McClelland & Stewart, 1966.

Worley, Ronald B. *The Wonderful World of W.A.C. Bennett.*
     Toronto: McClelland & Stewart, 1972.

Interviews:

The interviews for this book range from relatively short
discussions on specific points to many hours of tapes covering a
wide range of events during the Gaglardi era. All of the following
contributed to the book in various degrees, and I gratefully
acknowledge their help. Some have passed on and, regrettably,
are not here to read the results of their input:

Anderson, Gerry (1979); Baines, Ray (1980); Barrett, Bert
(1981); Barrett, Dave (1981); Bell, Fred (1991); Black, Randy
(1990); Black, Wesley (1980); Britton, Gordon (1987); Campbell,
Dan (1987); Capozzi, Herb (1981); Charlong, Lena (1980); Clark,
Ian (1984); Cowell, John (1990); Crosby, Dorothy (1981);
Cunliffe, S.J (1981); Dennett, Chris (1988); Dowding, Gordon
(1981); Gaglardi, Albert (1980); Gaglardi, Anthony (1980);
Gaglardi, Frank (1980); Gaglardi, Jennie (1981); Gaglardi, Phil
(1979–1991); Gaglardi, Robert (1981); Gibson, J. Gordon, Sr.
(1981); Guild, Don (1987); Gould, Jay (1990); Harding,
Randolph (1981, 1982); Holzworth, Dick (1991); Iverson, Lou
(1988, 1991); Kiernan, Ken (1980); Krushnisky, Jake (1981);
Latta, Mike (1982, 1987); Lea, Norman (1988); Luciani, Frank
(1990); McCallum, Neil (1980); McFarlane, Meredith M. (1988);
McLean, Fraser (1980); MacLeod, A.V. (1983); McLeod, Betty
(1988); McNeill, Jack (1988); Mazaros, Len (1981); Mercer, Bill
(1979); Merrick, Roy (1981); Miard, Tom (1980); Nesbitt, James
K. (1981); Nicholson, Babe (1990); Nimsick, Leo (1981); Odam,
Jes (1986); Perrault, Ray (1980); Perry, Sam (1986); Price, Bert
(1981); Price, Ron (1990); Sommers, Robert (1982); Smith, Della
(1982); Strohmeier, Helen (1980); Strohmeier, Joyce (1981);
Strohmeier, Larry (1981); Stephanishin, Norman (1990); Valen,
Edith (1979–80, 1988); Vincenzi, William (1988); Wanless, Rick
(1987); Wicks, Lyle (1980); Williston, Ray (1980); Willoughby,
John (1979); Wood, John (1990).

Periodicals:

Construction World

Coronet

Kamloops Daily News

Kamloops Sentinel

Kelowna Courier

Maclean's

Star Weekly

Toronto Globe and Mail

Vancouver Province

Vancouver Sun

Victoria Colonist

Victoria Times

Other:

Department of Rehabilitation and Social Improvement. B.C. Provincial Alliance of Businessmen Region Reports, 1970–71.

Department of Rehabilitation and Social Improvement. Report of the Department, 1970–71.

Department of Social Welfare, B.C.. Reports, 1968–69, 1969–70.

Gaglardi, P.A. "Calvary Temple 1944–1971." Kamloops (limited printing on occasion of 35th anniversary of Calvary Temple), 1980.

Keene, Roger. "Interview with W.A.C. Bennett." British Columbia Archives and Records Service, 1977.

Lea, Norman D. "The Deas Island Tunnel." *The Military Engineer*, July-August, 1959.

Lea, Norman D. and Brawner, C.O. "Highway Design and Construction Over Peat Deposits in the Lower Mainland Region of British Columbia." Highways Research Board, 1963.

Ministry of Transportation and Highways, "B.C. Deas Island Tunnel," unpublished manuscript. British Columbia Archives and Records Service.

Ministry of Transportation and Highways, "B.C. Frontier to Freeways," prepared by Raymond Baines. Queen's Printer for British Coumbia, 1971 and 1986.

Mitchell, David. J. "Interview with Philip A. Gaglardi," British Columbia Archives and Records Service. Oral History #1644, 1978.

Western Weekly Reports, N.S. Vol. 34. 1961, British Columbia Court of Appeal, Glazer v. Union Contractors Ltd. and Thornton and Gaglardi, B.C. Law Society, Vancouver, Burroughs & Co. Ltd., Law Publishers, Calgary, 1961.

A PERSONAL CHRONOLOGY
OF THE LIFE OF PHILIP ARTHUR GAGLARDI

BORN: January 13, 1913, Silverdale, B.C.

POSITIONS HELD:

1930s – 1940s: A born mechanic. Worked in construction and mechanics for such companies as A.R. Williams Machinery Co. Ltd., Vancouver; Bloedel, Stewart & Welch, Camps 3 and 8, Vancouver Island; Halenback Dollar Co. Ltd., Port Douglas, B.C.; General Construction Co. Ltd., Vancouver; and Thompson Clarke Timber Co., Harrison Mills.

1938 – 1944: Pastor and evangelist for Pentecostal Assemblies of Canada, Fraser Valley and elsewhere in B.C.

1944 – 1972: Pastor, Calvary Temple, Pentecostal Assemblies of Canada, Kamloops, B.C.

1952 – 1955: Minister of Public Works, Government of British Columbia, in charge of all government buildings and highways.

1955 – 1968: Minister of Highways, Government of British Columbia, in charge of all highways maintenance and construction, employing between six thousand and ten thousand. Said to have constructed more highways than anyone else in the world.

1968 – 1969: Minister Without Portfolio, Government of British Columbia.

1969 – 1972: Minister of Rehabilitation and Social Improvement, Government of British Columbia.

1972 – 1978: Advisor for Northland Properties Ltd. and Sandman Inns Ltd. (B.C. chain of inns and office structures).

1978 – 1988: Director, Northland Properties Ltd. Advisor for numerous companies.

1988 – 90: Mayor, City of Kamloops, B.C.

1990 – Present: Advisor for numerous companies.

ACHIEVEMENTS:

1944 – 1950
— Established and developed largest Sunday school in Canada, at Calvary Temple, Kamloops, and enlarged church seven times to accommodate growing congregation. The Sunday school remained the largest for eighteen years, and included thirteen buses. Wife Jennie trained teachers and administered the Sunday school.

1954 – 57
— Originated first–of–its–kind communication system for B.C. Department of Highways using mountaintop receivers and transmitters capable of contacting any office or automobile, or department airplane.

1956
— Constructed Agassiz–Rosedale Bridge, two-lane cantilever bridge across Fraser River ninety–six kilometres east of Vancouver.

1957

— Constructed Oak Street Bridge, connecting Vancouver to Lulu and Sea Islands.

— Constructed cantilever Nelson Bridge across West Arm of Kootenay Lake at Nelson.

— Constructed Northern Trans–Provincial Highway over a period of several years beginning in 1957.

1958

— Constructed Kelowna Bridge across Okanagan Lake between Westbank and Kelowna, a combination rock–fill causeway and floating pontoon bridge, replacing ferries. Princess Margaret officially opened the bridge.

1959

— Constructed six-lane Second Narrows Bridge across Burrard Inlet in Vancouver.

— Reconstructed Trans–Canada between Vancouver and Hope into four–lane freeway.

— Originated *Beautiful B.C.* pictorial magazine, sold worldwide.

1950s – 1960s

— Reconstructed Fraser Canyon highway, including two thousand–foot China Bar tunnel and other tunnels, and Alexandra Bridge.

1960

— Launched British Columbia Ferry Corporation with two ferries — *M.V. Sidney* and *M.V. Tsawwassen* — and two terminals — Swartz Bay on Vancouver Island and Tsawwassen on the mainland.

1961

— Constructed Upper Levels Highway from Vancouver to Horseshoe Bay. Highway was later extended to Squamish and then Whistler, making international skiing area possible.

1962

— Constructed Deas Tunnel Throughway (now called Vancouver–Blaine Freeway) between Vancouver and U.S. border. This route includes the Deas (Massey) Tunnel, the first of its kind in North America, which was officially opened by Queen Elizabeth II.

— Constructed world-famous Rogers Pass Highway through Rocky and Selkirk Mountains between Revelstoke and Golden, honouring a promise made in 1953 shortly after coming into office. Engineers had said for seventy-five years that it couldn't be done.

1963

— Constructed ten-mile "sawdust highway" as part of Burnaby freeway between Port Mann and Second Narrows Bridges, using special sawdust–based technique to overcome peat bogs, the first time this was used in construction of a major highway.

1964

— Constructed Port Mann Bridge between Surrey and Coquitlam, world's longest high–level, tie–arched bridge, first in North America to have an orthotropic plate deck.

— Constructed long-awaited Salmo–Creston cutoff, a sixty-seven-kilometre section of Southern Trans–Provincial Highway that attains highest elevation of any arterial highway in Canada.

— Constructed 194 miles of Yellowhead Highway between Kamloops and Vavenby (presented with Tete Jaune Award inscribed with words "he had a vision and did something about it").

1965
— Sponsored and constructed first high–rise senior citizens' residence in Canada, located in Kamloops. A second, eleven–storey tower was later added to the eight–storey tower. President of Silver Threads non–profit society operating this residence to provide low–rental housing for seniors.

— Constructed Richter Pass from Keremeos to Oliver, part of the Southern Trans–Provincial link from the coast to Alberta.

— Honoured by being made member of the Balch Collection of autographs of more than two thousand world leaders in Seattle Public Library.

1966
— Originated jet snowplow for Department of Highways using Pratt and Whitney turbojet engine; the world's first jet snowplow, used on the Salmo Creston cutoff and Rogers Pass.

1967
— "In recognition of outstanding qualities," was made honourary citizen and deputy high sheriff of Palm Springs, where he represented Canada for ten days raising funds for crippled children.

1952-1968
— Travelled on behalf of B.C. government to many cities worldwide — Europe, Asia, Africa, Australia, New Zealand, South America and the U.S.A., including Washington, D.C. Sent by B.C. Tourism Department to numerous cities to speak about and promote tourism in B.C. In Hollywood spoke to more than three hundred movie stars and was introduced by Canadian actor Raymond Massey as "the world's greatest Roman roadbuilder."

1981
— Invited to the inauguration celebration for Ronald Reagan, president of the United States of America. A document listing the names of those invited is in the Smithsonian Institute.

1989 – 90
— As mayor of Kamloops, played a crucial part in financing for new Riverside Coliseum. Instrumental in bringing chuckwagon races to Kamloops, an event that had been proposed for some twenty years. Played leadership role in improving the local economy.

OTHER:

— Name included in Edition Two of five thousand personalities of the World for exceptional achievement recognized by the American Biographical Institute.

— Leadership and achievements have merited mention in the First Edition published by the International Biographical Centre of Cambridge, England.

— Biography included in Canadian *Who's Who.*

— Appeared on *Front Page Challenge* three times.

Index

A

Aberhart, William, 27-29
Abilene Holdings, 180, 181
Action Team '88, 259-262, 264, 265
Active Petroleums, 181
Agassiz-Rosedale bridge, 58
Alaska Highway, 208
Alexandra Bridge, 112, 119
Anderson, David, 243
Anderson, Gerry, 245, 251-253, 255
Anderson, Pat, 262
Anscomb, Herbert, 26, 27, 29, 33, 35, 111
Arnish, Frank, 252
Ayres, James, 32

B

B and W Developments, 180
Backman, Donald, 143, 146
Baines, Ray, 52, 110
Barclay, Eric, 157
Barrett, Bert, 24
Barrett, Dave, 138, 139, 189, 190, 192, 224, 226, 227, 243, 252
Bate, Tom, 159
Beautiful B.C. magazine, 174
Beck, Ralph, 181, 182
Bell, Fred, 158
Bennett, Bill, 92, 234, 258
Bennett, Charlie, 182, 203-205, 225, 226
Bennett, R.J., 92
Bennett, W.A.C, 2, 27-29, 32, 34-37, 39, 41, 42, 47, 48, 50, 52, 61, 70, 74, 81, 82, 84-93, 96, 99, 108, 112, 113-116, 122, 123, 124-126, 128, 135, 138, 143, 144, 154, 159, 161, 170, 173-175, 186, 195-200, 203-206, 209, 211-217, 219, 220, 227-235, 238-243, 246, 249, 250, 252-254, 256, 258, 264
Bellotramo, Giuseppe, 15
Berger, Tom, 212-215, 243
Bethel Pentecostal Tabernacle, 209
Big Bend Highway, 58, 119
Bill 33, 233, 235
Bill 43 (Trade Union Act), 90
Bill 79 (Rolston Formula), 46
Bill 88, 233
Black, Randy, 259, 261, 265
Black, Wesley, 36, 38, 106, 144, 194, 205-207, 220, 228, 238, 242, 253, 254
Black Ball Ferries, 77, 95, 97
Bonanza Construction, 134
Bonner, Robert, 38, 44, 62, 81, 84-86, 93, 102, 154, 162, 174, 187, 201, 208
Bowden, Walter, 175, 176
Bowman, Harry, 35
Braithwood, Tom, 249
Branca, Angelo, 87, 155, 158

Briggs, H. Lee, 88, 93
B.C. Electric, 161, 162
B.C. Federation of Labour, 90, 91, 138
B.C. ferry system, 89, 93-97, 114, 116, 138, 174
B.C. Forest Products, 86, 87
B.C. Government Employees Union, 70
B.C. Hydro and Power Authority, 161, 232
B.C. Power Commission, 88
B.C. Social Credit League, 27, 28
B.C. Yukon Building and Construction Trades Council, 238
Britton, Gordon, 202
Broening, Wally, 145, 146
Brokenshire, Norman, 88, 89
Brotherhood of Carpenters and Joiners, 70
Brothers, Donald, 88, 89, 144, 159, 208, 229, 250, 253, 254
Brown, Fred, 157
Bryson, Mack, 212, 214
Burnaby sawdust highway, 117-119, 174

C

Cafferky, Emmet, 185, 186
Calder, Doc, 260
Calvary Temple, 19, 21-23, 25, 36, 60, 73, 100, 108, 131, 133, 134, 142, 145, 146, 148, 162, 179, 203, 209, 217, 227, 244, 245
Campbell, Dan, 71, 76, 91, 159, 217, 226, 228, 232, 253, 254
Campbell, Harvey "Slim," 131, 132
Canadian Labor Congress, 90
Canadian Merchant Services Guild, 77
Canadian Pacific Steamship Service, 77, 95
Caouette, Real, 176
Capozzi, Cap, 174
Capozzi, Herb, 174, 199, 210, 211, 220, 229, 242, 243
Cariboo College, 235
Carson, Ernie, 41, 60, 62, 111
Cassidy, Alex, 148, 162
Cartwright, Kenna, 260, 261
Chabot, Jim, 236, 238, 253, 261
Chant, William, 30, 91, 148, 228, 229
C.D. Schultz and Co. Ltd., 86
Charlong, Bud, 9
Charlong, Lena, 2, 9, 13
Chetwynd, Ralph, 34, 38
China Bar Tunnel, 119
Clancey, Bill, 93
Clark, Barrie, 189
Clark, Ian, 19, 33
Clark, Ken, 3
Clark, William, 3
Clarkson, Reg, 217, 218
Coalition government, 26, 29, 40-42, 124, 125, 141, 161, 243
Columbia River Bridge, 89

Index

Connaught Tunnel, 119-120

Cooperative Commonwealth Federation, 26, 31, 33-34, 47, 62, 71, 88, 90, 132, 138-139

Conservative Party, 26, 30, 31, 34, 35, 47, 62, 71, 88, 135, 139, 161-163, 174, 230, 243, 245, 251, 255

Constitution Act, 149

Construction Labour Relations Association, 236

Continental Contractors, 135

Coquihalla Highway, 112

Corbett, Irvine, 155, 158

Coronet magazine, 53

Cowell, John, 265

Cox, Cedric, 105

Creditistes, 176

Culver, Shirley, 261

D

Dawson Construction, 129, 133, 238

Dawson, Isabel, 226, 238, 253

Day, Colin, 262

Deas Island Tunnel, 66-68, 91, 114-116, 117, 174

Del Cielo, 182-184, 203, 225

Delmonico, Norm, 221

Dennett, Chris, 246-248

DeVito, F.E. 'Buddy,' 88, 89

Dewdney, Edgar, 110

de Wolfe. John. 212

Diefenbaker, John, 93, 122, 161

Dollar, Jim, 13

Donatelli, Dominic, 134

Dormer, John, 258, 259

Douglas, Clifford Hugh, 27, 28

Douglas, James, 41, 110

Douglas Social Credit Group, 28

Dowding, Gordon, 92, 153-155, 160, 162, 187

Driedeger, George, 225

Dufferin, 225, 226

Dunsdon Ray, 260

Duthie, Heather, 262

E

Eddie, Rae, 68

Elections, provincial, 1952 date set, 30; 1953 date set, 46; 1956 date set, 70; 1958 Rossland-Trail by-election, 87-89, 144; 1960 date set, 138; 1963 general election, 161-163; 1963 by-election, 161; 1966 general election, 173; 1969 by-election, 210; 1969 general election, 212-215; 1972 general election, 240-255

Emery, R.E., 33

Emil Anderson Construction, 129

Ernst, Jack, 202, 203, 212

Evergreen Lumber Sales, 86

Eversfield, Charles W., 84

F

Farris, John, 81

Ferber, C.J., 187

Finlayson, Deane, 46, 57, 70, 71, 89, 92, 139

Foundation of Canada Engineering Corporation, 66, 118

Francis, Harry, 44, 100

Fraser Canyon highway, 112

Friend, Shirley, 103, 104

Fulton, E. Davie, 33, 147, 161-163, 176, 211, 212

G

Gaglardi, Annie, 2, 8, 9

Gaglardi, Bert, 3, 6, 13, 134

Gaglardi, Bill, 19, 69, 177-180, 182, 183, 225, 257

Gaglardi, Bob, 18, 22, 69, 177-183, 185-188, 203, 205, 225, 256, 258, 260

Gaglardi, Chuck, 3, 20

Gaglardi, Domenica, 2, 4, 9, 13

Gaglardi, Frank, 2, 7, 13

Gaglardi, Helen, 3, 13

Gaglardi, Jennie, 12, 13, 17, 20-22, 32, 52, 60, 69, 134, 142, 158, 162, 177, 178, 203, 245

Gaglardi, Jim, 3

Gaglardi, Joe, 2, 9, 10

Gaglardi, John, 2, 4, 6, 8-11, 15

Gaglardi, Karen Gieser, 179, 188, 190, 191

Gaglardi, Phil, birth, 3; quits logging, 13; Northwestern Bible College, 15; move to Kamloops, 19; wins 1952 nomination, 32, 33; wins 1952 election, 35; loses party leadership election, 37; named public works minister, 38; wins 1953 election, 46; named highways minister, 61; criticized over 1955 flights, 68; wins 1956 election, 71; put in charge of building ferry service, 77; speeding tickets, 98-109; opens Rogers Pass, 122; opens bidding, 124-128; wins 1960 election, 139; convicted of contempt, 140; threatens to resign, 175; Lear scandal and resignation as highways minister, 189-201; appointed welfare minister, 217; loses 1972 election, 252-255; elected Kamloops mayor, 261

Gaglardi, Tony, 2, 6, 20, 75, 134

Gallaher, Bill, 203

Gardom, Garde, 174, 246

Geery, Glen, 130, 131, 150, 160

Gibbs, Archie, 47

Gibson, Gordon, 61, 62, 84, 85, 87, 149, 151, 151, 156, 184

Gigli, Beniamino, 24

Ginter, Ben, 125-129, 137, 207

Ginter Construction, 125, 133

Glazer, Burton, 130, 134, 140, 141

Godfrey, D.R., 165

Gould, Jay, 135, 141

Gray, H. Wilson "Wick," 84-87

Index

Gray, John, 86, 87
Gregory, George, 85, 139
Greer, George, 33
Gresty Bros., 131, 146
Gresty, Florence, 154, 155, 158
Gresty, Gloria, 155
Gresty, Vince, 131, 132, 137, 153, 158
Guild, Don, 184
Guild, Gordon, 184
Gunderson, Einar, 38, 44, 47

H

Hansell, Ernest, 29, 30, 31, 33
Harding, Randolph, 46, 132, 144, 159, 160
Harris, Sandy, 70
Hart, John, 40, 52
Highway 97, 112, 208, 235
Holzworth, Dick, 130, 131, 153-158, 160
Hope-Princeton Highway, 41, 110, 112, 164, 168
Hope Slide, 164-166
Hudson's Hope Bridge, 174
Huhn, Jacob, 159

I

International Brotherhood of Electrical Workers, 236
International Woodworkers of America, 90, 236
Irwin, Tom, 37, 44
Isherwood, Foster, 246
Iverson, Lou, 69, 166, 191, 192

J

Jacobs, Jim, 212
Jacques, Roy, 78
Jamieson Construction, 129
John Hart Highway, 41, 111
Johnson, Byron "Boss," 26, 27, 30, 35, 42, 52, 141
Johnson, Lyndon, 210
Johnston, Rita, 265
Jones, Evan, 50-52, 56, 64, 65, 67, 157, 168
Jones, P.S., 19
Jontz, Larry, 134
Jordan, Fritz and Lloyd, 137
Jordan, Pat, 226, 229, 237, 238, 253

K

Kalamen, A., 162
Kalyk, Nick, 173
Kamloops News Advertiser/ Kamloops News/ Kamloops Daily News, 224, 225, 251, 261
Karobil Enterprises, 181, 187
Keates, Stuart, 53
Kelowna Charter, 235, 241
Kennedy, Orvis, 31
Kent, Brian, 52
Kamloops Sentinel, 20, 252
Kenney, E.T., 46

Kiernan, Ken, 34, 38, 194, 227, 228, 229, 235, 237, 241, 242, 254
Kimberley-Radium highway, 120
Kinnaird, Jim, 238
Krause, H.E., 88, 89
Kriese, Beverley, 146
Krushnisky, Jake, 54, 56, 146, 201

L

L and M Logging, 129-131, 137, 153-155, 159
Labour Party, 26, 34, 47
Laing, Arthur, 46, 47, 60, 61, 69-71, 89, 92, 139, 194
Latta, Emily, 203
Latta, Mike, 180, 181, 203-205, 224, 225, 246, 258
Lea, Norm, 118
Lear jet, 170-174, 187-201
Legislature, 23rd Assembly, 44; prorogued 1962, 106
LeTourneau, Robert G., 74, 179
Lett, Sherwood, 81, 161
Liberal Party, 26, 30, 31, 34, 35, 46, 71, 88, 135, 139, 145, 161, 163, 173, 174, 176, 184, 185, 194, 201, 204, 210, 212, 214, 215, 230, 244, 246, 255
Lions Gate Bridge, 52, 53, 78, 122, 175
Little, Dudley, 193
Loffmark, Ralph, 205, 206, 229, 235, 250, 253
Lord, Arthur, 62
Luciani, Frank, 259, 265
Lyford, Chuck, 170-171
Lymburner, Burton, 129-131, 135, 151, 157, 158, 160, 184

M

McCallum, Neil, 42, 63-67, 80, 114
McCarthy, Grace, 174, 226, 229, 253
McDiarmid, Howard, 246
McDiarmid, Neil, 135
Macdonald, Alex, 148, 183, 185, 204
McDonald, D.M., 104, 105
McDonald, Murray, 83
Macdonell, C.B., 109
Macfarlane, Alan, 154, 171
McFarlane, M.M., 135, 140, 141
McGeer, Pat, 174, 189, 210, 212, 226
McKenzie, Lloyd, 155, 156,
McKibbon, John, 83
McLay, David, 103, 104, 106
McLean, Fraser, 54, 94, 133
Maclean's magazine, 53
MacLeod, Allan, 22
McLeod, Betty, 247, 248
McLeod, Roy, 167, 168
McNeill, Jack, 166, 167, 171, 191, 192
McNelly, Peter, 248, 249
McRann, Wayne, 259

Index

Main, Gerald, 182
Manitoba Social Credit League, 175
Manning, Ernest, 28, 29
Marchand, Len, 253
Marian, Pat, 8
Marriott, Syd, 129, 158
Marshall, Don, 229
Martin, Eric, 29, 30, 31, 37, 38, 41, 159, 173
Massey, George, 66
Massey, Raymond, 123
Mather, Camille, 105
Mauro, Vic, 70, 71
Mercer, Bill, 245, 253
Meredith, Ken, 134, 135
Merilees, Harold, 215
Merrick, Roy, 132, 146, 147
Miard, Tom, 57, 135, 158, 165, 201, 206
Mid-City Construction, 131, 158
Milobar, Tony, 260
Millikin, J.A., 68
Moran, Mickey, 132, 137
Morgan, Don, 180
Munro, Hector, 87
Murphy, Ed, 249, 251
Murray, W.H., 204
Mylrea, Katherine, 196

N
National Association of Marine Engineers, 77
Nesbitt, James K., 44, 52
New Democratic Party, 105, 145, 163, 173,
    184, 187, 201, 211-212, 214, 215, 230,
    244, 245, 252, 255
Newton, Orr, 44, 161
Nicholson, Babe, 258, 259, 265
Nicholson, John, 194, 220
Nimsick, Leo, 74-76, 159, 160
Nine Mile Canyon Bridge, 119
Nixon, Richard, 223
Norris, Tom, 135, 136, 140-141
Northland Properties Ltd., 180

O
Oak Street Bridge, 58, 66, 102
Odam, Jes, 185
Okanagan Lake (Princess Margaret) Bridge,
    58, 80, 81, 112
O'Neal, Pat, 91, 138
Orchard, C.D., 62
O'Rourke, Dennis, 224

P
Pacific Coast Services Ltd., 84-86
Pacific Press, 249
Page, Ron, 191
Parkinson, Ray, 215
Parsons, E.R., 43
Pattison, Jimmy, 24
Pattullo Bridge, 111, 113, 117, 122
Pattullo, T.D., 52

Paynter, Peer, 29, 31, 32, 36, 37
Peace River power plan, 138
Pearkes, George, 196, 199, 207
Pearson, Lester B., 192, 194
Pentecostal Assemblies of Canada, 18, 21,
    23, 31, 36, 146, 210
Peterson, Les, 96, 208, 220, 236, 237, 242, 253
Perini Pacific, 129
Perrault, Ray, 92, 139, 156, 157, 159-161,
    176, 189, 190, 192, 193, 204, 210
Peterson, Les, 74, 229, 236-238
Perkins, Charles, 55
Pifer, John, 252
Pollution Control Act, 232
Port Mann Bridge, 59, 112, 122, 123, 174
Powell, Claude, 37
Price, Bert, 37, 215, 221
Price, Ron, 219-221
Prince Philip, 91
Princess Margaret, 82
Project 819, 129-132, 134, 136, 138, 145,
    153-160
Project 1023, 156
Provenzano, A.F., 168
Provincial Alliance of Businessmen, 211,
    216, 217, 219, 220, 222, 247
Provincial Council of Carpenters, 236
Provincial Elections Act, 30, 150
Pybus, Ralph, 74

Q
Queen Elizabeth II, 91, 116

R
Radio CKNW, 249
Radio CHNL, 261
Randle, Lance, 173
Reid, J. Alan, 29, 31, 32, 37
Renk, Fred, 145, 146, 186, 187
Rhodes, Al, 133, 135, 158
Rhodes, James, 159
Richter, Frank, 228, 238, 253
Robinson, Don, 62
Rogers Pass, 119-122, 168, 174, 260
Rolston, Tilly, 27, 35, 38, 45, 47
Rosencrantz, Rodney, 130, 135
Ross, Frank, 74
Rothenburger, Mel, 251-253
Rudolph, Rudy, 30

S
Salmo Creston cutoff, 120
Sandman Inns, 182, 186, 256
Savemore Investment Associates Ltd., 181
Seafarers International Union, 77
Shantz, Hugh, 29, 34, 75
Shaw, Terry, 245
Schmidt, George, 80
Schultz, Charles D., 85-87
Schultz, Frieda, 13

Index

Second Narrows Bridge, 58, 78, 88, 112, 114, 116, 122
Shaw, Terry, 245
Shelford, Cyril, 193, 207, 228, 235, 238, 253, 254
Sherman, Paddy, 249
Shrum, Gordon, 88, 93
Silver Threads, 217
Silver Sage Ranch, 146, 181, 187, 190
Skillings, Waldo, 86, 159, 160, 205, 206, 218, 227, 229, 250, 253
Sloan, Gordon, 86, 87
Smith, Bud, 260
Smith, Don, 159
Smith, Syd, 30, 33, 34
Smith, Walter, 30, 131, 146-148
Social Credit Party, 28, 34, 35, 47, 71, 87-88, 139, 148, 161, 163, 173, 176, 192, 202, 210, 215, 224, 229, 230, 242-244, 249-255, 257
Sommers, Robert, 35, 38, 60, 84-89, 149, 150, 192
Southern Trans-Provincial Highway, 69, 111, 112, 120, 164, 165
Spaulding, Phil, 77, 94
Star Weekly *magazine*, 53
Stephanishin, Norm, 164, 165
Stewart, Doug, 221
Strachan, Robert, 35, 70, 80, 89, 92, 132, 133, 137, 139, 210 155, 158, 159, 161
Straith, W.T., 46
Strohmeier, Joyce, 55
Strohmeier, Larry, 55
Strom, Harry, 224
Sturdy, David, 84, 85
Swan, W.G., 78, 79

T
Taylor, E.P., 87
Taylor, Gordon, 122
Terry, Harry, 97
Thomas, A.I., 101
Thompson, Robert, 175
Thompson-Nicola Manufacturers Association, 259
Thornton, Clyde, 130, 131, 136, 140-141, 150, 151, 153, 155, 156, 184
Tisdalle, John, 85, 193
Toronto Globe and Mail, 53
Toronto Star, 246, 248, 253
Toye, Bert, 166, 167, 171, 188, 191-192, 195
Trail Times, 88
Trans-Canada Highway, 45, 56, 58, 116, 120-122, 129
Trudeau, Pierre, 223
Turcott, Les, 181, 182
Turnbull, Douglas, 35
Turner, Arthur, 68

Two Rivers Policy, 161, 231
U
Union Constractors, 131, 134, 135, 137, 140, 153, 155, 158
United Farmworkers of Alberta, 27
Uphill, Tom, 34, 47, 71, 139
Upper Levels Highway, 58, 116
V
Valen, Edith Scarff, 51, 52, 78, 108, 135, 196, 200, 204, 206, 207, 218, 262
Vancouver Province, 52, 196, 214, 248, 249, 253
Vancouver Sun, 52, 53, 80, 133, 134, 185, 186, 248
Vander Zalm, Bill, 243, 257, 258
Victoria Colonist, 52, 96, 214
Victoria Times, 52, 89
Vincenzi, Bill, 240, 243, 245
W
Wallace, Clarence, 38, 44, 46
Wallace, L.J., 199
Wallace, Scott, 229, 246
Wanless, Rick, 202, 203
Warren, Derril, 229, 241, 243
Wasserman, Jack, 249
Walton, Bill, 261
Watson, Ron, 261
Webster, Arnold, 46
Webster, Jack, 53
Webster, Ted, 157, 165
Wenman, Bob, 174
Wenner-Gren, Axel, 209
White Swan, 181
Wicks, Lyle, 28, 29, 31, 35, 37, 38, 41, 90, 96, 138, 139
Wilkins, Bert, 165
Williams, Bob, 226
Willis, Doug, 67
Willis, Lloyd, 67
Williston, Ray, 85, 108, 125, 196, 199, 227, 228, 234, 252, 253, 254
Willoughby, John, 244, 245, 251, 253, 255
Wills, Amy, 51
Wilson, Tom, 70, 71
Winch, Harold, 31, 33, 35, 46
Wood, John, 70, 156
Wooster, Anthony, 79
Worley, Ron, 40
Y
Yates, Jim, 181, 182
Yellowhead Highway, 56
Z
Zapf, Norm, 165